Attorney

A   ip

DISCARD

DEMCO

Other books in the *Rights* series:

Gay & Lesbian Rights
by Brette McWhorter Sember

Teen Rights
by Traci Truly

Traveler's Rights
by Alexander Anolik and John K. Hawks

Unmarried Parents' Rights, 2nd Ed.
by Jacqueline D. Stanley

Attorney Responsiblities & Client Rights

Your Legal Guide to the
Attorney-Client Relationship

Suzan Herskowitz Singer
Attorney at Law

SPHINX® PUBLISHING
AN IMPRINT OF SOURCEBOOKS, INC.®
NAPERVILLE, ILLINOIS
www.SphinxLegal.com

First Edition, 2003

Published by: Sphinx® Publishing, An Imprint of Sourcebooks, Inc.®

Naperville Office
P.O. Box 4410
Naperville, Illinois 60567-4410
630-961-3900
Fax: 630-961-2168
www.sourcebooks.com
www.SphinxLegal.com

This publication is designed to provide accurate and authoritative information in regard to the subject matter covered. It is sold with the understanding that the publisher is not engaged in rendering legal, accounting, or other professional service. If legal advice or other expert assistance is required, the services of a competent professional person should be sought.

From a Declaration of Principles Jointly Adopted by a Committee of the American Bar Association and a Committee of Publishers and Associations

This product is not a substitute for legal advice.

Disclaimer required by Texas statutes.

Library of Congress Cataloging-in-Publication Data
Singer, Susan Herskowitz.
    Attorney responsibilities and client rights : your legal guide to the attorney-client relationship / by Susan Herskowitz Singer.-- 1st ed.
        p. cm.
    ISBN 1-57248-347-4
    1. Attorney and client--United States. 2. Lawyers--Malpractice--United States. 3. Legal ethics--United States. I. Title.

KF311 .S56 2003
347.73'504--dc22
                                                            2003016482

Printed and bound in the United States of America.

BG Paperback — 10 9 8 7 6 5 4 3 2 1

ACKNOWLEDGMENTS

Thanks to Ernie Rubino for his assistance in
doing the initial research for this book.
As always, my thanks and love to my husband, Steve.

CONTENTS

Prejudice
Proving Ineffectiveness
Recognizing Ineffective Assistance of Counsel

INTRODUCTION

If you are reading this book you are probably having problems with a lawyer. You think the lawyer has wronged you in some way, and you want to know what you can do about it. Perhaps the lawyer charged you too much money; did not return your phone calls; did not complete the task you asked for; or, otherwise acted in a seemingly unethical manner.

A 1996 study by the American Bar Association (ABA) indicated that more than 27% of malpractice claims against attorneys were due to administrative errors. Another 20% of claims were because of missed deadlines. Yet the same study indicates that overall, claims in the 1990s shifted away from administrative errors (compared to prior years). The study surmises that the trend toward claims against substantive issues and away from administrative issues may be due to better office procedures, a more competitive environment among law firms and clients who are more educated and willing to *second guess* their lawyers in tougher economic times.

There is no doubt that malpractice suits against attorneys are on the rise, as are grievance procedures. This phenomenon has many causes. The general increase in lawsuits and the corresponding dependence on lawyers increases the likelihood of mistakes, both large and small, by those lawyers.

In addition, more and more lawyers are being licensed every year. For example, the Commonwealth of Virginia saw an increase of 30% from 1992 to 2002. Overall, between 1995 and 2001, the United States saw a 20% increase in the number of lawyers, from 870,000 to 1.1 million. That's approximately 40,000 more lawyers each year.

These lawyers are all trying to vie for the same clients. Some cut corners. Others may attempt to handle a matter for which they have little or no aptitude and leave themselves open for mistakes. Both of these factors are based on the percentage game. More lawyers equal more mistakes equal more malpractice claims.

Consumers are more educated about the legal process and are demanding quality service from their lawyers. A client is more likely to know when a lawyer has erred than ever before. When that lawyer makes a mistake, the client is more likely to sue. More malpractice suits have been filed in the last thirty years than in all prior years combined.

Some people think the term *ethical lawyer* is an oxymoron. Indeed, from what is portrayed daily in the media, you would think that finding a lawyer who is also ethical would be as likely as finding an ice cube in a 500° Fahrenheit oven.

This book's purpose is not to give the impression that all lawyers deserve labels like "slimy," "shark," "bottom feeder," "shyster," and other similarly derogatory comments or that all those lawyer jokes are true. Most lawyers in the United States are ethical and do their very best to assist their clients in a competent and professional manner. They remain within the law, treat others fairly and with respect, and try to do what is just and right.

Instead, the purpose of this book is to guide those who have encountered a lawyer they believe may have acted in an incompetent or unethical manner. It will inform you of the standards a lawyer is expected to uphold in his or her duty to the client and how a breach of those duties occurs.

TYPES OF CLAIMS AGAINST LAWYERS

Before you make a claim against your lawyer, you need to understand the different types of claims that can be made. It is important that you evaluate what your lawyer did wrong, and make the proper type of claim. Otherwise your claim may be dismissed because you do not have the proper legal basis. If your claim is totally without merit, you may even be forced to pay your lawyer's defense costs.

There are five types of claims that can be made against your lawyer: malpractice, breach of contract, conflict of interest, ineffective assistance of counsel and financial misconduct. These are summarized below and explained in detail in the following chapters.

- Malpractice. Your attorney negligently handled your case.
- Breach of contract. Your attorney did not follow the terms of your agreement for his or her services.
- Conflict of interest. Your case was harmed by your attorney having personal interests that conflicted with your interests.
- Ineffective assistance of counsel. Your attorney did not effectively represent you in a criminal matter.
- Financial misconduct. Your attorney mishandled funds that you entrusted to him or her.

EDUCATION AND LICENSING

To gain some appreciation for the complexity of the law, it may be helpful to know what a lawyer must do before he or she can hang a shingle outside the office door.

College

While the *American Bar Association* (ABA) requires only three years of college before someone can attend law school, most ABA accredited law schools require a student to have an undergraduate degree from an accredited college or university before admittance to law school will be granted. This means that most lawyers in the United States have attended college for a minimum of four years. Some states, such as California, require only two years of undergraduate preparation or its equivalent.

Law School

Most students will attend law school for three years as a full-time student, or four years for part-time study. This is also the ABA standard.

Almost all states require a law student to attend an ABA accredited school. California and Virginia are the notable exceptions. California allows students to attend any law school, whether accredited or not, as long as the students meet the educational requirements set by the bar examiners. In addition, anyone that went to a non-accredited law school must take a *pre-bar* on first year subjects before he or she will be considered qualified to sit for the regular bar examination.

In Virginia, approved individuals are entitled to study the law under qualified general practice lawyers to become eligible to sit for the bar examination after a prescribed period of study. This is called *reading for the law* or a *law reader program.*

A note about ABA accreditation: The American Bar Association, a private association and not a state agency, sets the standard for almost all law schools and bar examinations. The ABA's accreditation process looks at the quality and size of a school's faculty; its student body, library, and physical surroundings. The ABA requires any school it accredits to have a challenging curriculum for its students. The curriculum must indicate that a student will have attained a firm grasp of the fundamentals of legal subjects and the skills necessary to perform competently as a lawyer upon graduation. The ABA requires that each student successfully complete certain core classes. In some states, law schools are obliged to teach other certain supplementary subjects in addition to the courses the ABA requires.

Bar Examination

With some very restrictive exceptions, every state requires some type of examination before someone will be allowed to practice law in that state. The form of the exam will vary, but there are some generalities.

Most states require an exam given twice a year called the *Multistate Bar Examination (MBE)*. It is a 200 question exam covering constitutional law, criminal law and procedure, civil procedure, torts, contracts, and real property. It is given over a six hour period. The passing rate for each state varies. Most all states then require bar applicants to take another day (or more) of testing in essay format that usually covers state, federal, and general law principles. In addition to the bar examination proper, most states require an ethics exam, called the *Multistate Professional Ethics Exam (MPRE)*.

Some states, such as West Virginia, are requiring the *Multistate Performance Test (MPT)* as part of the bar exam proper. The MPT is a three hour exam with two performance test questions. The questions are designed to test an applicant's ability to use fundamental lawyering skills in a realistic situation.

California also requires applicants to undergo a performance examination. They are provided documents necessary to gather important facts and a mini-library of applicable cases, statutes, and rules. Using these materials, the applicants are required to prepare either a brief, memorandum of law, opinion, or other working paper.

Background Check

Applicants for the bar undergo a thorough background investigation. This investigation may include checks into the applicant's moral character and finances.

While the scope of what constitutes *unfit moral character* has come under fire in the past few years, the bar examiners hold considerable sway in determining if a bar applicant's character makes him or her a suitable candidate for practicing law. The examiners look toward the applicant's past conduct to determine how likely that past conduct will lead to future conduct considered incompatible with the responsibilities of being a lawyer. What is considered moral unfitness in one state, may not be so considered in another.

A short list of traits that the bar examiners may determine to be a barrier to law practice include:

- substance abuse;
- plagiarism;
- cheating;
- other acts of dishonesty;
- emotional illness or instability;
- questionable business or financial transactions; and,
- criminal convictions.

A shaky credit report showing three months past due on a credit card with a $500 limit will be scrutinized just as closely as someone with $15,000 of debt. Bankruptcy, however, will not automatically deem the applicant unfit.

In general, all questions about an applicant's fitness to practice law based on character is done on a case by case basis.

CONTINUING LEGAL EDUCATION

Continuing legal education (CLE) courses on a multitude of topics are given in every state by both state bar associations and private companies. Currently forty states require some amount of mandatory continuing education. Each state sets the amount of hours required, but the average is between ten to fifteen hours per year. Any lawyer that does not complete the required number of CLE hours within the prescribed time period is suspended from the practice of law until the coursework is completed. For a listing of state-by-state CLE requirements, go to:

www.cle.com/clerequirements.shtml

SPECIALIZATION

Many people believe that attorneys go to school to be a certain type of lawyer. For example, they believe that a person studied to become a divorce lawyer or a criminal lawyer. In fact, only a few states offer any type of *specialization* certification. If you live in a state that does certify an attorney for a particular practice area, that attorney generally has passed additional tests on the subject matter, practiced in the area for a number of years, and is deemed to be an expert in the area. However, an attorney may have just as much experience and skill in a subject as a specialist. And, if your state does not certify attorneys in particular practice areas, there is no rule preventing an attorney from claiming to be a divorce lawyer or tax lawyer to promote him or herself in that area of the law.

–1–
MALPRACTICE

A suit for *malpractice* is usually the first remedy a client thinks about when a lawyer has failed to perform his or her duties. Whether your attorney has *committed* malpractice will be the first avenue you will probably explore if you think your attorney has wronged you in some way. Statistics show that the average lawyer will have to defend against three malpractice claims during his or her legal career. To understand malpractice, an understanding of the legal concept of negligence becomes paramount.

NEGLIGENCE

The term *negligence* is tossed about freely in our society. It is not unusual to hear someone say, "that person was negligent" to describe a driver who ran a red light and almost hit somebody, or a the doctor who left a patient, wearing a drafty gown, sitting in an examining room for an hour, or a lawyer who *botched* a case. But what does the term mean legally? Legally negligent behavior may be different than what an average person considers negligent.

> **Example:** John leaves the keys in the car's ignition and locks the car door. In everyday terms, he was negligent, but does it rise to the occasion of legal negligence? Probably not.

Negligence is defined as a failure to use a reasonable or ordinary amount of care in a situation that causes harm to someone. You are negligent if you had a duty to do something and you were either careless or completely failed to do it.

Example: John is a lifeguard at the town pool. Clarissa is screaming for help, but John, oblivious that Clarissa may be drowning, chats with his buddies instead of offering assistance. In general, lifeguards have a legal duty to offer assistance to those under their care. In this case, John could be found *legally negligent.*

To be found negligent, a lawyer must *breach* or violate certain standards of conduct. This violation must also be shown to have *caused* you harm. What must you, as a wronged client, prove for your lawyer to be found guilty of malpractice?

Courts agree that a client must prove the following elements to be successful in a lawsuit for legal malpractice:

♦ an actual attorney-client relationship;
♦ a breach of duty to the client; and,
♦ injury caused by the breach.

Attorney-Client Relationship

An attorney-client relationship must exist. This basically means that the attorney took on the duty of giving legal representation to the client. This duty gives rise to certain standards of conduct on the part of the lawyer that will be discussed in a separate section below.

How is this relationship formed? It is possible for a relationship to exist although no contract is written. (See Chapter 2 for more about contracts between a lawyer and client.)

Example: In a Minnesota case, a woman consulted with a lawyer who told her he did not think her case was viable but that he would consult with another lawyer on her behalf and get a second opinion. No contract was entered into and no other consultation occurred. The woman, however, relied upon the lawyer's statement that he would talk to another lawyer for her. By the time she went to another lawyer on her own, the time limit for filing a claim had expired. The court found that the original lawyer was negligent.

As stated, no written agreement was involved. There was still, however, a duty on the lawyer's part to represent the woman in that matter, at least to the extent he said he would.

In addition, a lawyer-client relationship may exist even if no money is involved. When a lawyer takes a case *pro bono*, (which literally means "for the good," but generally refers to a case that the attorney handles for free), an attorney-client relationship still exists. If the lawyer represents you for free or at a low cost, a lawyer-client relationship exists.

Confidentiality. A by-product of the attorney-client relationship is *confidentiality*. This means that the attorney must hold anything said by the client in complete confidence or in secret. This concept of confidentiality is generally held to always apply with certain very narrow exceptions. Unless one of the following situations exists, a lawyer is prohibited from disclosing any information a client reveals.

- The client knowingly consents to disclosure of the information, such as telling the lawyer to tell a third party, or if the third party is present during the discussion between the lawyer and client.
  Example: Barbara visits Larry Lawyer regarding having a new will drawn up. Barbara brings her friend, Sara, with her to the appointment. While in the meeting, Barbara indicates that she wants to write a new will because she has decided to divorce her husband. Larry does not have to keep the confidence (although he most likely will) because of Sara's presence during the meeting.
- The client has stated an intent to commit a crime.
  Example: Tony tells his lawyer he intends to embezzle funds from his company where he is the accountant.
- The lawyer is trying to collect legal fees from the client.
  Example: Rob has refused to pay so Larry Lawyer sues to collect. Larry has a limited right to disclose certain information that would otherwise be confidential.

♦ The lawyer has been accused of wrongdoing, such as a mal-practice claim or grievance.

Example: Rhonda executes a deed giving property to her granddaughter, Beth. Rhonda's lawyer failed to record the deed in the land records. Rhonda sues him for malpractice. Her now former lawyer is permitted to disclose what would otherwise be confidential information.

NOTE: *Otherwise, a lawyer must maintain the confidence of the client whether a current or former client.*

Breach of Duty to the Client

A *breach of duty* occurs when the lawyer does something harmful to the client or fails to do what was required. Like Rhonda above, if you executed a deed in which you gave property to your grandchild and your lawyer failed to file the deed in the county records as required, your lawyer breached (or violated) your contract.

Injury Caused by the Breach

You must be able to prove that the harm you suffered was caused by your lawyer's conduct or misconduct

Example: Stephen hires Larry Lawyer to file a child custody suit. Stephen dos not tell Larry that he believes his children are in danger from his ex-wife's suspected drinking or that she has threatened to take the children away. Instead, he tells Larry that, after five years, he would like his children to live with him now that he has gotten remarried.

Larry gets to work on the suit but the day before he plans on filing the suit, Stephen's wife runs to another state with the children. If Larry delayed the filing, the delay may be con-sidered the primary cause of the harm Stephen suffered, i.e. the loss of his children. If, however, Larry's delay was not unreasonable, Larry will not be held accountable for Stephen's loss.

Had Stephen told Larry the situation was grave, a delay of only one day may have been unreasonable. Otherwise, Larry could not have been expected to foresee all consequences that may occur, such as a former spouse kidnapping her children, or considering the spouse's drinking, getting in a serious car accident with the children. Each situation will be different and must be considered on a case by case basis.

The purpose of the following section is to set out the standards for negligence as it relates to lawyers. (While these standards may be similar to medical or other negligence, consult another book for any other type of negligent behavior.)

STANDARDS OF CONDUCT

As was discussed in the introduction to this book, lawyers must jump through many hoops to become lawyers. They must have a college degree, go through three years of law school (a grueling as well as expensive experience for the majority of law students), study for and pass a difficult licensing exam (commonly known as the *bar exam*), and stay fresh with the law through *continuing legal education*.

All of these prerequisites set the stage for the standards to which all lawyers must adhere. They must follow any rules and regulations set by the bar associations of each state (discussed in Chapter 7) or other regulatory authority.

In addition, there are standards of conduct lawyers must maintain regardless of whether any rules and regulations exist. Failing to adhere to these standards opens the door to charges of legal malpractice or other negligence. Remember, however, courts are often more forgiving than the client. If the court believes the lawyer made decisions of strategy based on the law and after an intelligent, good faith assessment of all the applicable factors, the lawyer will not be found negligent. A bad result does not often mean the lawyer did something wrong, but out of two choices, picked the one that did not produce the best result.

In *Ziegelheim v. Apollo*, found in 128 N.J. 250, 607 A.2d 1298 (1992), the New Jersey Supreme Court stated, "The law demands that attorneys handle their cases with knowledge, skill, and diligence, but it does not demand that they be perfect or infallible, and it does not demand that they always secure optimum outcomes for their clients."

Standard of Care

The standard of care is composed of two components—*care* and *skill.* This refers to the care, skill, and knowledge a lawyer must use when representing a client. In general, a lawyer must use a reasonable degree of care and skill. How much care and skill is reasonable is determined by the standard of skills possessed by other attorneys practicing in that area of law in the immediate community. There is no national standard of reasonableness. What is reasonable in New York, may not be reasonable in California. This also means that the standard is determined on a *case by case* basis.

In general, a lawyer is liable for malpractice when he or she fails to exercise that reasonable degree of care and skill as is required to handle a particular case. You would not ask your doctor, a general practitioner, to perform brain surgery.

A lawyer who is not competent to perform certain tasks in a particular area of law must either learn it, ask for help from a more knowledgeable lawyer, or decline the representation. A real estate lawyer does not have a reasonable degree of skill and knowledge to handle a complex personal injury lawsuit. If a lawyer wanted to try to handle this matter, it should be disclosed to the client that the lawyer is not skilled in this area and that another lawyer, one skilled in personal injury, will be needed to assist with the case. Otherwise, the lawyer should decline.

Of course, there is a minimum standard of care that is understood to be required of all lawyers. This minimum standard is based on the educational and testing obligations that anyone called *attorney at law* is required to fulfill before becoming licensed to practice law. It is understood that if a lawyer takes the case, the task is supposed to be completed. All lawyers are expected to know the general principles of legal analysis and research learned in law school. They are required to know when their general knowledge is not sufficient.

No lawyer is required to be competent in all areas of law. All are required to know their limitations. Failure to know those limitations will usually give rise to negligence—a failure to competently represent a client with the proper care, skill and knowledge. The last section of this chapter lists certain tasks about which a lawyer, handling a particular type of case, may be required to be knowledgeable.

The following two specific areas may heavily contribute to a lawyer's negligence, or may be grounds for a charge of negligence.

Lawyer Impairment
Consider these facts.

◆ An Illinois survey found that 40-75% of discipline cases involve a chemically dependent or mentally ill practitioner.
◆ A Louisiana study found that 80% of Client Protection Fund cases involve chemical dependency or a gambling component.
◆ A study by John Hopkins Medical School found that of 28 occupations surveyed, lawyers are 3.6 times more likely to suffer depression than the average person.
◆ All fifty states have developed lawyer assistance programs or committees focused on quality of life issues, employing the use of intervention, peer counseling, and referral to Twelve Step Programs to assist in the lawyer's recovery process.

Lawyer impairment is tied to negligence, ethical violations, substance abuse, depression, and other factors (see Chapter 7). If a lawyer's impairment due to substance abuse or other instability is suspected, discharge him or her immediately.

Determine the following issues.

◆ Did the lawyer's substance abuse (or other impairment) cause harm? Did the lawyer violate the general standard of care? Some lawyers with less than perfect personal lives are still able to perform their duties, and these lawyers cannot be prosecuted.

Example: Anthony Attorney, despite his alcoholism, never missed a lawsuit deadline. Larry Lawyer, despite depression, drafted his client's wills completely to specification and the client's satisfaction.

If either Anthony or Larry mishandled a client matter, however, the client may show that the impairment was the cause. Usually, a charge of substance abuse or other impairment directly relates to the lawyer's *competence.* The client must show that the abuse made the lawyer's ability to render competent legal representation impossible, or at the very least, that the impairment may have influenced his or her ability to get the best possible outcome.

◆ Did the lawyer misappropriate the retainer money paid by the client? In other words, did the lawyer borrow or steal the money? Chapter 5 on client funds discusses how to reclaim that money and Chapter 7 on ethical violations discusses filing a grievance.

For more information about lawyers and substance abuse, see: www.vtbar.org/ezstatic/data/vtbar/journal/dec_2002/ Bumps_in_the_Road.pdf

Supervision of Employees

Lawyers must properly supervise their employees. The definition of employees includes secretaries, paralegals and investigators. These employees are held to the same standards as lawyers when confidentiality is involved.

In addition, any negligence or mistakes made by the employee, such as filing the wrong document or drafting a document improperly, will be *imputed* to the lawyer. This means that the employee's mistakes are the lawyer's mistakes and the lawyer may be sued for those mistakes. Ultimately, your lawyer's duty to you includes the obligation to adequately supervise his or her employees. Failure to supervise employees can cause an attorney to be punished by his or her state's bar.

Example 1: In October 2002, the Florida attorney was disbarred for, among other things, permitting his paralegal to engage in the unlicensed practice of law. The lawyer had permitted his paralegal to meet with clients without supervision.

Example 2: Another Florida attorney was suspended from practicing law for ninety days and placed on probation for one year because he had, among other things, failed to supervise his support staff.

As you can see, the punishment by the Bar may be quite different depending upon the apparent severity of the violations.

LIABILITY TO THIRD PARTIES

It used to be that a lawyer was immune to lawsuits for malpractice that were not brought directly by the client or on the client's behalf, with certain limited exceptions. This immunity was based on the concept of *privity*.

Privity refers to the contractual relationship between the attorney and his or her client. Without that attorney-client relationship, no lawsuit for malpractice could be brought against the lawyer. In other words, only the immediate client could bring a malpractice action.

This requirement was relied upon almost exclusively until a landmark decision in 1916. In that case, Judge Benjamin Cardozo (a very famous, respected, and influential judge) stated that "the source of the obligation" had to be put where it belonged—in the law. Judge Cardozo found that a car manufacturer did owe a duty to the car's buyer even though the buyer's contract was with the car dealer and not the manufacturer. The first case to hold that a professional may be held accountable for negligent services to a third party occurred in 1931. Yet it was not until 1958 that a court in California, and not until 1977 that a New York court, determined that a third party could recover for an attorney's negligence.

The test used to determine whether a third party could hold an attorney liable for negligence even without privity of contract is based on the 1958 California case. The court there found that a court must balance all the factors involved including:

- the extent to which the transaction was intended to affect the third party. For example, the attorney drafts a will that does not give property to the third party, who was the testator's (the person who had the lawyer write the will) choice as beneficiary;
- the foreseeability of harm to the third party. The attorney should realize that if the third party is the intended beneficiary but is not named, the third party would be harmed;
- the degree of certainty that the third party suffered injury;
- the closeness of the connection between the attorney's conduct and the injuries suffered. For example, the third party would have received an estate totalling $100,000 but for the attorney's failure to draft the will properly;
- the moral blame attached to the attorney's conduct; and,
- the public policy of preventing future harm.

Each lawsuit must be considered on a case by case basis. In general, the test is whether the third party was intended to *benefit* from the transaction between the attorney and client.

Example: Benny sues Uncle Oswald's lawyer for malpractice when Benny is not named in his uncle's will. Although Uncle Oswald was worth a great deal of money, he left specific instructions with his lawyer and stated on many occasions that, under no circumstances, did he intend to leave one thin dime to his nephew. In that instance, Benny would be barred from obtaining a recovery because he was not intended to benefit from Uncle Oswald's contractual relationship with the lawyer.

USE OF ETHICAL RULES
IN MALPRACTICE SUITS

Most states have adopted ethical rules that attorneys must follow. These are generally based on the *Model Rules of Professional Conduct* developed by the American Bar Association. A violation of these rules can subject an attorney to discipline by his or her state's attorney governing body.

The question of whether a violation of ethical rules and regulations (see Chapter 7) may be used in a malpractice suit is unsettled, however, they are being used more and more by clients suing their lawyers and are receiving greater acceptance by the courts. Ethical rules spell out, in fairly plain language, the standards by which a lawyer should conduct him or herself. It is more *black and white* than the *standard of care* criterion that is usually used in malpractice suits (discussed above). If a lawyer is labeled unethical because of an ethical violation, it will probably be a stigma that a jury may not be able to ignore. This makes using the rules regulating the bar as a part of the actual malpractice lawsuit a powerful tool.

The courts are divided on whether or not the ethical rules may be used as a standard in malpractice cases. Most courts have held that the use of ethical rules to set the standard for malpractice is inappropriate. However, there have been cases that have held the opposite. For example, in an Illinois case, the court said a jury instruction could be given stating that a lawyer may not violate an ethical rule and that the jury could consider the standards of professional ethics set forth in the rules regulating members of the bar when weighing all the evidence. The court also stated that jury instructions could quote the actual disciplinary rules, comparing them with statutes and codes.

The Model Rules of Professional Conduct most likely to assist with a malpractice claim are:

◆ Rule 1.5 (Fees).
◆ Rules 1.7, 1.8 and 1.9 (Conflict of Interest).

 ◆ Rule 1.13 (Organization as Client).
 ◆ Rule 1.15 (Safekeeping Client's Property).

(See Appendix D for the text of these particular rules.)

If it appears that your lawyer was not only negligent based on the standards of care, but also breached ethical duties, consideration should be given to using the rules and regulations for professional ethics as part of the case against the lawyer, if your state permits this information to be used. (See Chapter 7 for more on Ethical Violations.)

DIRECT DAMAGES

Direct damages are those damages which occur as the immediate consequence of the wrong your lawyer did to you. Direct damages may be *compensatory, punitive,* or *nominal.*

Courts typically look for an actual economic injury to the wronged party. This means that the court is going to assess your claim based on the actual financial loss you suffered as a result of your lawyer's negligence. The courts anticipate that you, as a wronged client, may be annoyed and inconvenienced by your attorney failing to file suit on time, filing the incorrect document with a court, or drafting some document incorrectly. Courts will assess these *inconveniences* and lapses of professional standards and determine (sometimes with the help of a jury), a monetary award that will be deemed to satisfy your loss. To determine this amount, courts look to the money the client would have received but for the attorney's negligence.

Compensatory Damages

Compensatory damages are an amount of money awarded to you based on what you lost. These are meant to help you regain what you lost through lawyer malpractice. Examples of compensatory damages are the value of property lost due to the attorney's negligence and attorney's fees paid to the opposing party.

Example: The Supreme Court of Connecticut upheld a lower court decision that awarded the wronged client damages totaling $1,500,000. This amount was arrived at by the jury in response to the evidence provided during the malpractice trial. The evidence showed that the attorney settled a marital dissolution dispute for the client in an amount totalling $450,000. The total amount of the marital estate, however, was $2,400,000.

The jury determined that it was likely that, but for the lawyer's incompetence, the client may have received up to 60% of the marital estate ($1,400,000) and alimony equalling between 35% and 50% of the client's and spouse's combined annual income. The Supreme Court of Connecticut agreed that it was reasonable for the jury to determine that the client should have received far more than she did in the marital settlement and that the monetary award of $1,500,000 against the lawyer was fair under the circumstances.

Punitive Damages

These damages are awarded to *punish* the lawyer for his or her negligence. Proving that the lawyer acted *deliberately* and *willfully* is usually required.

Nominal Damages

This is the plaintiff's nightmare. Receiving *nominal damages* (often only $1) shows that the client was correct and that the lawyer was negligent, but the court found that no money damages resulted. The client is left with the satisfaction of knowing he or she was right but not much else.

PAIN AND SUFFERING/ EMOTIONAL DISTRESS DAMAGES

In general, lawsuits asking for damages for pain and suffering as a result of an attorney's negligence are rarely successful. In order to recover such damages, the lawyer's actions must be more than negligent. They must be *extreme and outrageous, wanton and malicious,* or *coercive*. As long as the attorney's conduct does not involve fraud, some other intentional misconduct, a willful breach of duty, or physical contact (see Chapter 3 for discussion on sex with a client), it is highly unlikely that you will be able to recover damages for *emotional distress* from your lawyer. As one court stated, the attorney must be "certain or substantially certain that such distress would result from his conduct." Otherwise, a lawyer is not, in general, required to know that an error will cause emotional distress to a client.

However, it is not *impossible* to obtain damages for emotional distress.

> **Example:** A court awarded a client $400,000 for emotional distress. The client had been convicted of involuntary manslaughter. His conviction was overturned on appeal because the court found his attorney to be incompetent. On retrial, the client was acquitted of the charge. The court found that the client was entitled to money damages. These damages were awarded to compensate him for his emotional anguish at being incarcerated because of his lawyer's incompetence.

When determining the issue of awarding damages for emotional distress, the court will consider that most clients are emotionally involved in their lawsuits. That fact alone will not be enough to obtain an award for emotional distress. It appears from the few cases available, that a court will look to whether a personal, rather than a financial interest is involved before damages will be awarded for emotional distress. If the case revolves mostly around a financial interest, a request for damages due to emotional distress will most likely be denied.

NEGLIGENCE IN SPECIFIC AREAS OF LAW

The following is a list of possible causes of legal malpractice for specific areas of law. This list is not meant to be exhaustive but is indicative of the actions or omissions a lawyer may make.

Administrative Law

- Did not follow appropriate administrative procedures.
- Did not comply with the deadlines for an employee reinstatement hearing.
- Did not appear on behalf of the client in a hearing for the revocation of a corporate charter.
- Did not bring an available defense in a bar grievance hearing.
- Did not help the client get immigration permits.
- Did not appeal a disability claim denial.

Bankruptcy Law

- Did not properly file for a client's bankruptcy.
- Did not avoid conflicting interests: the lawyer represented multiple parties (see Chapter 3).
- Did not advise client about the proper type of bankruptcy under which to continue.
- Did not give notice to a preferred creditor.
- Did not initially include or later amend the petition to include a debt.
- Did not advise the client that a contract must be approved by bankruptcy court.
- Did not obtain a judgment that was immune from discharge.

Criminal Law

- Did not seek reduction of an excessive sentence.
- Did not appeal a conviction when one was warranted.
- Did not protect the client's rights during sentencing.
- Did not insure that the case could be properly appealed.
- Did not take a key witnesses deposition.
- Did not avoid conflicts of interest: the lawyer represented multiple parties (see Chapter 3).
- Did not call necessary witnesses at trial.
- Did not advise the client about how to plead.

Estate Planning and Probate

◆ Did not correctly identify the intended beneficiaries to a will.

◆ Did not advise the client about changes in the law that may alter documents previously executed.

◆ Did not foresee problems arising due to former spouses.

◆ Did not include possible future inheritances.

◆ Did not counsel regarding tax consequences.

◆ Did not correctly designate personal representatives, trustees, or guardians.

◆ Did not avoid conflicts of interest: the lawyer was a beneficiary, or the lawyer represented both the estate and a beneficiary, personal representative, or trustee, or the lawyer represented multiple beneficiaries with competing interests.

◆ Did not advise the client about potential litigation.

◆ Did not advise the personal representative about a possible wrongful death claim or medical malpractice claim.

Family Law

◆ Did not avoid conflicts of interest by representing both spouses in a divorce.

◆ Did not properly serve the other party to a lawsuit.

◆ Did not counsel client about possible interests in spouse's retirement benefits.

◆ Did not protect support or visitation rights.

◆ Did not get assignment of ownership in life insurance policies.

◆ Did not counsel about custody rights.

◆ Did not get the court's continuing jurisdiction for purposes of support or alimony.

◆ Did not prepare and file the final decree of divorce until final payment of legal fees.

◆ Did not counsel the client about the consequences of either a pre- or post-nuptial agreement.

Real Estate Law

- ◆ Did not avoid conflicts of interest by representing multiple parties with adverse interests.
- ◆ Did not accurately describe the real estate in documents.
- ◆ Did not find existing liens against the property.
- ◆ Did not counsel clients about tax consequences.
- ◆ Did not give informed opinions about the value of the property.
- ◆ Did not review documents before closing to insure correctness.
- ◆ Did not modify standard forms to correspond to the transaction.
- ◆ Did not insure that the title commitment was current at time of closing.
- ◆ Did not file closing documents.

Any Litigation Practice

These problems are in addition to any specific problems listed in the sections above if litigation is involved.

- ◆ Did not abide by applicable statutes of limitations, procedural deadlines, or time constraints.
- ◆ Guaranteed a result and then failed to achieve it. (Any time a lawyer guarantees a result, consider it a red flag.)
- ◆ Did not select the proper jurisdiction.
- ◆ Did not follow through on filing a claim.
- ◆ Did not avoid conflicts of interest by representing multiple parties.
- ◆ Did not complete or do any *discovery* when necessary. (Discovery refers to depositions, requests for admissions, and subpoenaing documents and other tangible items for examination and interrogatories.)
- ◆ Did not proceed in a timely manner because the client was lax in paying. (In this case, the lawyer should advise the client that he or she would not be able to continue without payment and allow the client the option of finding other counsel. Sometimes, however, a lawyer will be precluded from withdrawing as counsel if it would jeopardize the client's case.)

> **Example**: Larry Lawyer tries to withdraw two days before trial because Clyde Client has not paid any of his legal fees. If Larry is permitted to withdraw, it will likely be detrimental to Clyde's case. Courts try to protect clients like Clyde from this, as it often jeopardizes the client's position. Larry may not be permitted to withdraw at this late date. Larry will be required to put forth his best effort on the matter.

- Did not allege a worthy defense on the client's behalf.
- Did not appear in court on the client's behalf. (An appearance may be either in person or in the form of some document, such as an *answer*, showing that the client is aware of the lawsuit by responding to it in some manner.)
- Did not fight a motion for summary judgment. (If the opposing party gets a motion for summary judgment, you lose without a trial and without an opportunity to tell your side of the story.)
- Did not offer or object to evidence.
- Did not adequately investigate the client's claim.
- Did not file timely notice of appeal or perfect the appeal.

–2–
BREACHES OF CONTRACT

Suing your lawyer for *breach of contract* is a separate and distinct action from a lawsuit for malpractice. A breach of contract occurs when one of the contracting parties does not fulfill contractual promises made to you.

LEGAL DEFINITION OF A CONTRACT
The term *contract*, as most commonly used, refers to the written document containing all the terms and conditions to which the parties involved have agreed. In legal terms, however, a contract is a *promise* or set of promises that the law will enforce. The promise is a commitment made by someone to do (or not do) some act in the future. Fulfilling the promise, in legal terms, is called *performance*.

In most attorney-client situations, you have bought the services of an attorney and the attorney promises to perform certain legal services on your behalf. You likewise promise to pay a fee for those services when the lawyer bills you. The contract is fulfilled when your lawyer completes the job and you finish paying the bill.

CONTRACT PROCESS
The agreement process itself may be done:

- during face-to-face negotiations;
- by exchanging letters;
- by fax or telephone;
- by handshake; or,
- by signing a printed form spelling out all the terms.

A contract is formed whenever one person makes an *offer* and the other person *accepts* that offer. The following example of an electrician illustrates *offer and acceptance* as the basis for a contract.

> ***Example:*** You call the electrician, Mr. Jones, and ask for assistance with a wiring problem. The conversation may go something like this:
> **You:** "Mr. Jones, I seem to have a problem with the lights in the living room. They blink on and off. It's driving me crazy. What do you think it is?"
> **Jones:** "Sounds like a wiring problem. I can come over at 3 p.m. today to fix it, if you'll be there. I charge $45 per hour plus parts. I accept cash, local check, or credit card." [Jones has just offered his services for $45 per hour.]
> **You:** "Okay. I can be here. I'll write you a check for the amount."

You have just accepted Jones' offer. This entire transaction occurred over the telephone, yet a contract was just formed because there was an offer and an acceptance. If you had rejected Mr. Jones' fee or could not be available at 3 p.m., no contract would have been formed because you would not have accepted the offer. By agreeing, you have each made yourselves legally obligated to perform certain acts. You have agreed to be home at 3 p.m. and to let Mr. Jones into your home. He agreed to fix your wiring problem and you agreed to pay him his fee. You both now have a *legal duty* to complete these acts.

Similarly, when you seek legal services from an attorney, you agree to pay the attorney's fee and he or she agrees to do work for that fee. A contract has been formed.

CONTRACTING WITH YOUR LAWYER

When you go to a lawyer, he or she will likely have you sign a written document. This contract, which may also be called a *fee agreement, employment agreement, engagement letter,* or *representation letter,* will spell out all the terms and conditions under which the lawyer will perform services on your behalf. These terms and conditions are the legal duties and obligations to which you will both be bound. Some of the terms may include:

- fee charged (see Chapter 5 on client funds to learn more about the types of fees charged by lawyers) and how fees are to be paid;
- costs that may be charged, including court costs, photocopy charges, and long distance phone call fees;
- time that will be expended on your case;
- the exact services that will be performed, such as drafting a will, obtaining a divorce, writing a letter on your behalf, collecting or defending a debt, or filing bankruptcy for you;
- any retainer required (see Chapter 5 on client funds to learn more about retainers); and,
- terms by which the attorney may withdraw from employment. (You may discharge the lawyer at any time.)

Usually the attorney will require a written agreement. In fact, in many states, certain types of cases and fee arrangements are required by law to be in writing. (For example, in many states a *contingency fee arrangement* must be in writing.) A written contract is explicit in its terms. It is possible, however, that you and your attorney did not sign a written contract. In the electrician illustration above, no written contract was ever signed. Does this mean that you cannot have a suit for breach of contract? No.

Since a contract occurs when there is an offer and an acceptance of that offer, your agreement with the lawyer may very well have been oral. This is still a legitimate contract. Proof of an oral contract's terms is more difficult, but will not preclude the possibility that your attorney will be found to have breached the contract. The existence of a contract, and therefore an attorney-client relationship, will depend on the facts and circumstances of the situation.

Example: A Florida court found that, although there was no written contract between the attorney and client, an oral contract had been created. During the lawsuit, the client was able to produce office records with notes of appointments, phone records showing calls between her and the attorney, and testimony by a witness who said that the attorney claimed he was representing the client. The court found that the evidence was sufficient to support a claim of attorney-client relationship despite the lack of a written contract.

HOW A CONTRACT IS BREACHED

When people make agreements, they usually assume they will complete their obligations. In other words, when people make a contract, they probably do not intend to breach it.

How does someone *breach* a contract? A person breaches a contract when he or she does not uphold his or her end of the bargain. This is called *nonperformance*.

Example: Adam contracts with Bob Builder to construct a new house. Bob promises to build the house and Adam promises to pay Bob $175,000 upon completion of the project. If Bob does not complete the project, he has breached the contract and Adam does not have to pay. On the other hand, if Bob completes the project and Adam refuses to pay, Bob breached the contract. Adam's obligation to pay is conditioned on whether or not Bob completes the project. If Bob does not build, Adam does not have to pay.

What would happen if Adam had agreed to pay Bob a certain amount each month?

Example: Bob agrees to construct the house in five months for $175,000, with Adam paying $35,000 each month during construction. If Adam forgets to pay Bob the third installment, Bob may be able to assume Adam is breaching the contract. By the same token, if Adam pays the first three

$35,000 installments but Bob quits building in the fourth month, Adam may assume that Bob is breaching the contract.

Bob's duty is *discharged* when he builds Adam's house and Adam's duty to pay Bob is discharged when he completes the payment schedule. Any failure to perform by either of them is a *breach of contract*. If either fails to perform their respective obligations, they are not discharged. *Nonperformance* will prevent discharge.

Breach by Your Lawyer

Your lawyer will breach the contract if he or she fails to perform the services promised. Some examples of breach of contract by attorneys are:

- not prosecuting a workmen's compensation claim;
- failure to prepare a contract transferring the interest in real property to another person;
- failure to file a timely appeal;
- improperly examining and reporting on title to property;
- improperly drafting a will;
- failing to draft a will in the manner the client wanted it drafted; and,
- failure to make a claim for personal injuries within the time allotted by law.

This list is certainly not exhaustive and is only meant to illustrate that if your lawyer failed to perform the obligations he or she promised to do, you may have an action for breach of contract. It is important to determine what obligations your lawyer incurred when you hired him or her. Then you can determine what constitutes a breach of contract.

There are a few questions you should ask yourself when trying to decide if you are dealing with breach of contract.

- Was there a written contract? Remember that while a contract does not have to be written, it is much easier to prove a breach of contract if you have something in writing. If the contract was oral, you will need to gather as much information as possible that will prove that the lawyer had an obligation to represent you. Phone calls, a third party who will attest that the lawyer said he or she was your lawyer, and letters written on your behalf, will all lead toward the conclusion that a contract existed.

♦ Once you have established that there was a contract between you and your lawyer, determine what duties your lawyer owed you.

> **Example:** If your lawyer was going to draft a will for you and did not, you have an obvious breach of contract. If, however, your lawyer was supposed to handle a personal injury claim, the duties your lawyer owed you may not be so clear cut. You will have to find out what a personal injury lawyer must do to fulfill his or her obligations to a client.

Some of the expected action a personal injury lawyer will do is to find witnesses, take depositions, call the opposing side and try to achieve a settlement, and determine if the other party had insurance that would cover the injury. (This list, however, is by no means exhaustive of the duties a personal injury lawyer has when representing a client. You must decide if your lawyer failed to do the minimum that any lawyer practicing law in that specialty would have done.)

♦ What remedy or remedies do you think are available to you? (See the next section of this chapter to help you decide what remedies would be appropriate in your situation.)

♦ Do you want to take your lawyer to court? (see Chapter 6 on *Lawsuits*.)

♦ Do you want to file a grievance against the lawyer? (see Chapter 7 on *Ethical Violations*.)

Once you decide to file a lawsuit against your lawyer, the remedies available to you become important.

REMEDIES FOR BREACH OF CONTRACT

Remedies are either:

♦ legal or equitable;
♦ specific or substitutional; or,
♦ restitutionary.

Legal or Equitable

A court granting a *legal remedy* will award the injured person a sum of money.

> *Example:* When Bob Builder built Adam's home and Adam promised to pay $175,000, if Adam did not pay, the court could *order* him to pay. The award would be a legal remedy. It gives Bob the performance he was promised, in this case, a sum of money.

When a court grants an *equitable remedy*, it is enforcing a contract by requiring action (or to stop an action). This means that the court is going to require the person in the wrong to perform as he or she promised, or enjoin a person from doing something.

> *Example:* John asks his neighbor's son, Jim, to mow his yard and Jim agrees. Jim does not mow the lawn. If John took Jim to court for breach of contract (not a likely scenario), the court may require Jim to mow the yard. In other words, perform what he promised John.

> *Example:* Bill likes to play loud music during the day. No ordinance prohibits him from doing so. I work nights however, and the music keeps me awake. I offer to pay Bill $100 per week if he refrains from playing the loud music and he agrees. Two weeks later, Bill plays loud music at 2 p.m. A court may require Bill to refrain from playing the music as originally promised, or enjoin a person from doing something.

Specific or Substantial

In addition to being either legal or equitable, remedies are either *specific* or *substantial*. *Specific remedies* are intended to give the injured person the performance that was promised.

> **Example:** Jim promised to mow the lawn, but did not do it. A court may require him to mow the lawn.

This is called specific performance and it is both an equitable remedy and a specific remedy. A remedy is *substitutional* if it substitutes something for what the injured party originally wanted.

> **Example:** You ordered a new refrigerator from a department store and the store did not deliver it. Instead of ordering the store to give you a refrigerator (a specific remedy), the court may order the store to pay you monetary damages equal to the value of the refrigerator.

Restitutionary

The purpose of *restitution* is to place both parties in the position they were in before they entered into the contract. At one time, a client who had received services from an attorney could not bring an action for restitution. This is not true any longer.

If there is a total breach of contract, the wronged party may cancel the contract and seek restitution. This means that if your attorney breaches the contract he or she has with you, you can give the attorney notice that the contract is cancelled (in effect, you fire him or her) and seek to be returned as closely as possible to your pre-contract position. Your recovery will be for any sums already paid to the attorney, less the value of any services performed on your behalf. If any of the contract has been performed by the attorney, you will be unable to obtain restitution for the portion performed.

> **Example:** You hire Sam Lawyer to handle your divorce and a contract is signed. Martinez files a petition with the court on your behalf and has a copy served on your spouse as required. So far, Sam is doing what you hired him to do.

Your spouse's lawyer sends *interrogatories* (special questions that you are required to answer and return to the other party) along with the answer to the divorce petition. Sam neglects to have the interrogatories answered within the obligatory period of time. The court levies sanctions against you.

Unhappy with what transpired, you cancel the contract with Sam and request back the money you paid as a *retainer*. If a lawsuit for restitution occurs, Sam would be obliged to pay all of the money you forwarded to him less the value of the services he rendered (i.e., the filing of the petition and service on the opposing party).

You must choose the remedy you pursue, carefully. In general, you will be required to elect to either accept damages (discussed earlier in the chapter) or restitution because you will not be able to accept both restitution and damages.

Example: Consider the situation in which you had hired Sam Lawyer to handle your divorce. If, by Sam's failure to file the answers to the interrogatories, you lost your home or were not awarded alimony or child support, restitution would not appear to be an adequate remedy for the breach of contract. Restitution will not compensate you for those losses. Only a suit for damages will compensate you.

However, if Sam failed to file the petition in a timely manner and you cancel the contract, you may feel that the only thing you lost was time. It may be in your best interest to sue solely for restitution.

Keep in mind that a breach of contract may actually be easier to prove than a negligence action. You do not necessarily have to prove that the lawyer failed to keep a certain *standard of care* (see previous chapter on malpractice), but just that a violation of the contract occurred. You may also wish to consider filing both a negligence and breach of contract action against your lawyer.

–3–
CONFLICTS OF INTEREST

Lawyers have a duty to zealously represent their clients. This single-minded endeavor has certain limitation. A lawyer cannot break the law to represent a client, but one way lawyers stay focused is to avoid conflicts of interest. While a lawyer's attention may be divided among many clients, the interests of those clients must not directly be at odds with one another.

DEFINITION OF CONFLICT OF INTEREST

A *conflict of interest* occurs when someone's loyalties are divided and he or she is unable to render an unbiased, objective opinion or act in an objective manner. You have probably heard about doctors who will not operate on family members. The doctors do not want to have to make life and death decisions for loved ones. If your spouse (parent, sibling, child) was on the operating table and the doctor's choices were amputation or likely death, would you want to be the doctor making that decision? Could you? It is a difficult enough decision to make when you are not emotionally involved. Emotional involvement makes such a decision nearly impossible.

It is the same for lawyers. A lawyer should avoid conflicts of interest. There are ethical rules governing much of this (see Chapter 7). An attorney may also be sued for negligence if he or she crosses boundaries and renders an opinion that is not in the client's best interest due to a conflict of interest. The example dealing with doctors played on the conflict of emotions. Other potential areas of conflict are social and business related.

Lawyers are expected to perform duties for their clients in an impartial manner. It is so important for an attorney to remain essentially neutral because lawyers owe their clients:

- privacy and confidentiality (all secrets and confidences are preserved) and
- absolute loyalty.

It is difficult to preserve a client's confidentiality if the lawyer must tell the information to a second client in order to successfully represent the second client. An attorney cannot be absolutely loyal to one client if the attorney has conflicting loyalties or interests.

DUAL REPRESENTATION

Dual representation occurs when a lawyer simultaneously represents two clients with conflicting interests in the same matter. This, in and of itself, is not unusual. Lawyers often represent many clients at the same time. Dual representation only applies when the clients' interests conflict with each other.

In general, such simultaneous representation is either barred by ethics rules (see Chapter 7) or discouraged by them. Although there have been cases in which a lawyer was not barred from simultaneously representing two clients with adverse interests, it is not common or desirable.

As discussed above, a lawyer must hold a client's confidences and secrets totally and completely private as well as be absolutely loyal to that client's interests. When a lawyer is representing clients with conflicting interests, it is, at the very least, a tight-rope walk without a net for the lawyer. At the worst, it is disastrous and detrimental to one or both clients.

Example: Attorney Rob represents the local newspaper, *The Daily Newsrag*, whose editor-in-chief confides in Rob about its policies and procedures, including some that may be considered illegally discriminatory. Rob has, on many occasions, represented the newspaper against discharged employees, disgruntled readers and journalists, and the occasional celebrity suing for libel.

Polly Perk, a town socialite, goes to Rob and asks him to represent her. The newspaper printed a story in the gossip column alleging that Polly was having an affair with the owner of a local bar and grille. This story has upset both Polly and her husband. Polly wants to sue the newspaper and the gossip columnist for libel.

How can Rob represent Polly when he represents *The Daily Newsrag*? The newspaper's and Polly's interests are completely opposite. If he represents one zealously, as a good lawyer should, he will obviously be neglectful in his representation of the other. This is the ultimate danger in dual representation.

Other common examples of dual representation are:

◆ representing multiple criminal defendants for a crime in which more than one of these defendants played a part;
◆ representing an insured person against an insurance company that the lawyer currently represents; or,
◆ representing both parties in a divorce.

This may have particularly disastrous effects. In an Oregon case, for example, a lawyer represented both husband and wife in a divorce. The settlement agreement permitted the refinancing of the house so that it could be remodeled and sold. The attorney had the wife sign a document giving the husband the power to borrow the money using the house as collateral and obligate the wife to the loan's repayment. The husband borrowed money, kept it, and ran off. The lender foreclosed and the wife lost the equity in the house.

The Oregon Court of Appeals held that the lawyer did not protect the wife's interests in the divorce. The lawyer could not have fulfilled his duty to protect her interests, because he was also bound by a duty to protect the husband's interests. He knew the husband was having financial troubles and should have realized the husband might run off with the money.

SUCCESSIVE REPRESENTATION

A related potential area for conflict of interest is *successive representation*. This occurs when an attorney is representing a client whose interests are in opposition to a prior client's interests. A common situation is when a couple divorces and the client's previous spouse later asks the lawyer to represent him in a matter regarding the divorce.

> **Example:** Bob and Betty Jones decide to divorce. Betty goes to Ms. Smith and secures her legal services. One year after the divorce is finalized, Bob determines that the child custody arrangement must be changed. He liked Smith's demeanor and the way she handled Betty's case so Bob calls Smith and asks her to represent him in the child custody matter.
>
> Although Betty is no longer Smith's client, Smith cannot represent Bob. Since Smith represented Betty in the original lawsuit, any representation of Bob in the related child custody suit is a conflict of interest.

CONFLICTING BUSINESS INTERESTS

A lawyer must put aside all personal feelings and beliefs when a client needs representation. It may be difficult for the general public to understand, but lawyers are taught to do this in law school. Otherwise, many people would never receive the benefit of legal counsel. However, lawyers are people too, and occasions arise in which it is impossible for the lawyer to put aside those personal feelings. Sometimes a lawyer's business interests get in the way of the lawyer's ability to give a client impartial advice.

> **Example:** Bill asks Amy Attorney to sue ABC Corporation on his behalf and Amy is a major stockholder in ABC. Amy will be totally incapable of giving Bill the complete representation he should expect. Giving Bill proper representation may

mean that her earning potential (dividends, higher stock prices) would be decreased if the lawsuit was successful. It could, in the extreme, mean that the corporation could become bankrupt. These outcomes are not in Amy's best interest. She cannot possibly give Bill impartial, objective advice. It is presumed that she is looking out for her own interests.

PERSONAL INTERESTS

Any situation in which you and your lawyer may have opposing interests is one that your lawyer should avoid.

Example: You ask your lawyer to draft a document in which you state your wish that all life support be withheld if you are terminally ill and cannot make your wish known at the time due to physical or mental incompetence. This is known as a *living will.* This type of document, while legal in most states, goes against your lawyer's personal, ethical, moral, and religious beliefs. He or she is vehemently against these documents, but agrees to draft it for you.

As stated above, lawyers are trained to break faith with their personal feelings in an effort to assist and represent clients in the best way possible. Yet, a lawyer who is so fervent in his or her personal beliefs should avoid handling any type of case in which personal feelings may cloud his or her judgment. In addition, if the lawyer is required to be a witness in any action brought concerning this living will, he or she will be unlikely to defend or support the document. The client requires, and should expect, an unbiased opinion.

In the example just given, the lawyer is so vehemently against living wills that it is unlikely he will be capable of rendering an impartial opinion. His judgment will be tainted. This is not because he is a bad attorney, but because his personal feelings will prevent him from giving you the complete benefit of his legal expertise.

SEXUAL RELATIONSHIPS WITH CLIENTS

Until rather recently, there was little that specifically prohibited a lawyer from having sexual relations with a client. Law students were occasionally warned that it might cause problems with clients. Lawyers were reminded that it *didn't look good*. Some lawyers were reprimanded for the *appearances of impropriety*, lack of competence, or a lack of fitness to practice law. In the 1980s, we laughed when Arnie Becker, the divorce lawyer on L. A. Law, finagled his way into his clients' beds. Today, this behavior is largely considered a breach of ethical duty and a matter for discipline of the attorney.

How is having sex with a client a conflict of interest? This may be best illustrated by specific examples of cases in which lawyers were brought to task for having sexual relations with a client.

- ◆ A lawyer sexually touched and took semi-nude photographs of a female client, claiming the touching and photos were necessary to assess a personal injury claim.
- ◆ A lawyer initiated a sexual relationship with his client who wanted a divorce. He then initiated legal actions on her behalf without her knowledge or consent.
- ◆ A lawyer gave some clients the opportunity to waive their fees by posing nude or semi-nude for photographs.

This behavior may make it impossible for the lawyer to render the complete and competent assistance that is required. A California court probably said it best: "Emotional detachment is essential to the lawyer's ability to render competent legal services." It is almost impossible to be emotionally detached when a sexual relationship is involved.

In many states, having a sexual relationship with a client is a specific ethical violation. (This will be discussed in Chapter 7.)

WHEN THE LAWYER BECOMES A WITNESS

This potential conflict becomes an issue when the lawyer learns he or she may become a witness. A witness has a duty to tell the truth. A lawyer on the witness stand must therefore tell the truth also. His or her testimony may, however, be discounted by the *trier of fact* (usually the jury, but sometimes a judge) or create an appearance of impropriety. The jury may believe that the lawyer will lie in order to advance his or her client's position. In addition, the lawyer's testimony may diminish his or her credibility in the jury's eyes. Very often the jury will look at the lawyer with a jaundiced eye from that time forward, no matter how effectively he or she performs in the courtroom as a lawyer. Either of these situations may jeopardize the client's position and must therefore be avoided.

WAIVER OF CONFLICT

A client is in the position to *waive*, or give up, the conflict, but the waiver must be informed and completely voluntary. In some states such as Wisconsin, the waiver must be in writing. The requirement of *informed waiver* means that your attorney must have given you all the facts of the situation causing the conflict. Your lawyer may not leave anything out. Leaving out vital information because he or she thinks the information will be unpalatable to you and keep you from making the waiver will invalidate the waiver. Voluntariness means that your lawyer may not use any form of coercion to get a waiver from you. In some of the examples above, such as taking nude pictures of the client or having an affair with the client, it is unlikely that a client will be capable of giving a waiver that will not be construed as coerced, due to the sensitive nature of the relationship created with the lawyer.

—4—
INEFFECTIVE ASSISTANCE OF COUNSEL

The Sixth Amendment to the United States Constitution states "[I]n all criminal prosecutions, the accused shall...have the Assistance of Counsel for his defense." What that amendment actually means has been the subject of several court cases that have reached the United State's Supreme Court. Ineffective assistance of counsel only applies to criminal actions. If you hire an attorney for a civil action (divorce, wills, bankruptcy, etc), this is not a viable argument if you think your attorney did not do a good job.

HISTORY OF THE SUPREME COURT'S INTERPRETATION

Until 1932, this constitutional right was interpreted to mean that a defendant was entitled to receive assistance of counsel, but only if he or she could afford to hire an attorney. Someone who could not afford counsel received no help from the government. In *Powell v. Alabama*, however, the Supreme Court first recognized that an indigent defendant was entitled to have counsel appointed if a capital crime was involved. In 1938, the Supreme Court extended the right to include the appointment of counsel in any federal prosecution. Then in *Gideon v. Wainwright*, a 1963 case, the Supreme Court decided that this right to assistance of counsel was applicable to state prosecutions as well.

It is not enough for a defendant in a criminal action to be represented by any attorney, however. The Supreme Court decided that implicit in the right to counsel was the defendant's entitlement to an attorney that would provide *effective* representation; someone that would aid in assuring fairness in a necessarily adversarial process. This means that a defendant has a right to an attorney who has the degree of competence demanded of attorneys in criminal cases.

DETERMINING EFFECTIVENESS

Whether an attorney has provided effective assistance of counsel in a criminal case is not based on whether the attorney has committed any errors in his or her representation of a defendant. Instead, it is based on a two-step test that was set forth by the Supreme Court in *Strickland v. Washington*, a 1984 case. According to this test, the defendant must first prove that the attorney was incompetent and second, that due to that incompetence, the defendant's case was prejudiced.

INCOMPETENCE

In *ineffective assistance* of counsel cases, the test for *incompetence* is whether the lawyer's performance "fell below an objective standard of reasonableness." *Reasonableness* is based on professional standards at the time.

The Supreme Court, by refusing to establish specific guidelines, left the issue of whether an attorney was incompetent to the judges' discretion. In fact, the Supreme Court specifically said that the judge should be very mindful of the attorney's role and avoid being an armchair quarterback. In effect, the Supreme Court was saying that we all know that hindsight is 20/20 and holding a lawyer to that standard would be unfair. The judge must then evaluate the attorney's conduct from the attorney's viewpoint at the time of the representation. It is, therefore, presumed that the attorney's conduct was correct and perhaps nothing more than sound trial strategy gone awry. It is up to the defendant to prove otherwise.

PREJUDICE

The Supreme Court has ruled that the proper standard for measuring prejudice is whether it is reasonably probable that, but for the attorney's unprofessional errors, the trial's results would have been different. The question is then, were the lawyer's errors sufficient to weaken the reliance on the outcome of the case?

This does not mean that there was automatically prejudice where the attorney committed errors and the defendant lost the case. Instead, the judge is supposed to look at whether the trial's result was unfair.

PROVING INEFFECTIVENESS
The test to establish ineffective assistance of counsel is a difficult one to pass. An extensive study made by Professor James Liebman of Columbia University School of Law, *A Broken System: Error Rates in Capital Cases, 1973-1995*, found that the overall rate of prejudicial error in capital cases was 68%. Courts found serious errors in nearly 7 out of every 10 of the capital cases reviewed. This study was undertaken at the request of the U.S. Senate Committee on the Judiciary and covered the years 1973-1995. Janet Reno, the United States Attorney General at the time of the study stated, "Our system (of criminal justice) will work only if we provide every defendant with competent counsel." (It should be noted however, that another study shows that in reality, only about 25% of cases are overturned on appeal.)

What does this mean in regards to proving an ineffective assistance of counsel claim? It means that it is a very difficult standard to prove. The actions of your attorney, or in most cases the *inaction*, must be extreme and beyond reasonableness. Perfection or achieving an acquittal is not required.

However, as recently as 2003, an Ineffective Assistance case reached the Supreme Court. This case, *Wiggins v. Smith*, affirmed the Strickland Standard, but did find that the attorney failed to act reasonably under the circumstances of that case.

RECOGNIZING INEFFECTIVE ASSISTANCE OF COUNSEL
It may sound absurd to say this in a self-help legal book, and especially in a book about legal malpractice, but if you think you have an ineffective assistance claim, you should consider talking to an

appellate attorney who specializes in criminal law. The reason for this is simple. This is a tricky area. Proving the two-step test is not easy. A qualified lawyer may be able to make arguments in your favor that you may not have considered.

Barring your ability or desire to consult another lawyer, if you, a friend or loved one is in a situation where a criminal conviction is involved, follow the steps below to determine if you have any chance of advancing an ineffective assistance of counsel claim. These steps will not insure that you will prevail, but not following these steps will probably mean failure.

Investigating whether or not you should pursue a claim will require that you do the following.

- ◆ **Collect all relevant data.** You must be thoroughly familiar with the case. You should ask for the entire trial record. This will include the clerk's and court reporter's transcripts; the court clerk's file, and your former lawyer's file. If possible you will have to talk to your former lawyer about why he or she did or did not do certain things either in preparation for or during the trial. It is important not to alienate your former lawyer. If you do, he or she will probably be unwilling to talk to you.
- ◆ **Determine if the information collected indicates that your former lawyer was ineffective.** You will at this point be required to apply the first step of the test. Was the lawyer's conduct on par with current standards for the average criminal trial attorney? This test does not require flawlessness or vast experience. It just requires that he or she display reasonable conduct. (Remember that courts will presume that a lawyer's actions were reasonable.)

    This following list may give you some guidance when trying to decide if your lawyer was incompetent.
    - • Did your attorney meet with you to discuss the case without delay and as often as necessary?
    - • Did your attorney advise you of your rights promptly and take all necessary actions to preserve those rights?

- Did the attorney try to get you out on bail on your own recognizance pending trial or did he or she just let you sit in jail for six months before trial?
- Did the attorney make necessary motions for pretrial psychiatric examinations or try to have evidence suppressed?
- Did your attorney investigate all defenses available to you?
- Did the attorney interview all available witnesses? Did he or she try to discover all the information that the prosecutor or police had?
- Did your lawyer make a tactical decision that no other competent criminal lawyer would have made in a similar situation?
- Did the attorney volunteer information to the court that would be damaging to you? (A lawyer cannot do this.)

◆ **Determine if your lawyer's conduct prejudiced you.** Remember that the test requires you to show that, but for your lawyer's conduct, the trial's result would have been different.

◆ **Determine if pursuing this will ultimately be helpful.** If you can determine that your lawyer was indeed incompetent and that your trial was prejudiced, you should then decide if pursuing the issue will be helpful. If a successful, ineffective assistance of counsel claim lands the victorious defendant in jail for a longer sentence, it would not be helpful to pursue that claim. This occasionally happens when a plea bargain is involved. For example, if the plea bargain included throwing out a few other crimes in an effort to get the bargain, the prosecutor may want to pursue those claims after the defendant wins an ineffective assistance claim.

Another potential problem involves the *attorney-client privilege.* Usually, anything said between a client and his or her attorney is confidential. With few exceptions, the attorney is prohibited from telling anyone what the client said. An attorney who is being accused of ineffective assistance, however, may be able to divulge information to the court that would be damaging to the defendant. That information could get the defendant in more trouble. The attorney may not automatically get to tell the court everything, however.

It is important to research your state's laws concerning attorney-client privilege and the waiver of that privilege. If your state has determined that filing an ineffective assistance claim creates a waiver (abandonment), of the defendant's right to preserve confidential conversation with an attorney, it will be important to decide if anything you told your former attorney could hurt you. If that information will cause more harm than good, you may not want to pursue this claim.

–5–
FINANCIAL MISCONDUCT

Complaints about fees usually center on whether or not a lawyer charged too much, or having been fired, refused to return money advanced by the client. Trust account violations usually deal with either *commingling* of client funds with the attorney's funds or *outright theft* of funds.

TYPES OF FEES LAWYERS CHARGE

Flat Fees
A flat fee is a set amount for which the attorney agrees to render specified services. For example, it is not uncommon for a lawyer to charge a flat fee to draft a will, handle an uncontested divorce, or preside over a real estate closing. The lawyer will perform the services agreed to regardless of the length of time the services take to accomplish.

Hourly Rate
In this case, the client agrees to pay a set amount for each hour that the lawyer expends in performing legal services. The hourly rate may be different for each type of case and may greatly differ between lawyers, although there is usually a range of rates that lawyers in a geographic area charge.

> **Example:** Adam Attorney has an hourly rate of $300 per hour. His associate, Nelly Newattorney, has an hourly rate of $150 per hour. When Adam works on Joe Client's case, for a

total of 4 hours, Joe is charged $1200 for Adam's time. When Nelly works on the case at Adam's direction, for another 4 hours, Joe is charged an additional $600.

Contingency Fees

When a lawyer agrees to take a percentage of a settlement or judgment awarded to the client, the fee is *contingent*. The lawyer will not get a fee unless the client is given an amount of money from the case. The percentage the lawyer charges may be regulated by state law and may fluctuate depending upon the type of case involved. In general, the percentage is never more than one third of the award unless the case is taken up on appeal, in which case the percentage may be higher.

Your agreement with the lawyer should have specified a percentage. If it did not and the lawyer is asking for what seems to be an unreasonable amount, it probably is. Contingency fees are often prohibited in certain types of cases, including child custody, criminal matters, and divorce. Many states require the contingency agreement be in writing, as well.

Retainers

Most attorneys initially take fees through a *retainer*. The retainer is an amount paid when the lawyer is hired initially, to assure the client that the lawyer will perform work and assure the lawyer of payment for at least part of the services rendered. Very often part or all of the retainer is deemed *nonrefundable*.

Refundable v. nonrefundable. A *nonrefundable retainer* allows the attorney to keep money advanced to him or her, regardless of whether or not the attorney actually performs the agreed services.

This type of retainer is not to be confused with a *refundable retainer*, which is really payment in advance. Any funds which are part of a refundable retainer are credited against any services performed and any excess must be returned to the client when the attorney's obligation has been fulfilled.

Example: Attorney Smith collects a $500 refundable retainer from Joe Client when he agrees to handle a minor traffic violation problem for Joe. They agree that Smith's hourly rate will be $175 per hour plus costs (which Joe also pays up front). Smith handles the problem in two hours and bills Joe for $350. Since he has a $500 retainer, Smith deducts the $350 earned from the retainer and gives the $150 excess back to Joe. If the retainer was nonrefundable, however, Smith could keep the entire $500.

However, if Smith took 4 hours to complete the task and billed Joe $700, he would bill Joe for $200, the difference between the $500 retainer and the $200 balance.

General retainer. A fixed sum paid by the client to insure the attorney's availability is called a *general retainer*. When a lawyer is paid this sum, the lawyer promises to be available whenever the client needs the lawyer's services. This fee is in addition to whatever flat fee or hourly rate the lawyer will be paid for rendering the services. Such fees are not considered nonrefundable, although they are not returned to the client, because it has been interpreted that they are earned when paid.

In many respects, this type of retainer is similar to renting a house with an option to buy it. When the option is taken, an additional sum of money is paid up front. This sum gives the renter the first right to purchase the property if the owner decides to sell. If the holder does not purchase the property, he or she does not get the money back. The purpose of the payment was merely to hold the option open. Similarly, the purpose of paying a general retainer is to hold the attorney's time open for any matter that might arise for the client.

VALIDITY OF NONREFUNDABLE RETAINERS

While it is legal for an attorney to ask for a nonrefundable retainer in almost all jurisdictions, there are cases suggesting that these retainers are falling out of favor. Two separate New York courts have held that nonrefundable retainers are unethical and are, therefore, invalid. One of the courts went as far as to declare them illegal.

It is recognized in a majority of states that a client has the right to discharge an attorney at any time and without any cause. The client should be able to fire the attorney without penalty. This serves as a basis for finding nonrefundable retainers unethical or illegal as a client who wants to discharge a lawyer cannot do so without penalty if a nonrefundable retainer is involved. The retainer itself becomes a penalty because the client will be deprived of the amount of money retained by the lawyer.

Example: Amy gives Larry Lawyer at $2000 nonrefundable retainer. Amy is unhappy with Larry's services and decides to fire him after Larry has expended 3 hours of legal services at $150 an hour. If Amy has paid Larry a nonrefundable retainer, she is giving Larry $1550 more than he earned. That's a very large penalty for most people.

If, on the other hand, she gave him a refundable retainer, she would be getting back the $1550 remaining, less any fees and expenses Larry may have incurred on Amy's behalf.

It may be too soon in most states to make a claim that nonrefundable retainers are unethical or illegal. It may be entirely possible, however, to attempt an argument that the retainer, rather than being unethical or illegal, is excessive.

EXCESSIVE FEES

Attorneys may not charge clients excessive fees for legal work. All legal fees must be reasonable based on the circumstances.

Some companies have claimed that excessive attorney fees were making it difficult for them to emerge successfully from bankruptcy. (Companies in Chapter 11 bankruptcy try to reorganize instead of going out of business.) It was also reported that immigration lawyers were charging excessive fees for those people entering the country due to the visa lottery, and that corporations were cutting back on outside counsel and looking for other ways to reduce attorneys' fees. These are just a few of the incidents of fee abuse reported in major newspapers and magazines.

Whether the fee is excessive depends on the circumstances. What seems excessive, may actually be considered a reasonable fee. Based upon the lawyer's location, the community where the lawyer practices, the customary charges in the area, education, expertise, experience, and the size of the law firm, as well as the complexity of the matter, a lawyer's rates may seem exorbitant, but indeed be considered a reasonable fee.

Sometimes there is a specific statute or code provision prohibiting a lawyer from charging an excessive fee. However, in the absence of such a law, a lawyer may still be held accountable for charging an unreasonable fee. The standard to determine if the fee was excessive is based on asking if the fee charged was so exorbitant and disproportionate to the services rendered that a person's conscious would be shocked.

The following list of questions may help you determine if the fee charged was reasonable.

- How much time and labor was required? Could the lawyer complete the work in an hour or two, or did the job take ten, twenty, thirty or even one-hundred hours to complete?
- Was the task fairly easy to perform or was it difficult? Was the issue common or was it novel? What skills did the lawyer have to use to perform the task?
- Did your case require the lawyer to turn down other employment? Was it apparent to you that your legal problem required your lawyer to either give up all other legal employment or limit the amount of other work he or she could perform?
- What was the fee customarily charged in your area for similar legal services? Did your lawyer charge $1,000 for a living will when most other lawyers in the area charge $100?
- Was the attorney reputedly the top of the field so that a higher rate would be considered normal and customary? In other words, if Joe Client hired Johnnie Cochran to defend

his murder trial, would it seem unreasonable that Cochran's fee was $500 an hour, while Larry Lawyer would have charged Joe $150 an hour?)

◆   If it was a lawsuit involving money or damages—what was the amount of money involved and what results were obtained?

◆   Did you or the circumstances involved impose time limitations on your lawyer? In other words, did you call the lawyer on Monday at 4 p.m. and insist that the entire estate plan be completed by 8 a.m. Tuesday morning? Or, did you hire a lawyer two days before an important court hearing? A lawyer may charge more if the services must be performed in a very short period of time.

◆   What was the nature and length of your professional relationship with the lawyer?

◆   What was the lawyer's experience, reputation and ability? Was the lawyer new to the field or did the lawyer have years of experience? (If you hire F. Lee Bailey as your criminal lawyer, his reputation alone may raise the fees you are charged.)

◆   Was the fee *fixed* or *contingent*? (Your lawyer is not entitled to a fee if you had a contingency fee arrangement and you were not awarded a settlement or judgment.)

SHARING FEES WITH NONLAWYERS
In general, a lawyer may never share a fee with a nonlawyer. This occurs when a lawyer asks someone else, a nonlawyer, to supply legal business and agrees to pay a percentage of the fee to the nonlawyer. This type of arrangement is specifically prohibited. A lawyer may not pay any type of referral fee to a nonlawyer.

A reason lawyers are prohibited from splitting fees with non-lawyers is to prevent a lawyer from soliciting business, which is also prohibited. For example, lawyers may not solicit business, or as it is commonly known, *chase ambulances*. Ambulance chasing occurs when an attorney, seeing an opportunity to get a new client, inappropriately makes contact with that person. For example, Adam

Attorney reads about a car accident in the news and goes to visit the injured party uninvited. One of the most infamous incidents of ambulance chasing was after the chemical plant explosion in India in which a slew of lawyers travelled to India offering their services to the injured Indians. In John Grisham's *The Rainmaker*, the protagonist sat in the hospital cafeteria preying on the families of sick and injured patients.

In addition, lawyers should not encourage the unlicensed practice of law by unqualified personnel. As explained in the Introduction, lawyers are highly trained professionals. Even though a lawyer's staff may also be trained, the training is not identical or as comprehensive as that of the lawyer. A staff member may believe that he or she can make a legal determination on behalf of a client if the lawyer agrees to share a fee. For this reason, the practice of law by a nonlawyer is strictly prohibited.

This prohibition does not preclude the lawyer from paying staff-persons, however. If the lawyer is paying regular wages to members of the staff, then there is no prohibition. The lawyer may not, however, pay a percentage of your fee to the paralegal that worked on your case.

Even if you learn that your lawyer split a fee with a nonlawyer, you will probably not have grounds for a malpractice suit. You should look, however, at the chapter on filing grievances against attorneys.

PRESERVING CLIENT FUNDS

Preserving the client's funds properly may be the most important responsibility an attorney has in addition to providing competent representation. A lawyer is required to hold a client's money separately from his or her own. In fact, the minute a client's money comes into the attorney's possession that money must be held *in trust*.

A *trust* is a legal term to indicate that any property held is being so held for the benefit of someone else. Any money held in the lawyer's trust account is being held for the benefit of the lawyer's clients and nobody else. In essence then, a trust account is an *escrow account*. The lawyer may not spend the trust money to pay personal expenses, nor may the money be given to another client. The money is yours.

Commingling of Client Funds

In fact, any settlement or judgments collected on the client's behalf must be placed in trust. The lawyer may not, under any circumstances, put the money into a personal or general business account. Such *commingling* is strictly prohibited. Perhaps your lawyer did this, but told you that he or she intended to give you every last penny, and maybe all of the money was repaid. That does not matter. A lawyer's good intentions are not good enough. Your money must be kept separate and apart from the lawyer's money at all times.

> *Example:* Larry Lawyer has fallen on "hard times". Amelia comes in for an estate plan and gives Larry a $1000 refundable retainer that Larry puts in his general business account instead of his trust account. Larry proceeds to pay his electric bill and a week's salary to his secretary. This is prohibited. He cannot commingle his money with a client's money. He has not yet earned Amelia's money.
>
> At the end of the week, Larry drafts Amelia's estate plan and has then earned the money. Despite this, he had not at the time he paid his bills with the money. His actions are prohibited at the time he took the money and his earning it even one day later will not negate that.

Did your lawyer commingle the money and not give you any funds due you? If so you may want to consider a lawsuit to get your money back, as well as refer the incident to the prosecutor's office in your county and file a grievance. (See the next section on misappropriation of client funds.) If the lawyer gave you all of the money you were owed, you may not even be aware that the money was commingled. The only sure way to know is to look at the account on which the check was drawn. If it was drawn on a personal or general business (or operating) account, you have two choices. You can forget about it since you received your money, taking the attitude that no harm was done. Or you can refer the matter to the bar grievance committee. (See Chapter 7 for more information on grievances.)

Misappropriation of Client Funds

Commingling, discussed earlier, is one way an attorney misappropriates client funds. Any attorney who *borrows* a clients money (to pay bills perhaps) or embezzles the funds without any intent of returning the money is *misappropriating* the client's money. Even if the lawyer borrows the money and puts it back, the funds have been misappropriated.

A client's funds are always the client's and a lawyer may not take a personal loan from those funds without the client's express authorization. Misappropriation of client funds is not only grounds for sanctions from the bar (see the chapter on grievances), it is grounds for both civil lawsuits to recover the funds by the client and criminal prosecution by the state.

IOTA or IOLTA Accounts

All states require that attorneys place client funds into special interest-bearing trust accounts. The first state to adopt this type of account was Florida in 1981. Indiana was the last state to adopt this type of account in 1993.

Neither the clients nor the attorneys receive the interest in any form, however. The interest from these accounts, called either *IOTA (Interest on Trust Accounts)* or *IOLTA (Interest on Lawyers' Trust Accounts)* are given by the bank to the state bar or other designated organization to be used for charitable purposes. Some of the beneficiaries of these funds are legal services agencies for the needy, such as Legal Aid, legal education programs in junior and senior high schools, and agencies that serve the disabled and the poor.

Client Security Trust Funds

In many situations, the money from IOLTA goes to special client security trust funds. If the money does not derive from those accounts, the bar itself may appropriate a portion of each lawyer's annual dues to such a security fund. Every state as well as the

District of Columbia has these funds, which are client protection funds. (See Appendix B for contact information.)

If your attorney has stolen your money, you may not be able to get it back from the attorney. These client protection funds are set up for situations such as this. They were set up specifically to ensure a client can be reimbursed for the lawyer's theft of the client's money.

The amount of recovery under the funds may be limited and there may be a maximum allowable amount as well. For example, in Florida $50,000 is the maximum fund recovery payment allowed by the Florida Board of Governors. Consider that although there may be a maximum claim allowed, the security fund may only guarantee up to a certain amount of money.

Still, it makes sense to make a claim if your attorney misappropriated your money. This is one thing you can do for yourself for which you have nothing to lose. (A list of the agencies handling such claims is in Appendix E.)

FEE DISPUTE RESOLUTION

Many state bar associations now have fee dispute resolution procedures. In 2002, the ABA approved an arbitration clause for retainer agreements that require binding arbitration of fee disputes. This avenue provides an objective means by which a dispute over fees can be determined. See **www.mobar.net/law/fdrform.pdf** for an example of the type of paperwork a client will file to start the fee dispute resolution mechanism.

Many states are also either mandating or encouraging the practice of fee arbitration. Fee arbitration has one purpose, to determine the value of a lawyer's legal representation. It is not where claims of negligence, malpractice, or ethical misconduct are brought forth. If the client wishes to pursue those claims, the client must file a lawsuit or grievance procedure with the appropriate forum. If litigation is pending concerning fees, the arbitration will be stayed until such time that the lawsuit is deferred, often by court order. If a lawsuit has already been decided, arbitration will not be allowed.

Most importantly, both the lawyer and the client must agree to arbitrate unless the state has mandatory arbitration in which case, if the client requests arbitration, the lawyer must comply and participate. The arbitrator may determine that the lawyer's fees were unreasonable. The arbitrator will also determine an award amount that must be paid to the prevailing party. (See Chapter 8 for more information about arbitration, in general.) For an example of a fee arbitration petition see:

www.montanabar.org/membership/feearbpetitionform.html

–6–
LAWSUITS

Deciding to go to court is not an easy decision. Before filing a lawsuit you should first read the rest of this book. Learn more about legal malpractice. It is imperative that you determine if you have a valid claim. While you may feel you were treated badly by your lawyer, that factor alone may not be enough to file a lawsuit. Look at the appropriate chapter in this book to decide if your claim is sound. If necessary, go to the local law library and research the area of law for specific cases that were decided in your state. These cases may give you a better notion of whether or not your claim will have a good chance of being entertained by a court.

If you decide that your claim is valid, you need to determine the court most appropriate for filing an action against your lawyer. You may want to consider filing a grievance with the bar or appropriate regulatory agency first. (Grievances are discussed in Chapter 7.)

WHERE TO FILE
Most states have two types of trial courts: small claims and general trial. There are different factors to consider when determining if you are going to file in small claims or a general trial court. While the methods of filing in either of these courts is a broad area that cannot be fully covered in this book, a synopsis of both follows.

SMALL CLAIMS COURT
Small claims courts began as a method of settling disputes between neighbors without the need for lengthy lawsuits, delays, or legal jargon. Now such courts are common in every area of the country,

although they may be known by other names, such as *Justice, Justice of the Peace, Municipal, City,* and *Conciliation.*

The current purpose of small claims court is strikingly similar to their original purpose. These courts are set up to resolve disputes that involve small amounts of money, without long delay or formal court rules. While using lawyers is not prohibited in most small claims courts, it is often frowned upon and, in general, would not be cost effective. Most cases are brought by the people involved directly.

The requirements for small claims courts will vary from state to state. These differences include the amount you may sue for, who may sue, and the types of papers that must be filed. For example, your state may allow a small claim of up to $5,000 while another will allow one only up to $2,000. You can call your local small claims court to find out what the dollar limit is in your state.

Advantages to Small Claims Court
Small claims court has advantages including the following.

- ◆ *You do not have to pay a lawyer.* This is important when your claim is small. For example, if your claim is for $650 and you have to pay a lawyer $500, it is not really cost effective to hire one.
- ◆ *Most disputes are handled within a few months of filing the complaint.* The hearing itself takes less than twenty minutes in most cases.
- ◆ *Legal jargon and procedural forms are kept to a minimum.* Very often the complaint is a *fill-in-the-blank* form you can obtain at the clerk's office. The rules of evidence and procedure are either greatly relaxed or abandoned altogether.

Disadvantages to Small Claims Court
Following are some possible disadvantages to small claims court.

- ◆ *You may have to expend more effort than you are willing to exercise.* Remember that you will have to obtain the forms and fill them out. You will be responsible for finding out when your court hearing is, and you will have to prepare your case. Keep in mind that the court clerks will give you filing fee information, but they cannot assist you in completing the forms or give you any other advice.

- *Small claims court may not handle your claim.* If you have a potential for larger money damages, you give up the chance to obtain them if you file in small claims.
- *You may not collect any money.* If the attorney you are suing does not have malpractice insurance, you may go through the entire process, expending time, effort, and money and be unable to collect a penny.

This is not meant to discourage you. If you genuinely only want a small amount of money and no amount of negotiations with your lawyer have resolved the problem, small claims is a fairly easy and inexpensive method of making a claim. If you believe you have a claim you want to pursue in small claims court, consult a self-help book on how to file small claims court cases.

GENERAL TRIAL COURT

For the most part, any case for any amount may be filed in a state trial court. As in small claims court, the names of the court may vary by state. Some names include the terms *Circuit, District, Superior,* and *County.* In New York, the trial court is called the Supreme Court. No matter what the name, you must file your case in the trial court.

Advantages

The two main advantages of filing in a regular trial court, as opposed to small claims are:

- *There is no limit to the dollar amount for which you may sue.* This does not mean you will be awarded the original amount, but you will not be thrown out of court for asking for too much.

◆ *You can ask an attorney to represent you.* In fact, it will be preferred by the judge.

Disadvantages

There are disadvantages that should be considered as well.

◆ *Under the circumstances, you may not want to deal with another attorney.* While this is understandable, it will not be to your advantage to go to a regular trial court *pro se* (which literally means *for himself* and describes the person who goes to court without representation by a lawyer).

◆ *Delays.* From the time you file, it could be more than a year before you have your day in court.

◆ *Filing fees and other fees are generally higher.*

◆ *All the rules of evidence and procedure will be in force.* Unlike small claims court, a judge in a regular trial court will not cut you any slack for being unknowledgeable about court rules and procedures. You will be expected to conduct yourself like a lawyer. Everything will be much more formal.

◆ *There is much more paperwork involved.* Unlike small claims court, the *Complaint* is not simplified. In fact, it is unlikely that you will be able to pick one up at the court clerk's office. You will be expected to draft one from scratch.

None of these disadvantages are meant to discourage you from filing in a general trial court. You should, however, be aware of all the pitfalls before making your decision. It may be in your best interest to take a deep breath and file in a regular trial court. If you are considering this avenue, you should consult books about trial procedure and trial forms (at your local law library) and a self-help book on filing in a regular court. You should also consider hiring an attorney that will handle attorney malpractice cases. While there are not many, they are out there. Consult the bar grievance office in your state for a list. (See Appendix A for the addresses and phone numbers of the grievance office in your state.)

CHECKLIST FOR DETERMINING
THE APPROPRIATE COURT

❏ Call the court clerk for your county.

❏ Tell the clerk where you live, and tell the clerk where the lawyer either lives or works. This is important information because it sets up the court's jurisdiction. If the court does not have *jurisdiction* over either you or the lawyer, the case will be dismissed. You give the court jurisdiction over you voluntarily when you file the case. The court only gets jurisdiction over the lawyer by virtue of the place where the lawyer resides or works or where the negligence occurred.

❏ Tell the clerk the *amount* of money for which you wish to sue your lawyer. The amount of the claim may be the determining factor in whether the lawsuit is filed in small claims court or a general trial court.

❏ Ask what *documents* are needed. Remember that if you are filing in small claims court, the clerk will be better able to answer you. In some areas of the country, the clerk will not be very forthcoming at all. You may need to consult a legal book, such as a practice manual on filing lawsuits. These books, found at most county law libraries, usually have copies of the forms required to file a lawsuit. County libraries are open to the public but are usually only open during business hours. If your area has a law school, call to see if the public may use the facilities. Law school libraries are usually open seven days a week.

❏ Ask for the courthouse and the clerk's office hours. Ask specifically when you may file a claim.

❏ Ask the clerk what the *filing fee* will be and what method of payment will be required. A personal check may not be permissible.

❏ Ask for directions to the courthouse and where you should park. Bring ample money for any parking meters.

❏ Be brief with the clerk. The clerk does not want to know everything about your case and will not have the time to discuss it with you at length. In addition, clerks are generally prohibited from giving too much information over the phone. Do not assume that because the clerk works in the courthouse, he or she knows a lot about law. Some do; some do not.

❑ After you decide in which court to file, you will have to decide if you want to hire another lawyer to handle your lawsuit. In small claims it is not necessary. You may want to consider doing so, however, if you are going to file a large lawsuit in a general trial court.

Know your own limitations. Remember that even though your lawyer was negligent, most lawyers are competent. Call the bar grievance committee to find a lawyer that is willing to sue other lawyers for malpractice.

–7–
ETHICAL VIOLATIONS

Although your attorney may not have committed malpractice, he or she may have done something the bar would consider unethical and that requires disciplinary action. If, when reading the other chapters, you determined that your lawyer's actions were malpractice but it is not financially feasible to sue, or if you determined that his or her actions were not negligent, you still may want to consider determining if filing a grievance with your state's bar or other appropriate regulatory agency would be appropriate. (From this point on, the term *bar* or *bar association* will include any agency that regulates lawyers.) The bar's grievance committee will investigate the matter and take the appropriate actions. So, while your lawyer may have escaped a malpractice claim, the lawyer's wrongful actions will not go unpunished if the grievance committee finds that the lawyer's actions were unethical.

Legal ethics are the standards of behavior to which members of an organized bar association must conform. This is often referred to as *professional responsibility*. Lawyers are bound by codes and rules regulating the behavior of the individual states' bar members. Regardless of these rules and regulations, however, some lawyers have done unethical things. (You would not be reading this book unless you believed your lawyer did something negligent or unethical.)

LAWYER REGULATION
State bar association members are regulated by an arm of government. In most states, this arm is the highest court in the state, but some states regulate their lawyers through an administrative agency,

such as a *Department of Professional Regulation*. Since most courts are ill-equipped to regulate thousands of lawyers on a daily basis, the courts usually assign the daily administration of the state's lawyers to an office or bar association. It is this office or association that sets up grievance committees.

Grievance Procedures

Each state's grievance procedures are different, but there are some similarities. In general, following these guidelines will be of assistance if you decide to file a grievance.

- Inquire about filing a grievance against your lawyer by checking Appendix A for the main office you need to contact. The main office *may* refer you to a local office.
- Send a letter or call the office and briefly explain why you want to file a grievance against your lawyer.
- Request a complaint form and instructions for filling it out.
- Follow all directions carefully. You may want to make a copy of the form or write your answers on a blank piece of paper before you set your pen to the actual form you will return to the grievance committee.
- Consider your words carefully. Writing "my lawyer is a liar and a thief" without elaboration will not get the same consideration as writing "my lawyer took a large retainer, did not do any work, and refused to give back the money." Try to remain as objective as possible. It is important that you do not tell the committee what rules the lawyer violated. The committee and its personnel are well-versed in the regulations and will apply the facts in your case to the rules.
- Attach any copies of contracts or correspondence you believe to be pertinent to your grievance. Do not send originals with the form unless the instructions tell you to send originals (in which case you should keep copies of the documents.)
- You may wish to send the form back by certified mail, return receipt requested.

Grievance Committee Action

When the committee receives the form, an investigator will read your complaint and decide if there is a possibility that an ethical rule or regulation was violated. If not, you will receive a letter explaining why. For example, if you send a complaint to the committee saying that the lawyer was rude to you, you will in all likelihood receive a letter stating that, while rudeness is frowned upon, it is not an ethical violation.

On the other hand, if there is a possibility that a violation occurred, the lawyer will be notified of the complaint and asked to respond to it within a reasonable length of time. (In general, a lawyer who does not comply will be subject to sanctions even if he or she is later cleared of any charge of ethical violations.)

The committee will review the lawyer's information and, if possible, decide whether or not the lawyer's actions were a breach of ethical duty to you. If no violation is found, you will get a letter explaining why. If a violation is probable, the lawyer may be requested to appear before a tribunal consisting of members of the grievance committee.

If a hearing is held, you will probably be asked to testify on your behalf. At that time, if the committee finds a violation, the lawyer will be sanctioned. This may come in the form of a formal charge filed with the court.

At the court proceeding, the lawyer is allowed to present defenses to his or her actions. The committee's recommendations may be approved, rejected, or modified. In general, the committee's recommendations are approved. Wait a reasonable length of time for a response to your claim before calling the committee. (Remember that the committee may have hundreds of grievances it must investigate.)

Points to Remember if You File a Grievance

- In most states, the grievance committee is made up entirely of lawyers.
- Both grievance procedures and sanctions are are on the rise.

- You may be sworn to secrecy (a *gag order*) if no public action is taken.
- The hearings themselves are usually held in private.
- You may not be allowed to appeal the decision if it is not in your favor.

Does this mean you should not file a grievance? No. Grievance procedures and sanctions are increasing. The collective bar associations, and lawyers too, are getting tired of some lawyers giving the rest a bad reputation. The public is demanding better legal counsel. If your lawyer has been the subject of previous complaints, the committee may be unable to ignore the pattern of ethical violations. Even if you do not get what you consider a satisfactory result, your complaint on file may save a future client the headaches you received.

SANCTIONS

What type of *sanctions*, or penalties, may a lawyer receive for an ethical violation? The definitions for the types of sanctions for unethical conduct are as follows.

- *Disbarment: Termination of the right to practice law.* Disbarment may be *permanent* or *temporary. Temporary disbarment* does not necessarily mean that the lawyer may practice after a certain length of time. If temporary, the attorney will have to apply for readmission to the Bar after a designated period of time. Even after reapplying, the Bar may decide not to readmit the lawyer if it finds that the lawyer's conduct was not up to standard. For example, the lawyer may have had a DUI conviction during the disbarment period.
- *Suspension: The lawyer is removed from the practice of law for a specific period of time.* In some states, the lawyer has to apply for reinstatement. In other states, the reinstatement is automatic.

- *Reprimand: Usually a public declaration that the lawyer's conduct was improper.* It does not affect a lawyer's right to practice law, however. It may also be called *censure.*

- *Admonition: A nonpublic declaration that the lawyer's conduct was improper.* This is the mildest form of punishment a lawyer can receive and does not affect the right to practice law. It may also be called a *private reprimand.*

- *Probation: The lawyer is allowed to practice law under certain conditions.* These usually include some form of supervision, drug treatment, or mental health counseling. If the conditions are not met, the lawyer will be subject to stronger sanctions.

Just what are these rules and regulations to which lawyers are required to adhere? They will vary to some degree from state to state but all are based on one of two models proposed by the *American Bar Association (ABA).*

MODEL CODE OF PROFESSIONAL RESPONSIBILITY

In 1969, the ABA adopted the *Model Code of Professional Responsibility* (Model Code). What distinguished this from the ABA's prior ethical instructions (The 1908 Canons of Ethics), was that for the first time, a lawyer's duties to the client could make the lawyer subject to disciplinary action by the Bar. The ABA itself could not bring disciplinary actions against an attorney, since the ABA is just a service organization, albeit a powerful one. What gave the Model Code *teeth* was that it was adopted in some form or another by the individual states could enforce the rules.

Each state, by adopting this Model Code, gave the arm of government responsible for the legal profession the right and duty to discipline any attorney who violated the Model Code. Over time, the Model Code, as interpreted through ethics opinions made by the ABA and the individual state agencies and courts, became the cornerstone of lawyer regulation today.

The Model Code was split into three main parts. The first was called *canons*. *Canons* were a general statement of standards expected of lawyers. The second part was called *ethical considerations (ECs)*. *ECs* were standards to which a lawyer should try to aspire. They were not, however, mandatory upon the lawyer, and any violation of an EC was not grounds for disciplinary action. The third part was called *disciplinary rules (DRs)*. These rules were mandatory. Couched in terms of *must* or *must not*, a lawyer was bound by the obligations the DRs set forth. Any deviation or violation of a DR made a lawyer subject to discipline.

As discussed below, the Model Code has been replaced, for the most part, by Model Rules of Professional Conduct. A few states do still have the Model Code on their book. Ohio is one such state. A copy of Ohio's version of the Model Rules (which is very similar to the ABA version) can be found in Appendix C.

MODEL RULES
OF PROFESSIONAL CONDUCT

In 1983, the ABA proposed the *Model Rules of Professional Conduct* (Model Rules). The Model Rules were a revision of the Model Code. The ABA currently recommends that the Model Rules be adopted and used instead of the Model Code.

The Model Rules are organized differently than the Model Code. Instead of canons, ECs and DRs, the Model Rules set out the exact standard to which a lawyer should adhere followed by comments explaining each rule. All rules must be followed, unlike the ECs of the Model Code that are only guidelines.

For more information on professional responsibility, as well as a list of Model Rules by state, visit:

www.abanet.org/cpr/links.html

When a state adopts the Model Rules it can make any changes it wants to them. But for the most part, the rules are uniform across the country. (Appendix D contains the Rules of Professional

Conduct for the State of West Virginia, which closely resembles the Model Rules.)

EXAMPLES OF ETHICAL VIOLATIONS

Lawyers may be held accountable for many behaviors which may or may not also be considered malpractice. For example, a lawyer who is convicted of cocaine possession is not necessarily negligent in his or her duty to a client, but such an action will be considered unethical and will be grounds for sanctions. In fact, commission of a felony in most states usually means long term suspension or disbarment.

Some specific ethical violations include the following.

♦ *Having sex with a client.* (See Chapter 3 on conflict of interest for more information about this topic.)
♦ *Mishandling client funds.* (See Chapter 5 on client funds.) (Rule 1.5)
♦ *Incompetence.* This follows the general ideas of the standard of conduct required of all lawyers to avoid a malpractice claim also. A lawyer must have the legal knowledge, skill, thoroughness and preparation reasonably necessary for the representation of a client. (Rule 1.1)
♦ *Candor to a tribunal.* A lawyer may not knowingly make false statements to any court or officer of a court, nor offer false evidence. (Rule 3.3)
♦ *Lack of supervision of nonlawyer assistants.* A lawyer must properly supervise all employees and is responsible for any employee conduct that would violate the Rules if the lawyer had knowledge of the actions or specifically ordered the actions. (Rule 5.3) (Rule 1.5)
♦ *Substance abuse.* As discussed in the chapter on negligence, substance abuse by lawyers is a problem of increasing importance. Almost every state has lawyer assistance programs that advertise regularly in the nation's bar journals. These programs actively recruit lawyers with substance problems, offering confidentiality and, for those turning in the abusing lawyer, immunity from civil liability for reporting the lawyer.

This means that the person who squeals cannot be sued by the lawyer for defamation or some other action as long as the information was given in good faith.

This problem does not fall under any particular Rule. A lawyer with a substance abuse problem may be suspended under Rule 1.1, which requires a lawyer to act competently. This proactive response assumes that the lawyer is incapable of acting in a competent manner due to the abuse problem. In addition, an attorney with an abuse problem may steal clients' money, lie, or violate any number of rules due to the faulty judgment that comes from a mind clouded by drugs or alcohol.

The examples above are just a few of the ways that a lawyer may violate the rules of conduct necessary to maintain a license to practice law. (Look in Appendix D for additional rules which may apply to your situation.)

NOTE: *A lawyer is always accountable to the agency or court that licenses him or her. Richard Nixon was disbarred in New York for lying about the Watergate tapes even though he was not actively practicing in New York at the time. As long as he held a license there, he could be held accountable for an ethical violation.*

While it has been shown that, in general, bar associations and courts have been less than effective in insuring lawyer competence, they are making a greater effort at disciplining lawyers who have strayed. This may be a very good way of getting some relief from a lawyer who has not lived up to the responsibilities and duties owed you.

–8–
ALTERNATIVES TO LAWSUITS

Filing a lawsuit is often seen as a last resort. While it may be your last option, there are alternatives that should be considered. Generally, exploring the alternatives of settlement, mediation, and arbitration will be to your advantage.

SETTLEMENT

Settlement usually occurs in one of two ways. Either the parties, in an effort to avoid costly litigation, agree to settle for a certain amount of money, or the settlement occurs on the brink of trial when both parties have a clearer view of what will probably occur at trial. While settling the matter quickly may seem very attractive to you, it is important to keep a few points in mind.

- ◆ If your lawyer seems overly eager to settle and offers what seems like a lot of money, he or she may be afraid of a conviction for negligence. A prompt settlement reduces the risk that you will file a grievance with the bar or start a malpractice action.

- ◆ It would be wise to consider your position very carefully before accepting a settlement or turning one down too quickly. If you think you have a very strong position, the settlement offer may be too little. Conversely, if you think your position is weak, the settlement may be generous. Consider what a jury might award you if you took your case to trial. Also consider that the trial process may take a few years of your time.

- ◆ It would also be wise to have another lawyer review any settlement documents before they are signed. It is important to know what your rights and responsibilities will be. In fact, the lawyer offering the settlement may have a duty to advise you to seek independent counsel.

Contents of a Settlement Agreement

A *settlement agreement* is a contract. The following items may be required in the agreement.

- ◆ A concise *description* of the facts of the dispute.
- ◆ A provision stating the *consideration* being paid. This will include cash as well as any other compensation being made.
- ◆ A *release* that will completely bar either you or the lawyer from bringing any action relating to the dispute being settled.
- ◆ A closing deadline that is, in effect, an escape from settlement. If for some reason, an unreasonably long delay in complying with the terms of the settlement occurs, both parties will be able to back out of the settlement.
- ◆ The settlement agreement should be *signed* under oath by the parties and before a notary public.
- ◆ A provision for the way in which the parties will *settle* disputes over the settlement agreement if one arises. This may be through a court or through arbitration.
- ◆ A *confidentiality clause* may be included. The lawyer may want this clause to keep you from talking to the press or from filing a grievance. (Remember that promising not to report does not protect other members of the public from future misconduct by the lawyer.)

Over 90% of all civil disputes are settled. Consider all your options before turning down a settlement offer based on the *principle* of the matter.

MEDIATION

Mediation is a cooperative process in which disputed issues are defined and a mutually acceptable resolution is reached with the assistance of a neutral professional *mediator*. In the mediation environment, the parties to a dispute have a safe place to meet, exchange offers, and compromise. It is private and highly informal. Either party can terminate the mediation process for any reason at any time.

Role of the Mediator

The mediator is trained to help parties solve problems in a cooperative manner. The mediator guides the communication process so that everyone is heard and personal feelings are set aside. The mediator often arranges meetings between the parties, listens, empathizes, encourages emotional outbursts when they would be helpful to the process, urges the parties to listen to one another, and commends the parties' efforts to accommodate each other. The mediator is a neutral third party in the process, but, unlike a situation with a judge in a courtroom or with an arbitrator, the result of the mediator's efforts is not binding on the parties. The final agreement, if one is reached, is always left up to the parties involved.

A list of mediators can be obtained from the American Arbitration Association at **www.adr.org**, as well as through local bar associations.

Timing of the Mediation Process

If the parties choose mediation voluntarily, they can also choose the timing. Unlike other kinds of dispute resolution (notably arbitration), mediation is available throughout the dispute process. Parties can choose mediation before a trial begins or even after it has begun. Choosing to mediate early or late in the process should be based on the particular circumstances of the matter. It may be more desirable to mediate early in the process before the parties' positions become hardened and substantial costs are incurred. However, it may make more sense to wait until after more information is gathered, allowing for more meaningful negotiations.

Mediation Participation

Mediation requires participation by all parties. In addition, the parties really control the process. In some states, the parties' lawyers are prohibited from attending the actual mediation conference, depending on the subject matter of the mediation (e.g. divorce.) Other states either require the presence of a party's lawyer (if the party is represented by counsel) or gives the mediator the authority to exclude the lawyers from the process.

The Mediation Process

The mediation process is extremely informal. The first contact with the mediator is generally by a phone call from one of the parties or their counsel. The mediator will want to talk to both parties before the mediation process begins. Often a mediator will hold separate meetings with the parties to establish a rapport and trust. During these pre-mediation conferences, the mediator may perform some or all of the following.

- ◆ Explain the rules about confidentiality.
- ◆ Give each party an agreement to mediate.
- ◆ Determine who has the authority to make decisions and advise that the decision maker must be present at the mediation.
- ◆ Decide what documents may be necessary to examine at the mediation.
- ◆ Discuss the role of counsel at the mediation. If either you or your lawyer has retained counsel, you may or may not want the lawyer to be present during the mediation.
- ◆ Explain the mediator's role. The mediator will not offer legal advice during the process.
- ◆ Help calm your fears about the process.

Why Should You Mediate?

Unless court ordered, mediation is totally voluntary and the process can be terminated at any time. The decision of the mediator is not binding on either party. It is however, a good method of coming to a compromise position. Consider that:

◆   90% of all civil cases are settled, most immediately before trial. Settling during mediation may avoid both the financial and emotional investment that is required when you engage in litigation and

◆   the American Arbitration Association reported that 85% of the voluntary mediations it participated in nationwide resulted in settlement.

Mediation may be to your advantage if:

◆   you have an ongoing relationship with the opposing party and want to continue the relationship;

◆   there is a mutual interest in resolving the dispute quickly;

◆   litigating the dispute will be a long and expensive proposition; or,

◆   time is of the essence. (Remember that litigation is very time-consuming.)

Mediation may *not* be advantageous if:

◆   you know you can easily get a judgment in court because your case is very solid;

◆   the lawyer is not dealing in good faith;

◆   the lawyer wants to delay the resolution of the dispute for as long as possible;

◆   you think you will be intimidated by the lawyer during mediation. (Keep in mind, however, that you are more likely to feel intimidated in a courtroom); or,

◆   either you or the lawyer have no real interest in settlement. (In such a case, mediation will not be successful.)

ARBITRATION

Arbitration is an ancient method of resolving disputes that has roots in early Greece and Egypt. It was used by tradesmen as a means of getting *quick justice* in a time when any kind of justice was not ordinarily found.

The immediate roots of arbitration in this country come from medieval England, as do most all American legal traditions. In England, merchants settled disputes at informal courts that were held in the marketplace itself. Decisions of arbitrators were not always followed, but in 1697, the English Parliament made arbitration awards binding and more enforceable.

In the United States, arbitration as we know it, was utilized mostly after the Civil War as a means of resolving labor disputes. By 1901, seventeen states passed laws that established state arbitration boards, but arbitration was still not heavily used. New York passed the first modern arbitration statute in 1920, which brought about two good things. First, the statute gave the courts the power to enforce arbitration agreements. Second, the American Arbitration Association (AAA) was formed. The AAA provided a forum in which disputes could be arbitrated and paved the way for increased use of arbitration in general.

What Is Arbitration?

Arbitration is a method of resolving disputes and its main purpose is to decrease the time and expense of traditional litigation. Arbitration can be brought about through three different methods:

1. voluntary agreement of the parties;
2. compulsory arbitration—required by statute; or,
3. a hybrid form called *remedial arbitration.*

In most cases, arbitration for legal malpractice will be voluntary, either based on a paragraph in the contract you had with the lawyer or by mutual consent. However, some states, like New Hampshire, require that all civil case parties participate in some kind of dispute resolution, whether it be mediation, *nonbinding arbitration* (similar to mediation but with more procedures similar to arbitration), or arbitration. The parties decide in which type of dispute resolution to engage. If they cannot agree, the court will require them to participate in the least binding and burdensome procedure chosen by either party.

Voluntary arbitration is the process by which the parties voluntarily submit their problem to an impartial third person (or panel of individuals) for a final and binding decision. This is where arbitration is very different from mediation. *Decisions of the arbitrator are binding upon both parties.*

Unlike mediation, which works best when it is likely the parties will be able to reach an agreement or when the parties want to continue in their relationship, arbitration is usually undertaken when there is no reasonable likelihood of a negotiated settlement and there will not be a continuing relationship between the parties. Arbitration is much like litigation, only less formal, less costly, and less time consuming.

The Arbitration Process
Arbitration usually has six stages: initiation, preparation, prehearing conferences, hearing, decision making, and award.

- ◆ *Initiation.* The initiation stage consists of initiating the proceeding and selecting an arbitrator. If the arbitration is voluntary, starting the proceeding will be done in one of two ways. The first is called *submission.* In this process, both parties submit a signed agreement that contains:

  - about the arbitrator's authority;
  - procedures to be used at the hearing;
  - a statement of the disputed matter;
  - amount of money in controversy; and,
  - the remedy sought. Submission is used when there is no previous agreement to arbitrate.

The second method of initiating the arbitration process occurs when a clause in the attorney-client agreement requires arbitration. One party will serve a written *demand* or *notice* upon the other party. Often, however, parties will agree to draft a submission after the demand has been made.

As part of the initiation process, an *arbitrator* must be chosen. Selection of an arbitrator is a matter of choice. You will want to choose someone who has shown impartiality and if possible, has expertise in the area of legal negligence if you are suing for malpractice, or breach of contract if your dispute deals directly with the contract.

While many writers on the subject of arbitration have recommended that the arbitrator be an attorney (or if the arbitration is conducted by a panel, that the chairperson be a lawyer), you may want to consider choosing someone who is not a lawyer. Your first concern should be the *impartiality* of the arbitrator. It is a given that a lawyer-arbitrator will be quite knowledgeable about the process and the law. If you cannot be certain, however, that a lawyer-arbitrator will be completely *unbiased*, you should select someone who is not a lawyer.

Information concerning the qualifications of the more active arbitrators is in the *Directory of Arbitrators*, and *Who's Who* (of Arbitration). In addition, both the *Federal Mediation and Conciliation Service*, the *National Mediation Board* and the *American Arbitration Association* have biographical information about arbitrators.

♦ *Preparation.* Both parties must fully prepare for arbitration. Each party must understand his or her case and be able to convey that information to the arbitrator. It is important to prepare because the arbitrator's decision will be based upon the information presented during the hearing.

In addition, the arbitrator will prepare for the hearing by designating the time and place for the hearing, signing an oath if required, and determining if either or both parties will be represented by another person, such as a lawyer, during the hearing.

- *Prehearing conference.* Even though you can consider arbitration to be like a relaxed, or mini-trial, the need to prepare witnesses, present evidence, and testify still exist. Proper preparation is a key to potential success. The arbitrator may decide to hold prehearing conferences if the situation seems complex enough to warrant it. Usually these conferences are administrative in nature. Any discussion about the merits of the claims being advanced are usually avoided. The arbitrator will not speak with one party if the other party is not present.

- *Hearing.* While the parties may waive oral hearings and only submit documents to the arbitrator, oral hearings are much more advantageous since oral hearings allow both parties to present evidence to the arbitrator. Arbitration hearings are not public, so, unlike a courtroom situation, you will be alone with your attorney, the arbitrator and anyone representing either of you. Very often a court reporter is not even used, so there is usually no written record of the proceedings.

  The party complaining (in a malpractice action that is the client) usually presents his or her position first. The formal rules of evidence required in a courtroom are generally relaxed, but there may still be rules and procedures that must be followed during arbitration. The arbitrator is judge and jury during an arbitration proceeding and can provide you with whatever rules will be followed during the process. Obtain these rules as soon as possible and become familiar with them.

- *The Decision.* If the situation is not considered complex, the arbitrator may give the parties a decision immediately. If the arbitrator needs time to make a decision, however, it could take several weeks before you hear the arbitrator's result.

- *The Award.* The arbitrator's decision determines the award. While it may be given orally, it is usually written and signed by the arbitrator. An arbitrator's decision is usually final.

Advantages of Arbitration

Certain advantages to arbitration include:

- *Less costly.* Arbitration is assumed to be less costly than a trial because formal rules of evidence are not used. There is no formal discovery, such as depositions, interrogatories and production requests, that drive the cost of litigation up. It should be noted, however, that in some cases, the lawyers representing the parties have insisted that the arbitrator grant the same type of liberal discovery that a court of law grants. In fact, one article called these proposals "innovative". When arbitrators have allowed this, however, the cost of the arbitration has soared, greatly defeating the benefit of arbitration as a low cost means of settling disputes. (It is something to be strenuously avoided.)

- *No legal counsel.* In many situations, lawyers are not required for arbitration. In fact, even when a party is represented by a lawyer, the arbitrator often asks the party to present his or her argument directly, without the aid of counsel.

- *Speed of resolution.* Unlike trials, which can take a long time because of crowded court dockets and a barrage of paperwork, arbitrations often are resolved within a very short period of time. In addition, the parties themselves determine the timetable and thus are not at the mercy of a court that usually has sole discretion about timing of a trial.

- *Hearings are more informal.* This is greatly advantageous to a non-lawyer. If you are handling your own case, you will not be required to be informed of the formal rules of evidence. In fact, evidence that would normally be excluded in a courtroom may be permissible during arbitration.

- *Expertise of arbitrator.* All too often, a judge in a trial situation will have little or no experience in the matter at hand. The judge will rely on research done by his or her staff and on the evidence presented during the trial. An arbitrator, however, can be chosen as an expert in the disputed area. Finding an arbitrator with significant legal malpractice or breach of contract experience may be to your advantage.

Disadvantages of Arbitration

While the advantages are obvious and beneficial to a client suing for malpractice, the disadvantages that are usually enumerated by those in the legal profession may actually be advantages for a client as well.

- *Arbitration's informality may not be protective of your rights.* When you are dealing with a court, the judge has broad powers with which to protect you even if you are unaware that you have rights that need protecting. An arbitrator may not protect your rights as scrupulously.
- *The arbitrator's decision is reviewable on rather narrow grounds.* When you go to court, you have the option of appealing to a higher court if the decision does not go in your favor. You may be unable to do this if you go to arbitration.
- *Arbitrators are not bound by precedent or rules of law, making some decisions unpredictable.* The arbitrator may place great weight on social, moral, and fairness considerations when making a decision. Those issues that the arbitrator will focus on may make a lawyer uncomfortable since the lawyer is used to looking at facts and their application to the law as written. It can work in your favor, however, since the arbitrator will likely weigh those other issues that a judge may be obliged to ignore.
- *Arbitrators decide disputes on a middle ground.* This probably will not result in a win-win situation for both parties like a mediation may, and in fact some legal scholars say that this means the results will not be satisfactory to either party. However, studies have shown that a higher percentage of plaintiffs recover awards in arbitration, than they do in litigation.
- *The award may be smaller than that received in litigation.* During arbitration you will not have an emotional jury to sway. The arbitrator will be a dispassionate judge and will be less likely to award a very large sum.

◆ *The cost of arbitration is rising and it is also becoming more time-consuming.* If it appears that it will be as time-consuming and as costly as litigation, you may want to consider the litigation route.

Arbitration Clauses in the Attorney-Client Agreement

It is important to note that, even if your lawyer puts an arbitration clause into your agreement and is trying to hold you to it, you may not be bound by the clause. While there is no express ethical prohibition regarding the use of arbitration clauses, Model Rule 1.8(h) (see Appendix D) forbids the use of such a clause unless it is permitted by law and the client was independently represented. This means that *unless you had another lawyer counsel you about the clause, it will not be enforced.* (But who even considers hiring a lawyer to advise them about hiring another lawyer for the primary task?) However, more and more states are establishing and encouraging arbitration as a way to ease clogged court dockets, paving the way for these clauses to be enforceable.

–9–
DECIDING WHAT TO DO

Making the decision whether to file suit or not is important and should not be considered lightly. This book has explained the different areas in which an attorney may be considered negligent. Look at the appropriate chapters carefully. One of the hardest things you will need to do is take an objective look at the situation. Deciding what to do will depend on that objectivity. You may want to ask yourself, what would a lawyer think? Would a lawyer, looking at my situation, think that a valid claim exists?

If you have a problem with your attorney that you believe rises to malpractice, you must decide from the following options what course of action to take.

- Try to resolve the matter directly with your attorney.
- Request arbitration or mediation.
- Try to obtain a settlement.
- File a grievance with the bar.
- File a lawsuit for malpractice based on the negligence.
- File a lawsuit for breach of contract seeking restitution damages.

You must also decide what types of fees and costs may be required to go forward with each option. These include:

- the cost to file a lawsuit;
- attorney's fees, if you hire another attorney;
- cost for depositions, mediators, arbitrators, and expert witnesses;

- ◆ any costs of an appeal. If your lawyer loses, he or she very well may appeal the decision to a higher court. (Can you afford the time, money, and delay involved in the appeal? Consider that this may add years to your court battle, not to mention considerable cost.);
- ◆ possible travel expenses; and,
- ◆ your time.

Lastly, it is important to determine if you will be able to recover the money the court awards you. Many people believe that once a court awards you a sum of money, the losing party, in this case your attorney, just hands you a check. That may not be true, however. For example, if someone sued you for $250,000 and you lost the suit, would you have the money to pay? Probably not. This means that the person who sued you has a *paper judgment* (a piece of paper saying you owe money, the equivalent of a judicial I.O.U.). It will be the same if you have to collect from your lawyer. He or she may not be able to satisfy the judgment.

Turning the paper judgements into actual dollars in your hand is done by *enforcing* the judgment. This process itself can be very expensive, time consuming, and still result in little or no actual cash. The best way to determine if your lawyer will be able to satisfy a judgment is to find out if your lawyer carries *malpractice insurance*. This is really the only way to insure that any sum of money awarded to you will be paid.

Lawyers are not generally required to carry malpractice insurance or may only have a minimal amount. If your lawyer has little or no insurance, your judgment may only be a piece of paper for many years.

In addition, if your attorney does carry malpractice insurance, you should consider that the malpractice carrier may put the full weight of its own legal team into action to protect your lawyer from your claim of malpractice. This is understandable because the carrier does not want to pay out any sum of money. Insurance companies only make money when they are not paying claims. You should decide if you want to go up against a large insurance company without legal representation of your own.

Finally, it is possible that your lawyer may file bankruptcy in an effort to avoid paying the malpractice judgment. If this happens, you will become just another creditor of the attorney. This is another instance in which you may just get another paper judgment or be awarded a very small percentage of the original judgment by the bankruptcy court, if you receive any amount at all.

When you finish weighing all these options, you will have a much clearer picture of your situation and be able to determine with what you are willing to live. Remember that lawyers are human too and a less than perfect result does not always spell malpractice. You may decide that the risks are worth it. You may decide they are not.

Ultimately, only you can make that decision.

GLOSSARY

A

acceptance. Occurs when someone agrees to an offer. This creates a contract.

alternate dispute resolution (ADR). A generic term signifying any of the methods used to resolve disputes, including mediation, settlement, and arbitration.

anticipatory breach. Occurs when one party lets the other know that he or she will not or cannot complete a contract. This occurs before performance of the contract is legally required.

appeal. Procedure by which the decision of a lower court is brought to a higher court for review.

arbitration. The process by which an outside party (arbitrator) settles a dispute between parties. Use of this procedure usually binds all parties to whatever decision is rendered.

arbitrator. The outside party who settles disputes between parties during arbitration.

B

bankruptcy. The process by which a debtor's assets are sold to pay off creditors. In some forms of bankruptcy, the debtor is allowed time to restructure so that business may become viable again.

bilateral contract. A contract in which both parties make promises.

breach of contract. Failure to perform any promise that is the basis for a contract. A violation of a contract.

burden of proof. The duty of a party to prove a fact in dispute.

C

cause of action. Grounds on which a lawsuit is brought.

consideration. The price, motive, cause, or influence inducing a party to enter into a contract.

contingent fee. Arrangement between an attorney and client in which the attorney agrees to represent the client based on a percentage of any amount recovered on the client's behalf.

contract. A binding agreement between parties that spells out the terms and conditions each is bound to do or not do.

D

damages. Monetary compensation to a party when wronged by another.

decree. An order of a court.

defamation. Libel (written) or slander (spoken); when someone is ridiculed, scorned, or lied about in a public manner.

deposition. Questions and answers given before a court reporter in preparation for a lawsuit.

discovery. The methods used to find out information that would be useful in a lawsuit. Discovery includes depositions, interrogatories and requests for production.

duty. A legal or moral obligation; also the obligation to follow all laws or court directives.

E

equity. When a decision is rendered by a court based on fairness.

evidence. Information that may be properly admitted in a court that assists the court or jury to determine the outcome of the issue in dispute. This includes discovery devices and testimony of witnesses.

F

fiduciary. A person who manages money or property for another person and in whom a great deal of responsibility and trust is put.

fraud. A false representation which deceives another causing that person to act to his or her own injury.

I

interrogatories. A set of written questions used to examine a witness.

J

judgment. The official decision made by a court in response to a lawsuit.

L

legal assistant. *See paralegal.*

legal ethics. Customs used by the legal profession concerning moral and professional duties.

litigation. The procedure by which a lawsuit is had.

M

malpractice. Professional negligence.

mortgage. A written document that gives an interest in real property as security for payment of a note. Generally, when a bank gives you a loan for the property, it holds the mortgage and gains an interest in the property until you pay off the note.

N

negligence. Either doing or not doing an act that a reasonable person would have done or not done.

O

oath. A sworn statement by a person that he or she is telling the truth; given when affirmation of the truth is required.

offer. A promise. Acceptance of an offer completes the formation of a contract.

offeree. The person to whom an offer is made.

offeror. The person who makes the offer

opinion. A court's written explanation of its decision.

P

paralegal. Someone with legal skills who works under a lawyer's supervision; generally has fewer skills than a lawyer, but more than a secretary. A paralegal is not authorized to practice law.

pecuniary. Monetary.

precedent. A ruling by an appeals court that is binding upon lower courts in subsequent cases.

pro bono. For the good; used when describing work done by a lawyer free of charge.

proof. Anything that is used to convince a judge or jury of the truth or falsity of an allegation.

R

reasonable fee. Fee that is not excessive when the amount of time, complexity, and expertise involved and the customary charges of the community's other lawyers are considered.

rescission. An equitable action in which one party seeks to be relieved of a contractual obligation.

revocation. Taking back something; in contractual terms, it is voiding a contract.

S

specific performance. Carrying out a contract's terms to the letter. A court requiring specific performance will require a party to do everything the contract says to do.

T

trustee. The person who manages a trust.

trustor. The person who creates the trust.

V

void. Of no legal effect.

W

will. A document stating how a person's property shall be distributed upon death.

–Appendix A–

ATTORNEY DISCIPLINARY AGENCIES

This appendix contains the contact information for reporting a problem with your attorney. Specific grievance procedures can be obtained from each of the organizations listed.

ALABAMA

Alabama State Bar
Center for Professional Responsibility
415 Dexter Avenue
Post Office Box 671
Montgomery, AL 36101-0671
251-269-1515
www.alabar.org

ALASKA

Alaska Bar Association
510 L Street, Suite 602
Anchorage, AK 99501
907-272-7469
www.alaskabar.org

ARIZONA

State Bar of Arizona
111 West Monroe, Suite 1800
Phoenix, AZ 85003-1742
602-340-7241
www.azbar.org

ARKANSAS

Committee on Professional Conduct
Supreme Court of Arkansas
Justice Building
625 Marshall, Room 110
Little Rock, AR 72201-1054
501-376-0313

CALIFORNIA

State Bar of California
1149 South Hill Street, 10th Floor
Los Angeles, CA 90015-2299
213-765-1000
www.calbar.org

State Bar of California
180 Howard Street, 6th Floor
San Francisco, CA 94105-1614
415-538-2000

COLORADO

Colorado Supreme Court
Office of Attorney Regulation
Dominion Plaza Building
600 - 17th Street, Suite 200 South
Denver, CO 80202-5435
303-893-8121

CONNECTICUT

Statewide Grievance Committee
Second Floor, Suite Two
287 Main Street
East Hartford, CT 06118-1885
860-568-5157

DELAWARE
Delaware Office of Disciplinary Counsel
200 West Ninth Street, Suite 300-A
Wilmington, DE 19801
302-577-7042

DISTRICT OF COLUMBIA
District of Columbia
Board on Professional Responsibility
515 - 5th Street, NW
Building A, Room 127
Washington, DC 20001-2797
202-638-1501

FLORIDA
The Florida Bar
650 Apalachee Parkway
Tallahassee, FL 32399-2300
850-561-5600
www.flabar.org

GEORGIA
State Bar of Georgia
104 Marietta Street, NW
Suite 100
Atlanta, GA 30303
404-527-8720
www.gabar.org

HAWAII
Supreme Court of Hawaii
Office of Disciplinary Counsel
1132 Bishop Street, Suite 300
Honolulu, HI 96813
808-521-4591

IDAHO

Idaho State Bar
525 West Jefferson
Boise, ID 83702
208-334-4500
www.state.id.us-isb

ILLINOIS

(Chicago and Northern Illinois)
Illinois Attorney Registration and
Disciplinary Commission
130 East Randolph Street, Suite 1500
Chicago, IL 60601
312-565-2600; 800-826-8625

(Central and Southern Illinois)
Illinois Attorney Registration and
Disciplinary Commission
700 East Adams Street
Springfield, IL 62701-1625
800-252-8048

INDIANA

Indiana Supreme Court Disciplinary Commission
115 West Washington Street, Suite 1165
Indianapolis, IN 46204-3417
317-232-1807

IOWA

Iowa Supreme Court
Board of Professional Ethics and Conduct
521 East Locust Street, 3rd Floor
Des Moines, IA 50309-1939
515-243-0027

KANSAS

Supreme Court of Kansas
701 SW Jackson, 1st Floor
Topeka, KS 66603
785-296-2486

KENTUCKY

Kentucky Bar Association
514 West Main Street
Frankfort, KY 40601-1883
502-564-3795
www.kybar.org

LOUISIANA

Office of the Disciplinary Counsel
4000 S. Sherwood Forest Boulevard, Suite 607
Baton Rouge, LA 70816
225-293-3900

MAINE

Maine Board of Overseers of the Bar
Post Office Box 527
97 Winthrop Street
Augusta, ME 04332-0527
207-623-1121
www.mebaroverseers.org

MARYLAND

Attorney Grievance Commission of Maryland
100 Community Place, Suite 3301
Crownsville, MD 21032-2027
410-514-7051

MASSACHUSETTS

Office of the Bar Counsel
75 Federal Street
Boston, MA 02110
617-728-8750
ww.state.ma.us-obcbbo

MICHIGAN

Michigan Attorney Grievance Commission
Marquette Building, Suite 256
243 West Congress
Detroit, MI 48226-3259
313-961-6585
www.agcmi.com

Attorney Disciplinary Board
211 West Fort Street
Suite 1410
Detroit, MI 48226
313-963-5553
www.adbmich.org

MINNESOTA

1500 Landmark Towers
345 St. Peter Street
St. Paul, MN 55102-1218
651-296-3952
www.courts.state.mn.us-lprb

MISSISSIPPI

Mississippi State Bar
643 North State Street
P.O. Box 2168
Jackson, MS 39225-2168
601-948-4471
www.mslawyer.org

MISSOURI
Missouri Supreme Court
Office of Chief Disciplinary Counsel
3335 American Avenue
Jefferson City, MO 65109-1079
573-635-7400

MONTANA
Disciplinary Counsel
301 South Park Avenue
Suite 334
P.O. Box 203007
Helena, MT 59620-3007
406-841-2980

NEBRASKA
Nebraska State Bar Association
Post Office Box 81809
Lincoln, NE 68501
402-471-1040

NEVADA
State Bar of Nevada
600 East Charleston Boulevard
Las Vegas, NV 89104
702-382-2200
www.nvbar.org

NEW HAMPSHIRE
New Hampshire Supreme Court
Professional Conduct Committee
4 Park Street, Suite 304
Concord, NH 03301
603-224-5828

NEW JERSEY
Office of Attorney Ethics
Supreme Court of New Jersey
Post Office Box 963
840 Bear Tavern Road
West Trenton, NJ 08628
609-530-4008

NEW MEXICO
Disciplinary Board of the Supreme Court of New Mexico
400 Gold SW, Suite 800
Albuquerque, NM 87102-3261
505-842-5781

NEW YORK
(New York City: 1st Department)
First Judicial Department
Departmental Disciplinary Committee
61 Broadway, 2nd Floor
New York, NY 10006
212-401-0800

(New York City: 2nd Department)
Second Judicial Department
2nd & 11th Judicial District Grievance Committees
Renaissance Plaza, Suite 2400
335 Adams Street
Brooklyn, NY 11201
718-923-6300

(New York State: 2nd Department)
Second Judicial Department
9th Judicial District Grievance Committee
Suite 200
399 Knollwood Road
White Plains, NY 10603
914-949-4540

(New York State: 2nd Department)
Second Judicial Department
10th Judicial District Grievance Committee
6900 Jericho Turnpike, Suite 102LL
Syosset, NY 11791
516-364-7344

(New York State: 3rd Department)
Third Judicial Department
Committee on Professional Standards
40 Steuben Street, Suite 502
Albany, NY 12207-2109
518-474-8816

(New York State: 4th Department-5th District)
Fourth Judicial Department
5th District Attorney Grievance Committee
465 South Salina Street, Suite 106
Syracuse, NY 13202-2467
315-471-1835

(New York State: 4th Department-7th District)
Fourth Judicial Department
7th District Attorney Grievance Committee
50 East Avenue, Suite 404
Rochester, NY 14604-2206
716-530-3180

(New York State: 4th Department-8th District)
Fourth Judicial Department
Attorney Grievance Committee
295 Main Street, Room 1036
Buffalo, NY 14203-2560
716-858-1190

NORTH CAROLINA

North Carolina State Bar
208 Fayetteville Street Mall
Raleigh, NC 27611-2904
919-828-4620

NORTH DAKOTA

Disciplinary Board of the Supreme Court of North Dakota
P.O. Box 2297
Bismarck, ND 58501-2297
701-328-3925

OHIO

Office of the Disciplinary Counsel of the Supreme Court of Ohio
175 South Third Street, Suite 280
Columbus, OH 43215-5196
614-461-0256

Board of Commissioners on Grievances and Discipline
41 South High Street, Suite 3370
Columbus, OH 54327-6104
614-644-5800

(Akron/Summit County)
Akron Bar Association
7 West Bowery, Suite 1100
Akron, OH 44308
330-253-5007

(Cincinnati/Hamilton County)
Cincinnati Bar Association
35 East 7th Street, Suite 800
Cincinnati, OH 45202-2411
513-381-8213

(Cleveland/Cuyahoga County)
Cleveland Bar Association
113 St. Clair Avenue, NE, 2nd Floor
Cleveland, OH 44114-1252
216-696-3525

(Columbus/Franklin County)
Columbus Bar Association
175 S. Third Street
Columbus, OH 43215-5193
614-225-6053

(Dayton/Montgomery County)
Dayton Bar Association
600 One First National Plaza
Dayton, OH 45402-1501
513-222-7902

(Toledo/Lucas County)
The Toledo Bar Association
311 N. Superior Street
Toledo, OH 43604
419-242-9363

OKLAHOMA
Oklahoma State Bar Association
1901 North Lincoln Boulevard
Post Office Box 53036
Oklahoma City, OK 73152
405-416-7000
www.oba-net.org

OREGON
Oregon State Bar
P.O. Box 1689
5200 SW Meadows Road
Lake Oswego, OR 97035-0889
503-620-0222
www.osbar.org

PENNSYLVANIA
Disciplinary Board of the Supreme Court of Pennsylvania
501 Grant Street, Suite 400
Pittsburgh, PA 15219
412-565-3173

RHODE ISLAND
Disciplinary Board of the Supreme Court of Rhode Island
Fogarty Judicial Annex
24 Weybosset Street
Providence, RI 02903
401-222-3270

SOUTH CAROLINA
South Carolina Board of Commissioners
Grievances and Discipline
P.O. Box 12159
Columbia, SC 29211
803-734-2038

SOUTH DAKOTA
State Bar of South Dakota
222 E. Capitol
Pierre, SD 57501
605-224-7554

TENNESSEE

Board of Professional Responsibility
Supreme Court of Tennessee
The Oaks Tower, Suite 730
1101 Kermit Drive
Nashville, TN 37217
615-361-7500

TEXAS

State Bar of Texas
6300 La Calma Drive, Suite 300
Austin, TX 78752
512-463-1463
www.texasbar.com

UTAH

Utah State Bar
Office of Professional Conduct
645 South 200 East, Suite 205
Salt Lake City, UT 84111-3834
801-531-9110
www.utahbar.org

VERMONT

Professional Conduct Board
Supreme Court of Vermont
32 Cherry Street, Suite 213
Burlington, VT 05401-7305
802-859-3000

VIRGINIA

Virginia State Bar
Eighth and Main Building
707 East Main Street, Suite 1500
Richmond, VA 23219-2803
804-775-0500
www.vsb.org

WASHINGTON
Washington State Bar Association
2101 Fourth Avenue, 4th Floor
Seattle, WA 98121-2330
206-727-8255
www.wsba.org

WEST VIRGINIA
Office of Disciplinary Counsel
2008 Kanawha Boulevard, East
Charleston, WV 25311
304-558-7999

WISCONSIN
Office of Lawyer Regulation
110 East Main Street, Suite 315
Madison, WI 53703-3383
608-267-7274
www.courts.state.wi.us

WYOMING
Wyoming State Bar
P.O. Box 109
500 Randall Avenue
Cheyenne, WY 82003-0109
307-632-9061
www.wyomingbar.org

–Appendix B–

CLIENT SECURITY FUNDS

Client Security Funds are established to reimburse individuals whose lawyer's improperly retained their money. The contact information is given for all 50 states and the District of Columbia. Contact the Fund in your state to learn its specific rules and guidelines.

ALABAMA

Client Security Fund
Alabama State Bar
415 Dexter Avenue
P.O. Box 671
Montgomery, AL 36101
334-269-1515
www.alabar.org

ALASKA

Lawyers' Fund For Client Protection
Alaska Bar Association
510 L Street
Suite 602
Anchorage, AK 99501
907-272-7469

ARKANSAS
Client Security Fund
Justice Building
Room 110
625 Marshall Street
Little Rock, AR 72201
501-376-0313

ARIZONA
Client Protection Fund
State Bar of Arizona
111 West Monroe
Suite 1800
Phoenix, AZ 85003
602-340-7286
www.azbar.org

CALIFORNIA
Client Security Fund
State Bar of California
1149 South Hill Street
Los Angeles, CA 90015
213-765-1144

COLORADO
Clients' Security Fund
Colorado Supreme Court
Office of Attorney Regulation
600 17th Street
Suite 200 South
Denver, CO 80202-5435
303-893-8121

CONNECTICUT

Office of the Clients Security Fund Committee
287 Main Street
Second Floor
Suite One
East Hartford, CT 06118-1885
860-568 - 3450
www.jud.state.ct.us

DELAWARE

Lawyers' Fund For Client Protection
of the Bar of Delaware
200 West Ninth Street
Suite 300B
Wilmington, DE 19801
302-577-7034
www.courts.state.de.us

DISTRICT OF COLUMBIA

D.C. Bar Clients' Security Fund
1250 H Street NW
Sixth Floor
Washington, DC, 20005-5937
202-737-4700

FLORIDA

Clients' Security Fund
The Florida Bar
650 Apalachee Parkway
Tallahassee, FL 32399-2300
850-561-5812
www.flabar.org

GEORGIA

Clients' Security Fund
State Bar of Georgia
800 The Hurt Building
50 Hurt Plaza
Atlanta, GA 30303
800-334-6865
www.gabar.org

HAWAII

Lawyers' Fund for Client Protection
Hawaii State Bar Association
1132 Bishop Street
Suite 300
Honolulu, HI 96813
808-599-2483
www.hsba.org

IDAHO

Client Security Fund
Idaho State Bar
P.O. Box 895
Boise, ID 83701
208-334-4500
www.state.id.us

ILLINOIS

Client Protection Program
Attorney Registration & Disciplinary
Commission of the Illinois Supreme Court
One Prudential Plaza
130 East Randolph Drive
Suite 1500
Chicago, IL 60601
312-565-2600

INDIANA

Clients' Financial Assistance Fund
Indiana State Bar Association
230 East Ohio Street
Fourth Floor
Indianapolis, IN 46204
317-639-5465
www.inbar.org

IOWA

Client Security Trust Fund
Supreme Court of Iowa
State Capitol
Des Moines, IA 50319
515-246-8076

KANSAS

Kansas Lawyers' Fund Client Protection
Kansas State Bar
Kansas Judicial Center
Room 374
301 S.W. Tenth Avenue
Topeka, KS 66612-1507
785-296-3229

KENTUCKY

Clients' Security Fund
Kentucky Bar Association
514 West Main Street
Frankfort, KY 40601-1883
502-564-3795
www.kybar.org

LOUISIANA
Client Protection Fund
Louisiana State Bar
601 Saint Charles Avenue
New Orleans, LA 70130
504-619-0107
www.lsba.org

MAINE
Lawyers Fund for Client Protection
Maine State Bar Association
P.O. Box 216
Islesboro, Maine 04848
207-734-6712
www.mainebar.org

MARYLAND
Client Security Fund
Bar of Maryland
Robert S. Sweeney District Court Building
Client Security Trust Fund
251 Rowe Boulevard Suite 341
Annapolis, MD 21401-2804
410-260-1950
www.cstf.org

MASSACHUSETTS
Clients' Security Board
75 Federal Street
Boston, MA 02110
617-388-0677
www.massbar.org

MICHIGAN

Client Protection Fund
State Bar of Michigan
Michael Franck Building
306 Townsend Street
Lansing, MI 48933
517-346-6379

MINNESOTA

Client Security Fund
Minnesota Judicial Center
25 Constitution Avenue
Suite 105
St. Paul, MN 55155
651-296-8406
www.courts.state.mn.us

MISSISSIPPI

Client Security Fund
The Mississippi Bar
643 North State Street
P.O. Box 2168
Jackson, MS 39225-2168
601-948-4471
www.msbar.org

MISSOURI

Client Security Fund
Missouri Bar
326 Monroe Street
P.O. Box 119
Jefferson City, MO 65102
573-635-4128
www.mobar.org

MONTANA

Lawyers' Fund for Client Protection
State Bar of Montana
P.O. Box 577
Helena, MT 59624-0577
406-442-7660

NEBRASKA

Client Protection Fund
Nebraska State Bar Association
635 South 14th Street
P.O. Box 81809
Lincoln, NE 68501
402-475-7091
www.nebar.com

NEVADA

Client's Security Fund
State Bar of Nevada
600 East. Charleston Blvd.
Las Vegas, NV 89104-1563
800-254-2797
www.nvbar.org

NEW HAMPSHIRE

Clients' Indemnity Fund
New Hampshire Bar Association
112 Pleasant Street
Concord, NH 03301
603-224-6942
www.nhbar.org

NEW JERSEY

Lawyers' Fund for Client Protection
Richard J. Hughes Justice Complex
P.O. Box 961
Trenton, NJ 08625-0961
609-984-7179

NEW MEXICO

Client Protection Fund
State Bar of New Mexico
P.O. Box 25883
Albuquerque, NM 87125
505-797-6000
www.jud.state.ct.us

NEW YORK

Lawyers' Fund for Client Protection
119 Washington Avenue
Albany, NY 12210
518-434-1935
Toll Free: 800-442-3863
www.nylawfund.org

NORTH CAROLINA

Client Security Fund
North Carolina State Bar
P.O. Box 25908
Raleigh, NC 27611
919-828-4620
www.ncbar.com

NORTH DAKOTA

Client Protection Fund
North Dakota State Bar
515 1/2 E. Broadway
Suite 101
Bismarck, ND 58502-2136
701-255-1404
www.sband.org

OHIO

Clients' Security Fund
1700 Lake Shore Drive
Columbus, OH 43204 Suite 285
800-282-6556
www.ohiobar.org

OKLAHOMA

Client Security Fund
Oklahoma Bar Association
P.O. Box 53036
1901 North Lincoln Boulevard
Oklahoma City, OK 73152-3036
405-416-7000
www.okbar.org

OREGON

Clients' Security Fund
Oregon State Bar
5200 S.W. Meadows Road
P.O. Box 1689
Lake Oswego, OR 97035
503-620-0222
www.osbar.org

PENNSYLVANIA

Pennsylvania Lawyers' Fund
for Client Security
5035 Ritter Road
Suite 900
Mechanicsburg, PA 17055-4823
800-962-4618
www.palawfund.com

RHODE ISLAND

Client Protection Fund
Rhode Island Bar Association
115 Cedar Street
Providence, RI 02903
401-421-5740
www.ribar.com

SOUTH CAROLINA

Lawyers' Fund for Client Protection
South Carolina Bar
950 Taylor Street
P.O. Box 608
Columbia, SC 29201-0608
803-799-6653
www.scbar.org

SOUTH DAKOTA

Client Security Fund
State Bar of South Dakota
222 East Capitol Street
Pierre, SD 57501
605-224-7554
www.sdbar.org

TENNESSEE

Lawyers' Fund for Client Protection
221 Fourth Avenue North
Suite 300
Nashville, TN 37219
615-741-3097
www.tsc.state.tn.us

TEXAS

Client Security Fund
State Bar of Texas
P.O. Box 12487
Austin, TX 78711-2487
512-453-5535

UTAH

Lawyers' Fund for Client Protection
Utah State Bar
645 South 200 East
Suite 310
Salt Lake City, UT 84111-3834
801-531-9095
www.utahbar.org

VERMONT

Client Security Fund
Vermont Bar Association
P.O. Box 100
Montpelier, VT 05601-0100
802-223-2020
www.vtbar.org

VIRGINIA

Clients' Protection Fund
Virginia State Bar
Eighth & Main Building
707 East Main Street
Suite 1500
Richmond, VA 23219-2803
804-775-0524
www.vsb.org

WASHINGTON

Lawyers' Fund For Client Protection
Washington State Bar Association
2101 Fourth Avenue
Fourth Floor
Seattle, WA 98121-2300
206-727-8232
www.wsba.org

WEST VIRGINIA

Clients Protection Fund
West Virginia State Bar
2006 Kanawha Boulevard East
Charleston, WV 25311
304-558-2546
www.wvbar.org

WISCONSIN

Clients' Security Fund
State Bar of Wisconsin
P.O. Box 7158
Madison, WI 53707-7158
608-257-3838
www.wisbar.org

WYOMING

Clients' Security Fund
Wyoming State Bar
P.O. Box 109 Drawer 5059
Cheyenne, WY 82003-0109
307-632-9061

-Appendix C-

CODE OF PROFESSIONAL RESPONSIBILITY

As stated in the text of this book, the American Bar Association developed both the Model Rules and Model Code of Professional Conduct. Most states have adopted some form of either the Rules or the Code. While some states have made substantial changes to the ABA's versions, many states versions have been adopted with little or no changes whatsoever. The state presented here, Ohio is an example of a state that has adopted a comparable version.

Table of Contents

Canon 8. A Lawyer Should Assist in Improving the Legal System

Canon 9. A Lawyer Should Avoid Even the Appearance of
Professional Impropriety Definitions

PREFACE

The Canons of this Code are statements of axiomatic norms, expressing in general terms the standards of professional conduct expected of lawyers in their relationships with the public, with the legal system, and with the legal profession. They embody the general concepts from which the Ethical Considerations and the Disciplinary Rules are derived.

The Ethical Considerations are aspirational in character and represent the objectives toward which every member of the profession should strive. They constitute a body of principles upon which the lawyer can rely for guidance in many specific situations.

The Disciplinary Rules, unlike the Ethical Considerations, are mandatory in character. The Disciplinary Rules state the minimum level of conduct below which no lawyer can fall without being subject to disciplinary action.

CANON 1

A Lawyer Should Assist in Maintaining the Integrity and Competence of the Legal Profession.

ETHICAL CONSIDERATIONS

EC 1-1. A basic tenet of the professional responsibility of lawyers is that every person in our society should have ready access to the independent professional services of a lawyer of integrity and competence. Maintaining the integrity and improving the competence of the bar to meet the highest standards is the ethical responsibility of every lawyer.

EC 1-2. The public should be protected from those who are not qualified to be lawyers by reason of a deficiency in education or moral standards or of other relevant factors but who nevertheless seek to practice law. To assure the maintenance of high moral and educational standards of the legal profession, lawyers should affirmatively assist courts and other appropriate bodies in promulgating, enforcing, and improving requirements for admission to the bar. In like manner, the bar has a positive obligation to aid in the continued improvement of all phases of pre-admission and post-admission legal education.

EC 1-3. Before recommending an applicant for admission, a lawyer should satisfy himself that the applicant is of good moral character. Although a lawyer should not become a self-appointed investigator or judge of applicants for admission, he should report to proper officials all unfavorable information he possesses relating to the character or other qualifications of an applicant.

EC 1-4. The integrity of the profession can be maintained only if conduct of lawyers in violation of the Disciplinary Rules is brought to the attention of the proper officials. A lawyer should reveal voluntarily to those officials all unprivileged knowledge of conduct of lawyers which he believes clearly to be in violation of the Disciplinary Rules. If in the course of an investigation by a grievance or ethics committee of a bar association or by the office of disciplinary counsel it is found that persons involved in the investigation may have violated federal or state criminal statutes, it is the duty of the investigatory agency to notify the appropriate law enforcement or prosecutorial authority of such alleged criminal violation. A lawyer should, upon request, serve on and assist committees and boards having responsibility for the administration of the Disciplinary Rules.

EC 1-5. A lawyer should maintain high standards of professional conduct and should encourage fellow lawyers to do likewise. He should be temperate and dignified, and he should refrain from all illegal and morally reprehensible conduct. Because of his position in society, even minor violations of law by a lawyer may tend to lessen public confidence in the legal profession. Obedience to law exemplifies respect for law. To lawyers especially, respect for the law should be more than a platitude.

EC 1-6. An applicant for admission to the bar or a lawyer may be unqualified, temporarily or permanently, for other than moral and educational reasons, such as mental or emotional instability. Lawyers should be diligent in taking steps to see that during a period of disqualification such person is not granted a license or, if licensed, is not permitted to practice. In like manner, when the disqualification has terminated, members of the bar should assist such person in being licensed, or, if licensed, in being restored to his full right to practice.

DISCIPLINARY RULES

DR 1-101. MAINTAINING INTEGRITY AND COMPETENCE OF THE LEGAL PROFESSION.

(A) A lawyer is subject to discipline if he has made a materially false statement in, or if he has deliberately failed to disclose a material fact requested in connection with, his application for admission to the bar.

(B) A lawyer shall not further the application for admission to the bar of another person known by him to be unqualified in respect to character, education, or other relevant attribute.

DR 1-102. MISCONDUCT.

(A) A lawyer shall not: (1) Violate a Disciplinary Rule or, as a judicial candidate as defined in Canon 7 of the Code of Judicial Conduct, the provisions of the Code of Judicial Conduct applicable to judicial candidates. (2) Circumvent a Disciplinary Rule through actions of another. (3) Engage in illegal conduct involving moral turpitude. (4) Engage in conduct involving dishonesty, fraud, deceit, or misrepresentation. (5) Engage in conduct that is prejudicial to the administration of justice (6) Engage in any other conduct that adversely reflects on the lawyer's fitness to practice law.

(B) A lawyer shall not engage, in a professional capacity, in conduct involving discrimination prohibited by law because of race, color, religion, age, gender, sexual orientation, national origin, marital status, or disability. This prohibition does not apply to a lawyer's confidential communication to a client or preclude legitimate advocacy where race, color, religion, age, gender, sexual orientation, national origin, marital status, or disability is relevant to the proceeding where the advocacy is made.

DR 1-103. DISCLOSURE OF INFORMATION TO AUTHORITIES.

(A) A lawyer possessing unprivileged knowledge of a violation of DR 1-102 shall report such knowledge to a tribunal or other authority empowered to investigate or act upon such violation.

(B) Any knowledge obtained by a member of a committee or subcommittee of a bar association, or by a member, employee, or agent of a nonprofit corporation established by a bar association, designed to assist lawyers with substance abuse or mental health problems shall be privileged for all purposes under DR 1-103, provided the knowledge was obtained while the member, employee, or agent was performing duties as a member, employee, or agent of the committee, subcommittee, or nonprofit corporation.

(C) Any knowledge obtained by a member of a committee or subcom-

mittee of a bar association, or by a member, employee, or agent of a non-profit corporation established by a bar association, designed to assist lawyers with substance-abuse problems shall be privileged for all purposes under DR 1-103, provided the knowledge was obtained while the member, employee, or agent was performing duties as a member, employee, or agent of the committee, subcommittee, or non-profit corporation.

DR 1-104. DISCLOSURE OF INFORMATION TO THE CLIENT.

(A) A lawyer shall inform a client at the time of the client's engagement of the lawyer or at any time subsequent to the engagement if the lawyer does not maintain professional liability insurance in the amounts of at least one hundred thousand dollars per occurrence and three hundred thousand dollars in the aggregate or if the lawyer's professional liability insurance is terminated. The notice shall be provided to the client on a separate form set forth following this rule and shall be signed by the client.

(B) A lawyer shall maintain a copy of the notice signed by the client for five years after termination of representation of the client.

(C) The notice required by division (A) of this rule shall not apply to a lawyer who is engaged in either of the following:

(1) Rendering legal services to a governmental entity that employs the lawyer;

(2) Rendering legal services to an entity that employs the lawyer as in-house counsel.

NOTICE TO CLIENT
Required by DR 1-104
Ohio Code of Professional
Responsibility

Pursuant to DR 1-104 of the Ohio Code of Professional Responsibility, I am required to notify you that I do not maintain professional liability (malpractice) insurance of at least $100,000 per occurrence and $300,000 in the aggregate.

_____
Attorney's Signature

CLIENT ACKNOWLEDGE-MENT

I acknowledge receipt of the notice required by DR 1-104 of the Ohio Code of Professional Responsibility that [insert attorney's name] does not maintain professional liability (malpractice) insurance of at least $100,000 per occurrence and $300,000 in the aggregate.

_____
Client's Signature

_____
Date

CANON 2

A Lawyer Should Assist the Legal Profession in Fulfilling Its Duty to Make Legal Counsel Available

ETHICAL CONSIDERATIONS

EC 2-1.The need of members of the public for legal services is met only if they recognize their legal problems, appreciate the importance of seeking assistance, and are able to obtain the services of acceptable legal counsel. Hence, important functions of the legal profession are to educate laymen to recognize their legal problems, to facilitate the process of intelligent selection of lawyers, and to assist in making legal services fully available.

Recognition of Legal Problems

EC 2-2. The legal profession should assist laymen to recognize legal problems because such problems may not be self-revealing and often are not timely noticed. Therefore, lawyers acting under proper auspices should encourage and participate in educational and public relations programs concerning our legal system with particular reference to legal problems that frequently arise. Such educational programs should be motivated by a desire to benefit the public rather than to obtain publicity or employment for particular lawyers. Examples of permissible activities include preparation of institutional advertisements and professional articles for lay publications and participation in seminars, lectures, and civic programs. But a lawyer who participates in such activities should shun personal publicity.

EC 2-3. Whether a lawyer acts properly in volunteering advice to a layman to seek legal services depends upon the circumstances. The giving of advice that one should take legal action could well be in fulfillment of the duty of the legal profession to assist laymen in recognizing legal problems. The advice is proper only if motivated by a desire to protect one who does not recognize that he may have legal problems or who is ignorant of his legal rights or obligations. Hence, the advice is improper if motivated by a desire to obtain personal benefit, secure personal publicity, or cause litigation to be brought merely to harass or injure another.

EC 2-4. Since motivation is subjective and often difficult to judge, the motives of a lawyer who volunteers advice likely to produce legal controversy may well be suspect if he receives professional employment or other benefits as a result. A lawyer who volunteers advice that one should obtain the services of a lawyer generally should not himself accept employment, compensation, or other benefit in connection with that matter. However, it is not improper for a lawyer to volunteer such advice and render resulting legal services to close friends, relatives, former clients (in regard to matters germane to former employment), and regular clients.

EC 2-5. A lawyer who writes or speaks for the purpose of educating members of the public to recognize their legal problems should carefully refrain from giving or appearing to give a general solution applicable to all apparently similar individual problems, since slight changes in fact situations may require a material variance in the applicable advice; otherwise, the public may be misled and misadvised. Talks and writings by lawyers for laymen should caution them not to attempt to solve individual problems upon the basis of the information contained therein.

Selection of a Lawyer: Generally

EC 2-6. Formerly a potential client usually knew the reputations of local lawyers for competency and integrity and therefore could select a practitioner in whom he had confidence. This traditional selection

process worked well because it was initiated by the client and the choice was an informed one.

EC 2-7. Changed conditions, however, have seriously restricted the effectiveness of the traditional selection process. Often the reputations of lawyers are not sufficiently known to enable laymen to make intelligent choices. The law has become increasingly complex and specialized. Few lawyers are willing and competent to deal with every kind of legal matter, and many laymen have difficulty in determining the competence of lawyers to render different types of legal services. The selection of legal counsel is particularly difficult for transients, persons moving into new areas, persons of limited education or means, and others who have little or no contact with lawyers.

EC 2-8. Selection of a lawyer by a layman often is the result of the advice and recommendation of third parties--relatives, friends, acquaintances, business associates, or other lawyers. A layman is best served if the recommendation is disinterested and informed. In order that the recommendation be disinterested, a lawyer should not seek to influence another to recommend his employment. A lawyer should not compensate another person for recommending him, for influencing a prospective client to employ him, or to encourage future recommendations.

Selection of a Lawyer: Professional Notices and Listings

EC 2-9. Methods of advertising that are false, misleading or deceptive should be and are prohibited.

However, the Disciplinary Rules recognize the value of giving assistance in the selection process through forms of advertising.
EC 2-10. The name under which a lawyer conducts his practice may be a factor in the selection process. The use of a trade name or an assumed name could mislead laymen concerning the identity, responsibility, and status of those practicing thereunder. Accordingly, a lawyer in private practice should practice only under his own name, the name of a lawyer employing him, a partnership name composed of the name of one or more of the lawyers practicing in a partnership, or, if permitted by law, in the name of a professional legal corporation, which should be clearly designated as such. For many years some law firms have used a firm name retaining one or more names of deceased or retired partners and such practice is not improper if the firm is a bona fide successor of a firm in which the deceased or retired person was a member, if the use of the name is authorized by law or by contract, and if the public is not misled thereby. However, the name of a partner who withdraws from a firm but continues to practice law should be omitted from the firm name in order to avoid misleading the public.
EC 2-11. A lawyer occupying a judicial, legislative, or public executive or administrative position who has the right to practice law concurrently may allow his name to remain in the name of the firm if he actively continues to practice law as a member thereof. Otherwise, his name should be removed from the firm name, and he should not be identified as a past or present member of the firm; and he should not hold himself out as being a practicing lawyer.
EC 2-12. In order to avoid the possibility of misleading persons with whom he deals, a lawyer should be scrupulous in the representation of his professional status. He should not hold himself out as being a partner or associate of a law firm if he is not one in fact, and thus should not hold himself out as a partner or associate if he only shares offices with another lawyer.
EC 2-13. In some instances, a lawyer confines his or her practice to a particular field of law. Except as provided in the Rules for the Government of the Bar of Ohio, a lawyer should not be permitted to hold himself or herself out as a specialist or as having special training or ability, other than in the historically excepted fields of admiralty, trademark, and patent law.
EC 2-14. The legal profession has developed lawyer referral systems designed to aid individuals who are able to pay fees but need assistance in locating lawyers competent to handle their particular problems. Use of a lawyer referral system enables a layman to avoid an uninformed selection of a lawyer because such a system makes possible the employment of competent lawyers who have indicated an interest in the subject matter involved. Lawyers should support the principle of lawyer referral systems and should encourage the evolution of other ethical plans

which aid in the selection of qualified counsel.

Financial Ability to Employ Counsel: Generally

EC 2-15. The legal profession cannot remain a viable force in fulfilling its role in our society unless its members receive adequate compensation for services rendered, and reasonable fees should be charged in appropriate cases to clients able to pay them. Nevertheless, persons unable to pay all or a portion of a reasonable fee should be able to obtain necessary legal services, and lawyers should support and participate in ethical activities designed to achieve that objective.

Financial Ability to Employ Counsel: Persons Able to Pay Reasonable Fees

EC 2-16. The determination of a proper fee requires consideration of the interests of both client and lawyer. A lawyer should not charge more than a reasonable fee, for excessive cost of legal service would deter laymen from utilizing the legal system in protection of their rights. Furthermore, an excessive charge abuses the professional relationship between lawyer and client. On the other hand, adequate compensation is necessary in order to enable the lawyer to serve his client effectively and to preserve the integrity and independence of the profession.

EC 2-17. The determination of the reasonableness of a fee requires consideration of all relevant circumstances, including those stated in the Disciplinary Rules. The fees of a lawyer will vary according to many factors, including the time required,

his experience, ability, and reputation, the nature of the employment, the responsibility involved, and the results obtained. Suggested fee schedules and economic reports of state and local bar associations provide some guidance on the subject of reasonable fees. It is a commendable and longstanding tradition of the bar that special consideration is given in the fixing of any fee for services rendered a brother lawyer or a member of his immediate family.

EC 2-18. As soon as feasible after a lawyer has been employed, it is desirable that he reach a clear agreement with his client as to the basis of the fee charges to be made. Such a course will not only prevent later misunderstanding but will also work for good relations between the lawyer and the client. It is usually beneficial to reduce to writing the understanding of the parties regarding the fee, particularly when it is contingent. A lawyer should be mindful that many persons who desire to employ him may have had little or no experience with fee charges of lawyers, and for this reason he should explain fully to such persons the reasons for the particular fee arrangement he proposes.

EC 2-19. Contingent fee arrangements in civil cases have long been commonly accepted in the United States in proceedings to enforce claims. The historical bases of their acceptance are that (1) they often, and in a variety of circumstances, provide the only practical means by which one having a claim against another can economically afford, finance, and obtain the services of a competent lawyer to prosecute his claim, and (2) a successful prosecution of the claim produces a res out of which the fee can be paid. Although a lawyer generally should decline to accept employment on a contingent fee basis by one who is able to pay a reasonable fixed fee, it is not necessarily improper for a lawyer, where justified by the particular circumstances of a case, to enter into a contingent fee contract in a civil case with any client who, after being fully informed of all relevant factors, desires that arrangement. Because of the human relationships involved and the unique character of the proceedings, contingent fee arrangements in domestic relations cases are rarely justified. In administrative agency proceedings contingent fee contracts should be governed by the same considerations as in other civil cases. Public policy properly condemns contingent fee arrangements in criminal cases, largely on the ground that legal services in criminal cases do not produce a res with which to pay the fee.

EC 2-20. A lawyer should not accept compensation or any thing of value incident to his employment or services from one other than his client without the knowledge and consent of his client after full disclosure.

EC 2-21. Without the prior consent of his or her client, a lawyer should not associate in a particular matter another lawyer outside his or her firm. A fee may properly be divided between lawyers properly associated if: (1) the division is in proportion to the services performed or, if agreed to in writing by the client, all of the lawyers assume responsibility for representing the client; (2) the terms of the fee division and the identity of all lawyers sharing in the fee are disclosed in writing to the client prior to obtaining the client's consent; and (3) the total fee is reasonable.

EC 2-22. A lawyer should be zealous in his efforts to avoid controversies over fees with clients and should attempt to resolve amicably any differences on the subject. He should not sue a client for a fee unless necessary to prevent fraud or gross imposition by the client.

Financial Ability to Employ Counsel: Persons Unable to Pay Reasonable Fees

EC 2-23. A layman whose financial ability is not sufficient to permit payment of any fee cannot obtain legal services, other than in cases where a contingent fee is appropriate, unless the services are provided for him. Even a person of moderate means may be unable to pay a reasonable fee which is large because of the complexity, novelty, or difficulty of the problem or similar factors.

EC 2-24. Historically, the need for legal services of those unable to pay reasonable fees has been met in part by lawyers who donated their services or accepted court appointments on behalf of such individuals. The basic responsibility for providing legal services for those unable to pay ultimately rests upon the individual lawyer, and personal involvement in the problems of the disadvantaged can be one of the most rewarding experiences in the life of a lawyer. Every lawyer, regardless of professional prominence or professional workload, should find time to participate in serving the disadvantaged. The rendition of free legal services to those unable to pay reasonable fees continues to be an obligation of each lawyer, but the efforts of individual lawyers are often not enough to meet the need. Thus it has been necessary for the profession to institute additional programs to provide legal services. Accordingly, legal aid offices, lawyer referral services, and other related programs have been developed, and others will be developed, by the profession. Every lawyer should support all proper efforts to meet this need for legal services.

Acceptance and Retention of Employment

EC 2-25. A lawyer is under no obligation to act as adviser or advocate for every person who may wish to become his client; but in furtherance of the objective of the bar to make legal services fully available, a lawyer should not lightly decline proffered employment. The fulfillment of this objective requires acceptance by a lawyer of his share of tendered employment which may be unattractive both to him and the bar generally.

EC 2-26. History is replete with instances of distinguished and sacrificial services by lawyers who have represented unpopular clients and causes. Regardless of his personal feelings, a lawyer should not decline representation because a client or a cause is unpopular or community reaction is adverse.

EC 2-27. The personal preference of a lawyer to avoid adversary alignment against judges, other lawyers, public officials, or influential members of the community does not justify his rejection of tendered employment.

EC 2-28. When a lawyer is appointed by a court or requested by a bar association to undertake representation of a person unable to obtain counsel, whether for financial or other reasons, he should not seek to be excused from undertaking the representation except for compelling reasons. Compelling reasons do not include such factors as the repugnance of the subject matter of the proceeding, the identity or position of a person involved in the case, the belief of the lawyer that the defendant in a criminal proceeding is guilty, or the belief of the lawyer regarding the merits of the civil case.

EC 2-29. Employment should not be accepted by a lawyer when he is unable to render competent service or when he knows or it is obvious that the person seeking to employ him desires to institute or maintain an action merely for the purpose of harassing or maliciously injuring another. Likewise, a lawyer should decline employment if the intensity of his personal feeling, as distinguished from a community attitude, may impair his effective representation of a prospective client. If a lawyer knows a client has previously obtained counsel, he should not accept employment in the matter unless the other counsel approves or withdraws, or the client terminates the prior employment.

EC 2-30. Full availability of legal counsel requires both that persons be able to obtain counsel and that lawyers who undertake representation complete the work involved. Trial counsel for a convicted defendant should continue to represent his client by advising whether to take an appeal and, if the appeal is prosecuted, by representing him through the appeal unless new counsel is substituted or withdrawal is permitted by the appropriate court.

EC 2-31. A decision by a lawyer to withdraw should be made only on the basis of compelling circumstances, and in a matter pending before a tribunal he must comply with the rules of the tribunal regarding withdrawal. A lawyer should not withdraw without considering carefully and endeavoring to minimize the possible adverse effect on the rights of his client and the possibility of prejudice to his client as a result of his withdrawal. Even when he justifiably withdraws, a lawyer should protect the welfare of his client by giving due notice of his withdrawal, suggesting employment of other counsel, delivering to the client all papers and property to which the client is entitled, cooperating with counsel subsequently employed, and otherwise endeavoring to minimize the possibility of harm. Further, he should refund to the client any compensation not earned during the employment.

EC 2-32. As a party of the legal profession's commitment to the principle that high quality legal services should be available to all, attorneys are encouraged to cooperate with qualified legal assistance organizations providing prepaid legal services. Such participation should at all times be in accordance with the basic tenets of the profession: independence, integrity, competence and devotion to the interests of individual clients. An attorney so participating should make certain that his relationship with a qualified legal assistance organization in no way interferes with his independent, professional representation of the interests of the individual client. An attorney should avoid situations in which officials of the organization who are not lawyers attempt to direct attorneys concerning the manner in which legal services are performed for individual members, and should also avoid situations in which considerations of economy are given undue weight in determining the attorneys employed by an organization or the legal services to be performed for the member or beneficiary rather than competence and quality of service. An attorney interested in maintaining the historic traditions of the profession and preserving the function of a lawyer as a trusted and independent advisor to individual members of society should carefully assess such factors when accepting employment by, or otherwise participating in, a particular qualified legal assistance organization, and while so participating should adhere to the highest professional standards of effort and competence.

DR 2-101. PUBLICITY.

(A) A lawyer shall not, on his or her own behalf or that of a partner, associate, or other lawyer affiliated with the lawyer or the lawyer's firm, use, or participate in the use of, any form of public communication, including direct mail solicitation, that: (1) Contains any false, fraudulent, misleading, deceptive, self-laudatory, or unfair statement; (2) Seeks employment in connection with matters in which the lawyer or law firm does not intend to actively participate in the representation, but that the lawyer or law firm intends to refer to other counsel, except that this provision shall not apply to organizations defined in DR 2-103(D)(1); (3) Contains any testimonial of past or present clients pertaining to the lawyer's capability; (4) Contains any claim that is not verifiable; (5) Contains characterizations of rates or fees chargeable by the lawyer or law firm, such as "cut-rate," "lowest," "giveaway," "below cost," "discount," and "special;" however, use of characterizations of rates or fees such as "reasonable" and "moderate" is acceptable.

(B) Subject to the limitations contained in these rules: (1) A lawyer or law firm may advertise services or the sale of a law practice through newspapers, periodicals, trade journals, "shoppers," and similar print media, outdoor advertising, radio and television, and written communication. (2) A lawyer or law firm may permit or purchase inclusion of information in a telephone or city directory, subject to the following standards: (a) The lawyer's or the firm's name, address, and telephone number may be listed alphabetically in the residential, business, or classified sections. (b) Listing or display advertising in the classified section shall be limited to one or more of the following: (i) under the general heading "Lawyers" or "Attorneys;" (ii) if a lawyer or a firm meets the requirements of DR 2-105(A)(1), under the classification or heading identifying the field or area of practice in which the lawyer or firm is so qualified; (iii) under a classification or heading that identifies the lawyer or firm by geographic location, certification as a specialist pursuant to DR 2-105(A)(4) or (5), or field of law as provided by DR 2-105(A)(6).

(c) Nothing contained in this rule shall prohibit a lawyer or law firm from permitting inclusion in reputable law lists and law directories intended primarily for the use of the legal profession, of such information as has traditionally appeared in those publications. (3) Brochures or pamphlets containing biographical and informational data that is acceptable under these rules may be disseminated directly to clients, members of the bar, or others.

(C) A communication is false or misleading if it satisfies any of the following: (1) Contains a material misrepresentation of fact or law, or omits a fact necessary to make the statement considered as a whole not materially misleading; (2) Is likely to create an unjustified expectation about results the lawyer can achieve, or states or implies that the lawyer can achieve results by means that violate the Code of

Professional Responsibility or other law; (3) Is subjectively self-laudatory, or compares a lawyer's services with other lawyers' services, unless the comparison can be factually substantiated.

(D) The following information with regard to lawyers, law firms, or members of firms will be presumed to be informational rather than solely promotional or self-laudatory, and acceptable for dissemination under these rules, if accurate and presented in a dignified manner: (1) Name or names of lawyer, law firm, and professional associates, together with their addresses and telephone numbers, with designations such as "Lawyer," "Attorney," "Law Firm"; (2) Field or fields of practice, limitations of practice, or areas of concentration, but only to the extent permitted by DR 2-105; (3) Date and place of birth; (4) Dates and places of admission to the bar of the state and federal courts; (5) Schools attended, with dates of graduation and degrees conferred; (6) Legal teaching positions held at accredited law schools; (7) Authored publications; (8) Memberships in bar associations and other professional organizations (9) Technical and professional licenses; (10) Military service;(11) Foreign language abilities; (12) Subject to DR 2-103, prepaid or group legal service programs in which the lawyer or firm participates; (13) Whether credit cards or other credit arrangements are accepted; (14) Office and telephone answering services hours.

(E)(1) Any of the following information with regard to fees and charges, if presented in a dignified manner, is acceptable for communication to the public in the manner stipulated by DR 2-101(B): (a) Fee for an initial consultation; (b) Availability upon request of either a written schedule of fees or of an estimate of the fee to be charged for specific services; (c) Contingent fee rates, subject to DR 2-106(C), provided that the statement discloses whether percentages are computed before or after deduction of costs and expenses and advises the public that, in the event of an adverse verdict or decision, the contingent fee litigant could be liable for payment of court costs, expenses of investigation, expenses of medical examinations, and costs incurred in obtaining and presenting evidence; (d) Fixed fee or range of fees for specific legal services or hourly fee rates, provided the statement discloses that; (i) Stated fixed fees or range of fees will be available only to clients whose matters are included among the specified services; (ii) If the client's matter is not included among the specified services or if no hourly fee rate is stated, the client will be entitled, without obligation, to a specific written estimate of the fee likely to be charged. (2)(a) If a lawyer or a law firm quotes a fee for a service in an advertisement or direct mail solicitation, the service must be rendered for no more than the fee advertised or quoted. (b) Unless otherwise specified in the advertisement, if a lawyer or a law firm includes any fee information in a publication that is published more frequently than one time per

month, the lawyer or law firm shall be bound by any representation made in the advertisement for a period of not less than thirty days after such publication. If a lawyer or law firm publishes any fee information in a publication that is published once a month or less frequently, the lawyer or law firm shall be bound by any representation made in the advertisement until the publication of the succeeding issue. If a lawyer or law firm advertises any fee information in a publication that has no fixed date for publication of a succeeding issue, the lawyer or law firm shall be bound by any representation made in the advertisement for a reasonable period of time after publication, but in no event less than one year. (c) Unless otherwise specified, if a lawyer or law firm broadcasts any fee information by radio or television, the lawyer or law firm shall be bound by any representation made in the broadcast for a period of not less than thirty days after the date of the broadcast.
(F)(1) A lawyer shall not make any solicitation of legal business in person or by telephone, except as provided in DR 2-103 and DR 2-104. (2) A lawyer or law firm may engage in written solicitation by direct mail addressed to persons or groups of persons who may be in need of specific legal service by reason of a circumstance, condition, or occurrence that is known or, upon reasonable inquiry, could be known to the soliciting lawyer or law firm, provided the letter of solicitation: (a) Discloses accurately and fully the manner in which the lawyer or law firm became aware of and verified the identity and specific legal need of the addressee; (b) Disclaims any prior acquaintance or contact with the addressee and avoids any personalization in approach unless the facts are otherwise; (c) Disclaims or refrains from expressing any predetermined evaluation of the merits of the addressee's case; (d) Conforms to standards required by these rules with respect to information acceptable for inclusion in media advertising by lawyers and law firms; (e) Includes in its text and on the envelope in which mailed, in red ink and in type no smaller than 10 point, the recital - "ADVERTISEMENT ONLY." (3) The provisions of division (F)(2) of this rule shall not apply to organizations defined in DR 2-103(D)(1). (4) Prior to mailing a written solicitation of legal business pursuant to division (F)(2) of this rule to a party who has been named as a defendant in a civil action, a lawyer or law firm shall verify that the party has been served with notice of the action filed against that party. Service shall be verified by consulting the docket of the court in which the action was filed to determine whether mail, personal, or residence service has been perfected or whether service by publication has been completed. Division (F)(4) of this rule shall not apply to the solicitation of a debtor regarding representation of the debtor in a potential or actual bankruptcy action. (G) A lawyer shall not directly or indirectly compensate or give any thing of value to representatives of the press, radio, television, or other communication

medium in anticipation of or in return for professional publicity in a news item. (H)(1) If a communication is sent by a lawyer to a prospective client or a relative of a prospective client within thirty days of an accident or disaster that gives rise to a potential claim for personal injury or wrongful death, the following "Understanding Your Rights" must be enclosed with the communication.

UNDERSTANDING YOUR RIGHTS*

If you have been in an accident, or a family member has been injured or killed in a crash or some other incident, you have many important decisions to make. We believe it is important for you to consider the following: 1. Make and keep records - If your situation involves a motor vehicle crash, regardless of who may be at fault, it is helpful to obtain a copy of the police report, learn the identity of any witnesses, and obtain photographs of the scene, vehicles, and any visible injuries. Keep copies of receipts of all your expenses and medical care related to the incident. 2. You do not have to sign anything - You may not want to give an interview or recorded statement without first consulting with an attorney, because the statement can be used against you. If you may be at fault or have been charged with a traffic or other offense, it may be advisable to consult an attorney right away. However, if you have insurance, your insurance policy probably requires you to cooperate with your insurance company and to provide a statement to the company. If you

fail to cooperate with your insurance company, it may void your coverage. 3. Your interests versus interests of insurance company - Your interests and those of the other person's insurance company are in conflict. Your interests may also be in conflict with your own insurance company. Even if you are not sure who is at fault, you should contact your own insurance company and advise the company of the incident to protect your insurance coverage. 4. There is a time limit to file an insurance claim - Legal rights, including filing a lawsuit, are subject to time limits. You should ask what time limits apply to your claim. You may need to act immediately to protect your rights. 5. Get it in writing - You may want to request that any offer of settlement from anyone be put in writing, including a written explanation of the type of damages which they are willing to cover. 6. Legal assistance may be appropriate - You may consult with an attorney before you sign any document or release of claims. A release may cut off all future rights against others, obligate you to repay past medical bills or disability benefits, or jeopardize future benefits. If your interests conflict with your own insurance company, you always have the right to discuss the matter with an attorney of your choice, which may be at your own expense. 7. How to find an attorney - If you need professional advice about a legal problem but do not know an attorney, you may wish to check with relatives, friends, neighbors, your employer or co-workers who may be able to recommend an attorney. Your local bar association may have a lawyer referral service that can be found in the Yellow Pages.

8. Check a lawyer's qualifications - Before hiring any lawyer, you have the right to know the lawyer's background, training, and experience in dealing with cases similar to yours.

9. How much will it cost? - In deciding whether to hire a particular lawyer, you should discuss, and the lawyer's written fee agreement should reflect: a. How is the lawyer to be paid? If you already have a settlement offer, how will that affect a contingent fee arrangement? b. How are the expenses involved in your case, such as telephone calls, deposition costs, and fees for expert witnesses, to be paid? Will these costs be advanced by the lawyer or charged to you as they are incurred? Since you are obligated to pay all expenses even if you lose your case, how will payment be arranged? c. Who will handle your case? If the case goes to trial, who will be the trial attorney? This information is not intended as a complete description of your legal rights, but as a checklist of some of the important issues you should consider.

*THE SUPREME COURT OF OHIO, WHICH GOVERNS THE CONDUCT OF LAWYERS IN THE STATE OF OHIO, NEITHER PROMOTES NOR PROHIBITS THE DIRECT SOLICITATION OF PERSONAL INJURY VICTIMS. THE COURT DOES REQUIRE THAT, IF SUCH A SOLICITATION IS MADE, IT MUST INCLUDE THE ABOVE DISCLOSURE. (2) The communication described in division (H)(1) of this rule must meet all of the other requirements of these rules. (3) The communication described in division (H)(1) of this rule applies to any communication sent by a lawyer, on the lawyer's behalf, or by the lawyer's firm, partner, associate, or any other lawyer affiliated with the lawyer or the lawyer's firm.

DR 2-102. PROFESSIONAL NOTICES, LETTERHEADS, AND OFFICES. (A) A lawyer or law firm may use or participate in the use of professional cards, professional announcement cards, office signs, letterheads, or similar professional notices or devices, that are in dignified form and comply with the following: (1)A professional card of a lawyer identifying the lawyer by name and as a lawyer and giving the lawyer's addresses, telephone numbers, law firm name, and any information permitted under DR 2-105. A professional card of a law firm may also give the names of members and associates and may be used for identification. (2)A brief professional announcement card stating new or changed associations or addresses, change of firm name, sale of a law practice, or similar matters pertaining to the professional offices of a lawyer or law firm. It shall not state the nature of the practice except as permitted under DR 2-105. (3) A sign on or near the door of the office and in the building directory identifying the law office. The sign shall not state the nature of the practice, except as permitted under DR 2-105. (4)A letterhead of a lawyer identifying the lawyer by name and as a lawyer, and giving the lawyer's addresses, telephone numbers, law firm name, associates, and any information permitted under DR 2-105. A letterhead of a law firm may also give the names of members and associates, and names and dates relating to deceased and retired members. A lawyer may be designated "Of Counsel" on a letterhead if the lawyer has a continuing relationship with a lawyer or law firm, other than as a partner or associate. A lawyer or law firm may be designated as "General Counsel" or by similar professional reference on stationery of a client if the lawyer or the firm devotes a substantial amount of professional time in the representation of that client. The letterhead of a law firm may give the names and dates of predecessor firms in a continuing line of succession.

(B) A lawyer in private practice shall not practice under a trade name, a name that is misleading as to the identity of the lawyer or lawyers practicing under the name, or a firm name containing names other than those of one or more of the lawyers in the firm, except that the name of a professional corporation or association, legal clinic, limited liability company, or registered partnership shall contain symbols indicating the nature of the organization as required by Gov. Bar R. III. If otherwise lawful, a firm may use as, or continue to include in, its name the name or names of one or more deceased or retired members of the firm or of a predecessor firm in a continuing line of succession. A lawyer who assumes a judicial, legislative, public executive, or administrative post or office shall not permit his or her name to remain in the name of a law firm or to be used in professional notices of the firm during any significant period in which the lawyer is not actively and regularly practicing law as a member of the firm, and during this period other members of the firm shall not use the lawyer's name in the firm name or in professional notices of the firm.

(C) A lawyer shall not hold himself or herself out as having a partnership with one or more other lawyers or professional corporations unless they are in fact partners.

(D) A partnership shall not be formed or continued between or among lawyers licensed in different jurisdictions unless all enumerations of the members and associates of the firm on its letterhead and in other permissible listings make clear the jurisdictional limitations on those members and associates of the firm not licensed to practice in all listed jurisdictions; however, the same firm name may be used in each jurisdiction.

(E) A lawyer who is engaged both in the practice of law and another profession or business shall not so indicate on the lawyer's letterhead, office sign, or professional card, nor shall the lawyer identify himself or herself as a lawyer in any publication in connection with his or her other profession or business.

(F) Nothing contained in this rule shall prohibit a lawyer from using or permitting the use, in connection with the lawyer's name, of an earned degree or title derived from an earned degree indicating the lawyer's training in the law.

(G) A legal clinic operated by one or more lawyers may be organized by the lawyer or lawyers for the purpose of providing standardized and multiple legal services. The name of the law office shall consist only of the names of one or more of the active practitioners in the organization, and may include the phrase "legal clinic" or words of similar import. The use of a trade name or geographical or other type of identification or description is prohibited. The name of any active practitioner in the clinic may be retained in the name of the legal clinic after the lawyer's death, retirement or inactivity because of age or disability, and the name must otherwise conform to other provisions of the Code of Professional Responsibility and The Supreme Court Rules for the Government of the Bar of Ohio. The legal clinic cannot be owned by, and profits or losses cannot be shared with, non-lawyers or lawyers who are not actively engaged in the practice of law in the organization.

DR 2-103. RECOMMENDATION OF PROFESSIONAL EMPLOYMENT.

(A) A lawyer shall not recommend employment, as a private practitioner, of himself or herself, his or her partner, or associate to a non-lawyer who has not sought the lawyer's advice regarding employment of a lawyer, except as provided in DR 2-101.

(B) A lawyer shall not compensate or give any thing of value to a person or organization to recommend or secure the lawyer's employment by a client, or as a reward for having made a recommendation resulting in the lawyer's employment by a client, except that the lawyer may pay the usual and reasonable fees or dues charged by any of the organizations listed in DR 2-103(D).

(C) A lawyer shall not request a person or organization to recommend or promote the use of the lawyer's services or those of the lawyer's partner or associate, or any other lawyer affiliated with the lawyer or the lawyer's firm, as a private practitioner, except that:

(1) The lawyer may request referrals from a lawyer referral service that refers the lawyer to prospective clients but only if the lawyer referral service conforms to all of the following: (a) Operates in the public interest for the purpose of referring prospective clients to lawyers, pro bono and public service programs, and government, consumer, or other agencies who can provide the assistance the clients need in light of their financial circumstance, spoken language, any disability, geographical convenience, and the nature and complexity of their problem; (b) Calls itself a lawyer referral service or a lawyer referral and information service; (c) Is open to all lawyers who are licensed and admitted to the practice of law in Ohio who maintain an office in the geographi-

cal area to be served by the service and who meet reasonable, objectively determined experience requirements established by the service; pay the reasonable registration and membership fees established by the service; and maintain in force a policy of errors and omissions insurance in an amount established by the service; (d) Establishes rules that prohibit lawyer members of the service from charging prospective clients to whom a client is referred, fees and or costs that exceed charges the client would have incurred had no lawyer referral service been involved;

(e) Establishes procedures to survey periodically clients referred to determine client satisfaction with its operations and to investigate and take appropriate action with respect to client complaints against lawyer members of the service, and the service and its employees;

(f) Establishes procedures for admitting, suspending, or removing lawyers from its roll of panelists and promulgates rules that prohibit the making of a fee generating referral to any lawyer who has an ownership interest in, or who operates or is employed by the lawyer referral service, or who is associated with a law firm that has an ownership interest in, or operates or is employed by the lawyer referral service; (g) Establishes subject-matter panels, eligibility for which shall be determined on the basis of experience and other substantial objectively determinable criteria; (h) Does not, as a condition of participation in the referral service, limit the lawyer's selection of co-counsel to other lawyers listed with the referral service; (i) Does not make a fee-generating referral to any lawyer who has an ownership interest in or who operates or is employed by the lawyer referral service or who is associated with a law firm that has an ownership interest in or operates or is employed by a lawyer referral service. (j) Reports regularly to the Supreme Court Committee for Lawyer Referral and Information Services and complies with the record-keeping and requirements of and regulations adopted by the Committee. (2) A lawyer participating in a lawyer referral service that meets the requirements of divisions (C)(1)(a) to (j) of this rule may: (a) Be required, in addition to payment of a membership or regitration fee as provided in divisions (C)(1)(c) of this rule, to pay a fee calculated as a percentage of legal fees earned by any lawyer panelist to whom the lawyer referral service has referred a matter. The income from the percentage fee shall be used only to pay the reasonable operating expenses of the service and to fund public service activities of the service or its sponsoring organization, including the delivery of pro bono public services; (b) As a condition of participation in the service, be required to submit any fee disputes with a referred client to mandatory fee arbitration; (c) Participate in moderate and no-fee panels and other special panels established by the service that respond to the referral needs of the consumer public, eligibility for which shall be determined on the basis of experience and other substantial objectively determinable criteria. (3) The lawyer may cooperate with the legal service activities of any of the offices or organizations enumerated in divisions (D)(1) to (4) of this rule and may perform legal services for those to whom the lawyer was recommended by it to do such work if both of the following apply: (a) The person to whom the recommendation is made is a member or beneficiary of such office or organization; (b) The lawyer remains free to exercise independent professional judgment on behalf of the lawyer's client.

(D) A lawyer shall not knowingly assist a person or organization that furnishes or pays for legal services to others to promote the use of the lawyer's services or those of the lawyer's partner or associate or any other lawyer affiliated with the lawyer or the lawyer's firm except as permitted in DR 2-101(B). However, this does not prohibit a lawyer or the lawyer's partner or associate or any other lawyer affiliated with the lawyer or the lawyer's firm from being recommended, employed, or paid by, or cooperating with, assisting, and providing legal services for, one of the following offices or organizations that promote the use of the lawyer's services or those of the lawyer's partner or associate or any other lawyer affiliated with the lawyer or the lawyer's firm if there is no interference with the exercise of independent professional judgment on behalf of the lawyer's client: (1) A legal aid office or public defender office: (a) Operated or sponsored by a duly accredited law school. (b) Operated or sponsored by a bona fide non-profit community organization. (c) Operated or sponsored by a governmental agency. (d) Operated, sponsored, or approved by a bar association. (2) A military legal assistance office. (3) A lawyer referral service that complies with division (C) of this rule. (4) Any bona fide organization that recommends, furnishes, or pays for legal services to its members or beneficiaries provided all of the following conditions are satisfied: (a) The organization, including any affiliate, is organized and operated so that no profit is derived by it from the rendition of legal services by lawyers, and that, if the organization is organized for profit, the legal services are not rendered by lawyers employed, directed, supervised, or selected by it except in connection with matters where the organization bears ultimate liability of its member or beneficiary. (b) Neither the lawyer, the lawyer's partner, associate, or any other lawyer affiliated with the lawyer or the lawyer's firm, nor any non-lawyer, shall have initiated or promoted the organization for the primary purpose of providing financial or other benefit to the lawyer, partner, associate, or affiliated lawyer.

(c) The organization is not operated for the purpose of procuring legal work or financial benefit for any lawyer as a private practitioner outside of the legal services program of the organization. (d) The member or beneficiary to whom the legal services are furnished, and not the organization, is recognized as the client of the lawyer in the matter. (e) Any member or beneficiary who is entitled to have legal services furnished or paid for by the organization, if such member or beneficiary so desires, may select counsel other than that furnished, selected or approved by the organization; provided, however, that the organization shall be under no obligation to pay for the legal services furnished by the attorney selected by the beneficiary unless the terms of the legal services plan specifically provide for payment. Every legal services plan shall provide that any member or beneficiary may assert a claim that representation by counsel furnished, selected, or approved by the organization would be unethical, improper, or inadequate under the circumstances of the matter involved. The plan shall provide for adjudication of a claim under division (D)(4)(c) of this rule and appropriate relief through substitution of counsel or providing that the beneficiary may select counsel and the organization shall pay for the legal services rendered by selected counsel to the extent that such services are covered under the plan and in an amount equal to the cost that would have been incurred by the plan if the plan had furnished designated counsel. (f) The lawyer does not know or have cause to know that the organization is in violation of applicable laws, rules of court, and other legal requirements that govern its legal service operations. (g) The organization has filed with the Supreme Court of Ohio, on or before the first day of January

of each year, a report with respect to its legal service plan, if any, showing its terms, its schedule of benefits, its subscription charges, agreements with counsel, and financial results of its legal service activities or, if it has failed to do so, the lawyer does not know or have cause to know of the failure. (E) Nothing in this rule prohibits a lawyer from accepting employment received in response to the lawyer's own advertising, provided the advertising is in compliance with DR 2-101.

DR 2-104. SUGGESTION OF NEED OF LEGAL SERVICES.

(A) A lawyer who has given unsolicited advice to a nonlawyer that the nonlawyer should obtain counsel or take legal action shall not accept employment resulting from that advice, except that: (1) A lawyer may accept employment by a close friend, relative, former client, if the advice is germane to the former employment, or one whom the lawyer reasonably believes to be a client. (2) A lawyer may accept employment that results from the lawyer's participation in activities designed to educate nonlawyers to recognize legal problems, to make intelligent selection of counsel, or to utilize available legal services if the activities are conducted or sponsored by any of the offices or organizations enumerated in DR 2-103(D)(1) through (4), to the extent and under the conditions prescribed in these rules.

(3) A lawyer who is recommended, furnished or paid by a qualified legal assistance organization enu-

merated in DR 2-103(D)(1) through (4) may represent a member or beneficiary of the organization, to the extent and under the conditions prescribed in these rules. (4) Without affecting the lawyer's right to accept employment, a lawyer may speak publicly or write for publication on legal topics so long as the lawyer does not emphasize the lawyer's own professional experience or reputation and does not undertake to give individual advice. (5) If success in asserting rights or defenses of the lawyer's client in litigation in the nature of a class action is dependent upon the joinder of others, a lawyer may accept, but shall not seek, employment from those contacted for the purpose of obtaining their joinder.
(B) Nothing in this rule prohibits a lawyer from accepting employment received in response to the lawyer's own advertising, provided the advertising is in compliance with DR 2-101.

DR 2-105. LIMITATION OF PRACTICE.

(A) A lawyer shall not hold himself or herself out publicly as a specialist or as limiting his or her practice, except as follows:(1) A lawyer admitted to practice before the United States Patent Office may use the designation "Patents," "Patent Attorney," or "Patent Lawyer," or any combination of those terms, on his letterhead and office sign. A lawyer engaged in the trademark practice may use the designation "Trademarks,"   "Trademark Attorney," or "Trademark Lawyer," or any combination of those terms, on his letterhead and office sign, and a lawyer engaged in the admiralty practice may use the designation "Admiralty," "Proctor in Admiralty," or "Admiralty Lawyer," or any combination of those terms, on his letterhead and office sign. (2) A lawyer may permit his name to be listed in lawyer referral service offices according to the fields of law in which he will accept referrals. (3) A lawyer available to act as a consultant to or as an associate of other lawyers in a particular branch of law or legal service may distribute to other lawyers and publish in legal journals a dignified announcement of such availability, but the announcement shall not contain a representation of special competence or experience. (4) A lawyer who is certified as a specialist in a particular field of law pursuant to the Supreme Court Rules for the Government of the Bar of Ohio may hold himself or herself out as a specialist only in accordance with those rules. (5) A lawyer who has received certification from a private organization of special training, competence, or experience in a particular field of law may communicate the fact of the certification only if the certifying organization is bona fide, certification is issued only to lawyers who meet objective and consistently applied standards relevant to practice in that field of law that are higher than those required for admission to the practice of law, and certification is available to all lawyers who meet the standards. Any communication regarding certification shall comply with DR

2-101 and, unless the certifying organization is so approved, shall contain a statement that the certifying organization is not approved by the Supreme Court Commission on Certification of Attorneys as Specialists. (6) A lawyer may state that his or her practice consists in large part or is limited to a field or fields of law. Except as provided in DR 2-105(A)(1), (4), and (5), a lawyer may not claim or imply special competence or experience in a field of law through use of the term "specialize" or otherwise.

DR 2-106. FEES FOR LEGAL SERVICES.
(A) A lawyer shall not enter into an agreement for, charge, or collect an illegal or clearly excessive fee.
(B) A fee is clearly excessive when, after a review of the facts, a lawyer of ordinary prudence would be left with a definite and firm conviction that the fee is in excess of a reasonable fee. Factors to be considered as guides in determining the reasonableness of a fee include the following:
(1) The time and labor required, the novelty and difficulty of the questions involved, and the skill requisite to perform the legal service properly. (2) The likelihood, if apparent to the client, that the acceptance of the particular employment will preclude other employment by the lawyer.
(3) The fee customarily charged in the locality for similar legal services. (4) The amount involved and the results obtained. (5) The time limitations imposed by the client or by the circumstances. (6) The nature

and length of the professional relationship with the client. (7) The experience, reputation, and ability of the lawyer or lawyers performing the services. (8) Whether the fee is fixed or contingent.
(C) A lawyer shall not enter into an arrangement for, charge, or collect a contingent fee for representing a defendant in a criminal case.

DR 2-107. DIVISION OF FEES AMONG LAWYERS.
(A) Division of fees by lawyers who are not in the same firm may be made only with the prior consent of the client and if all of the following apply: (1) The division is in proportion to the services performed by each lawyer or, if by written agreement with the client, all lawyers assume responsibility for the representation; (2) The terms of the division and the identity of all lawyers sharing in the fee are disclosed in writing to the client; (3) The total fee is reasonable.
(B) In cases of dispute between lawyers arising under this rule, fees shall be divided in accordance with mediation or arbitration provided by a local bar association. Disputes that cannot be resolved by a local bar association shall be referred to the Ohio State Bar Association for mediation or arbitration.
(C) This rule does not prohibit payment to a former partner or associate pursuant to a separation or retirement agreement or payments made in conjunction with the sale of a law practice in accordance with DR 2-111.

DR 2-108. AGREEMENTS RESTRICTING THE PRACTICE OF A LAWYER.

(A) A lawyer shall not be a party to or participate in a partnership or employment agreement with another lawyer that restricts the right of a lawyer to practice law after the termination of a relationship created by the agreement, except as a condition to payment of retirement benefits or the sale of a law practice in accordance with DR 2-111.

(B) In connection with the settlement of a controversy or suit, a lawyer shall not enter into an agreement that restricts his right to practice law.

DR 2-109. ACCEPTANCE OF EMPLOYMENT.

(A) A lawyer shall not accept employment on behalf of a person if he knows or it is obvious that such person wishes to: (1) Bring a legal action, conduct a defense, or assert a position in litigation, or otherwise have steps taken for him, merely for the purpose of harassing or maliciously injuring any person. (2) Present a claim or defense in litigation that is not warranted under existing law, unless it can be supported by good faith argument for an extension, modification, or reversal of existing law.

DR 2-110. WITHDRAWAL FROM EMPLOYMENT.

(A)   In General.
(1) If permission for withdrawal from employment is required by the rules of a tribunal, a lawyer shall not withdraw from employment in a proceeding before that tribunal without its permission. (2) In any event, a lawyer shall not withdraw from employment until the lawyer has taken reasonable steps to avoid foreseeable prejudice to the rights of his or her client, including giving due notice to his or her client, allowing time for employment of other counsel, delivering to the client all papers and property to which the client is entitled, and complying with applicable laws and rules. (3) A lawyer who withdraws from employment shall refund promptly any part of a fee paid in advance that has not been earned, except when withdrawal is pursuant to DR 2-111.

(B)   Mandatory Withdrawal. A lawyer representing a client before a tribunal, with its permission if required by its rules, shall withdraw from employment, and a lawyer representing a client in other matters shall withdraw from employment if the lawyer: (1) Knows or it is obvious that the client is bringing the legal action, conducting the defense, or asserting a position in the litigation, or is otherwise having steps taken for the client, merely for the purpose of harassing or maliciously injuring any person. (2) Knows or it is obvious that his or her continued employment will result in violation of a Disciplinary Rule.

(3)   Has a mental or physical condition that renders it unreasonably difficult for the lawyer to carry out the employment effectively.

(4)   Is discharged by the client.

(C)   Permissive Withdrawal. If DR 2-110(B) is not applicable, a lawyer may not request permission to withdraw in matters pending before a tribunal, and may not withdraw in other matters, unless the request or withdrawal is because: (1) The client: (a) Insists upon presenting a claim or defense that is not warranted under existing law and cannot be supported by good faith argument for an extension, modification, or reversal of existing law. (b) Personally seeks to pursue an illegal course of conduct. (c) Insists that the lawyer pursue a course of conduct that is illegal or that is prohibited under the Disciplinary Rules. (d) By other conduct renders it unreasonably difficult for the lawyer to carry out his or her employment effectively. (e) Insists, in a matter not pending before a tribunal, that the lawyer engage in conduct that is contrary to the judgment and advice of the lawyer but not prohibited under the Disciplinary Rules. (f) Deliberately disregards an agreement or obligation to the lawyer as to expenses or fees. (2) The lawyer's continued employment is likely to result in a violation of a Disciplinary Rule. (3) The lawyer's inability to work with co-counsel indicates that the best interests of the client likely will be served by withdrawal. (4) The lawyer's mental or physical condition renders it difficult for him to carry out the employment effectively. (5) The client knowingly and freely assents to termination of the lawyer's employment. (6) The lawyer believes in good faith, in a proceeding pending before a tribunal, that the tribunal will find the existence of other good cause for withdrawal. (7) The lawyer sells the law practice in accordance with DR 2-111.

DR 2-111. SALE OF LAW PRACTICE

(A)(1) Subject to the provisions of this rule, a lawyer or law firm may sell or purchase a law practice, including the good will of the practice. The law practice shall be sold in its entirety, except where a conflict of interest is present that prevents the transfer of representation of a client or class of clients. This rule shall not permit the sale or purchase of a law practice where the purchasing lawyer is buying the practice for the sole or primary purpose of reselling the practice to another lawyer or law firm. (2) As used in this rule: (a) "Purchasing lawyer" means either an individual lawyer or a law firm; (b) "Selling lawyer" means an individual lawyer, a law firm, the estate of a deceased lawyer, or the representatives of a disabled or disappeared lawyer.

(B) The selling lawyer and the prospective purchasing lawyer may engage in general discussions regarding the possible sale of a law practice. Before the selling lawyer may provide the prospective purchasing lawyer with information relative to client representation or confidential material contained in client files, the selling lawyer shall require the prospective purchasing lawyer to execute a confidentiality agreement. The confidentiality agreement shall bind the prospective purchasing lawyer to preserve the confidences and secrets of the clients of the selling lawyer, consistent with DR 4-101, as if those clients were clients of the prospective purchasing lawyer.

(C) The selling lawyer and the purchasing lawyer may negotiate the terms of the sale of a law practice, subject to all of the following: (1) The sale agreement shall include a statement by selling lawyer and purchasing lawyer that the purchasing lawyer is purchasing the law practice in good faith and with the intention of delivering legal services to clients of the selling lawyer and others in need of legal services. (2) The sale agreement shall provide that the purchasing lawyer will honor any fee agreements between the selling lawyer and the clients of the selling lawyer relative to legal representation that is ongoing at the time of the sale. The purchasing lawyer may negotiate fees with clients of the selling lawyer for legal representation that is commenced after the date of the sale. (3) The sale agreement may include terms that reasonably limit the ability of the selling lawyer to reenter the practice of law, including, but not limited to, the ability of the selling lawyer to reenter the practice of law for a specific period of time or to practice in a specific geographic area. The sale agreement shall not include terms limiting the ability of the selling lawyer to practice law or reenter the practice of law if the selling lawyer is selling his or her law practice to enter academic, government, or public service or to serve as in-house counsel to a business.

(D)(1) Prior to completing the sale, the selling lawyer and purchasing lawyer shall provide written notice of the sale to the clients of the selling lawyer. For purposes of this rule, clients of the selling lawyer include all current clients of the selling lawyer and any closed files that the selling lawyer and purchasing lawyer agree to make subject of the sale. The written notice shall include all of the following: (a) The anticipated effective date of the proposed sale; (b) A statement that the purchasing lawyer will honor all existing fee agreements for legal representation that is ongoing at the time of sale and that fees for legal representation commenced after the date of sale will be negotiated by the purchasing lawyer and client; (c) The client's right to retain other counsel or take possession of case files; (d) The fact that the client's consent to the sale will be presumed if the client does not take action or otherwise object within ninety days of the receipt of the notice; (e) Biographical information relative to the professional qualifications of the purchasing lawyer, including but not limited to applicable information set forth in DR 2-101(D)(1) to (11), information regarding any disciplinary action taken against the purchasing lawyer, and information regarding the existence, nature, and status of any pending disciplinary complaint certified by a probable cause panel pursuant to Gov. Bar R. V, Section 6(D)(1).

(2) If the seller is the estate of a deceased lawyer or the representative of a disabled or disappeared

lawyer, the purchasing lawyer shall provide written notice to the clients, and the purchasing lawyer shall obtain written consent from each client to act on the client's behalf. The client's consent shall be presumed if no response is received from the client within ninety days of the date the notice was sent to the client at the client's last known address as shown on the records of the seller or the client's rights would be prejudiced by a failure to act during the ninety day period. (3) If a client cannot be given notice, the representation of that client may be transferred to the purchaser only upon entry of an order authorizing the transfer by a court having jurisdiction. The seller may disclose to the court, in camera, information relating to the representation only to the extent necessary to obtain an order authorizing the transfer of the representation. (4) The written notice to clients required by division (D)(1) and (2) of this rule shall be provided by certified mail, return receipt requested. In lieu of providing notice by certified mail, either the selling lawyer or purchasing lawyer, or both, may personally deliver the notice to a client. In the case of personal delivery, the lawyer providing the notice shall obtain written acknowledgement of the delivery from the client. (E) Neither the selling lawyer nor the purchasing lawyer shall attempt to exonerate the lawyer or law firm from or limit liability to the former or prospective client for any malpractice or other professional negligence. DR 6-102 shall be

incorporated in all agreements for the sale or purchase of a law practice. The selling lawyer or the purchasing lawyer, or both, may agree to provide for the indemnification or other contribution arising from any claim or action in malpractice or other professional negligence.

(F) The selling lawyer and the purchasing lawyer shall comply with the limitations, restrictions, or prohibitions contained in the Attorney's Oath of Office, the Supreme Court Rules for the Government of the Bar of Ohio, and the Code of Professional Responsibility, including but not limited to, DR 2-103, 3-102, 4-101, and 5-105.

CANON 3
A Lawyer Should Assist in Preventing the Unauthorized Practice of Law

ETHICAL CONSIDERATIONS
EC 3-1. The prohibition against the practice of law by a layman is grounded in the need of the public for integrity and competence of those who undertake to render legal services. Because of the fiduciary and personal character of the lawyer-client relationship and the inherently complex nature of our legal system, the public can better be assured of the requisite responsibility and competence if the practice of law is confined to those who are subject to the requirements and regulations imposed upon members of the legal profession.

EC 3-2. The sensitive variations in the considerations that bear on legal determinations often make it difficult even for a lawyer to exercise appropriate professional judgment, and it is therefore essential that the personal nature of the relationship of client and lawyer be preserved. Competent professional judgment is the product of a trained familiarity with law and legal processes, a disciplined, analytical approach to legal problems, and a firm ethical commitment.

EC 3-3. A non-lawyer who undertakes to handle legal matters is not governed as to integrity or legal competence by the same rules that govern the conduct of a lawyer. A lawyer is not only subject to that regulation but also is committed to high standards of ethical conduct. The public interest is best served in legal matters by a regulated professional committed to such standards. The Disciplinary Rules protect the public in that they prohibit a lawyer from seeking employment by improper overtures, from acting in cases of divided loyalties, and from submitting to the control of others in the exercise of his judgment. Moreover, a person who entrusts legal matters to a lawyer is protected by the attorney-client privilege and by the duty of the lawyer to hold inviolate the confidences and secrets of his client.

EC 3-4. A layman who seeks legal services often is not in a position to judge whether he will receive proper professional attention. The entrustment of a legal matter may well involve the confidences, the reputation, the property, the freedom, or even the life of the client. Proper protection of members of the public demands that no person be permitted to act in the confidential and demanding capacity of a lawyer unless he is subject to the regulations of the legal profession.

EC 3-5. It is neither necessary nor desirable to attempt the formulation of a single, specific definition of what constitutes the practice of law. Functionally, the practice of law relates to the rendition of services for others that call for the professional judgment of a lawyer. The essence of the professional judgment of the lawyer is his educated ability to relate the general body and philosophy of law to a specific legal problem of a client; and thus, the public interest will be better served if only lawyers are permitted to act in matters involving professional judgment. Where this professional judgment is not involved, non-lawyers, such as court clerks, police officers, abstracters, and many governmental employees, may engage in occupations that require a special knowledge of law in certain areas. But the services of a lawyer are essential in the public interest whenever the exercise of professional legal judgment is required.

EC 3-6. A lawyer often delegates tasks to clerks, secretaries, and other lay persons. Such delegation is proper if the lawyer maintains a direct relationship with his client, supervises the delegated work, and has complete professional responsibility for the work product. This delegation enables a lawyer to render legal service more economically and efficiently.

EC 3-7. The prohibition against a non-lawyer practicing law does not prevent a layman from representing himself, for then he is ordinarily exposing only himself to possible injury. The purpose of the legal profession is to make educated legal representation available to the public; but anyone who does not wish to avail himself of such representation is not required to do so. Even so, the legal profession should help members of the public to recognize legal problems and to understand why it may be unwise for them to act for themselves in matters having legal consequences.

EC 3-8. Because a lawyer should not aid or encourage a nonlawyer to practice law, a lawyer should not practice law in association with a nonlawyer or otherwise share legal fees with a nonlawyer. This does not mean, however, that the pecuniary value of the interest of a deceased lawyer in his or her firm or practice may not be paid to his estate or specified persons such as a surviving spouse or heirs through the sale of a law practice or otherwise. In like manner, profit-sharing retirement plans of a lawyer or law firm that include nonlawyer office employees are not improper. These limited exceptions to the rule against sharing legal fees with nonlawyers are permissible since they do not aid or encourage nonlawyers to practice law.

EC 3-9. Regulation of the practice of law is accomplished principally by the respective states. Authority to engage in the practice of law conferred in any jurisdiction is not per se a grant of the right to practice elsewhere, and it is improper for a lawyer to engage in practice where he is not permitted by law or by court order to do so. However, the demands of business and the mobility of our society pose distinct problems in the regulation of the practice of law by the states. In furtherance of the public interest, the legal profession should discourage regulation that unreasonably imposes territorial limitations upon the right of a lawyer to handle the legal affairs of his client or upon the opportunity of a client to obtain the services of a lawyer of his choice in all matters including the presentation of a contested matter in a tribunal before which the lawyer is not permanently admitted to practice.

DISCIPLINARY RULES

DR 3-101. AIDING UNAUTHORIZED PRACTICE OF LAW.

(A) A lawyer shall not aid a non-lawyer in the unauthorized practice of law.

(B) A lawyer shall not practice law in a jurisdiction where to do so would be in violation of regulations of the profession in that jurisdiction.

DR 3-102. DIVIDING LEGAL FEES WITH A NON-LAWYER.

(A) A lawyer or law firm shall not share legal fees with a nonlawyer, except that: (1) An agreement by a lawyer with his or her firm, partner, or associate may provide for the payment of money, over a reasonable period of time after the lawyer's death, to the lawyer's estate or to one or more specified persons. (2) An agreement to purchase the practice of a deceased, disabled, or disappeared lawyer in accordance with DR 2-111 may provide for the payment of money, over a reasonable period of time, to a nonlawyer. (3) A lawyer who undertakes to complete unfinished legal business of a deceased lawyer may pay to the estate of the deceased lawyer a proportion of the total compensation that fairly represents the services rendered by the deceased lawyer. (4) A lawyer or law firm may include nonlawyer employees in a retirement plan, even though the plan is based in whole or in part on a profit-sharing arrangement.

(5)   A lawyer participating in a lawyer referral service that satisfies the requirements of DR 2-103(C) may pay to the service a fee calculated as a percentage of legal fees earned by the lawyer in his or her capacity as a lawyer to whom the service has referred a matter. This percentage fee is in addition to any reasonable membership or registration fee established by the service.

DR 3-103. FORMING A PARTNERSHIP WITH A NON-LAWYER.

(A) A lawyer shall not form a partnership with a non-lawyer if any of the activities of the partnership consist of the practice of law.

CANON 4

A Lawyer Should Preserve the Confidences and Secrets of a Client

ETHICAL CONSIDERATIONS

EC 4-1. Both the fiduciary relationship existing between lawyer and client and the proper functioning of the legal system require the preservation by the lawyer of confidences and secrets of one who has employed or sought to employ him. A client must feel free to discuss whatever he wishes with his lawyer and a lawyer must be equally free to obtain information beyond that volunteered by his client. A lawyer should be fully informed of all the facts of the matter he is handling in order for his client to obtain the full advantage of our legal system. It is for the lawyer in the exercise of his independent professional judgment to separate the relevant and important from the irrelevant and unimportant. The observance of the ethical obligation of a lawyer to hold inviolate the confidences and secrets of his client not only facilitates the full development of facts essential to proper representation of the client but also encourages laymen to seek early legal assistance.

EC 4-2. The obligation to protect confidences and secrets obviously does not preclude a lawyer from revealing information when his client consents after full disclosure, when necessary to perform his professional employment, when permitted by a Disciplinary Rule, or when required by law. Unless the client otherwise directs, a lawyer may disclose the affairs of his client to partners or associates of his firm. It is a matter of common knowledge that the normal operation of a law office exposes confidential professional information to nonlawyer employees of the office, particularly secretaries and those having access to the files; and this obligates a lawyer to exercise care in selecting and training his employees so that the sanctity of all confidences and secrets of his clients may be presented. If the obligation extends to two or more clients as to the same information, a lawyer should obtain the permission of all before revealing the information. A lawyer must always be sensitive to the rights and wishes of his client and act scrupulously in the making of decisions which may involve the disclosure of information obtained in his professional relationship. Thus, in the absence of consent of his client after full disclosure, a lawyer should not associate another lawyer in the handling of a matter; nor should he, in the absence of consent, seek counsel from another lawyer if there is a reasonable possibility that the identity of the client or his confidences or secrets would be revealed to such lawyer. Both social amenities and professional duty should cause a lawyer to shun indiscreet conversations concerning his clients.

EC 4-3. Unless the client otherwise directs, it is not improper for a lawyer to give limited information from his files to an outside agency necessary for statistical, bookkeeping, accounting, data processing, banking, printing, or other legitimate purposes, provided he exercises due care in the selection of the agency and warns the agency that the information must be kept confidential.

EC 4-4. The attorney-client privilege is more limited than the ethical obligation of a lawyer to guard the confidences and secrets of his client. This ethical precept, unlike the evidentiary privilege, exists without regard to the nature or source of information or the fact that others share the knowledge. A lawyer should endeavor to act in a manner which preserves the evidentiary privilege; for example, he should avoid professional discussions in the presence of persons to whom the privilege does not extend. A lawyer owes an obligation to advise the client of the attorney-client privilege and timely to assert the privilege unless it is waived by the client.

EC 4-5. A lawyer should not use information acquired in the course of the representation of a client to the disadvantage of the client and a lawyer should not use, except with the consent of his client after full disclosure, such information for his own purposes. Likewise, a lawyer should be diligent in his efforts to prevent the misuse of such information by his employees and associates. Care should be exercised by a lawyer to prevent the disclosure of the confidences and secrets of one client to another, and no employment should be accepted that might require such disclosure.

EC 4-6. The obligation of a lawyer to preserve the confidences and secrets of clients continues after the termination of employment. A lawyer should also provide for the protection of the confidences and secrets of clients following the termination of the practice of the lawyer, whether termination is due to death, disability, or retirement.

For example, a lawyer might provide for the personal papers of the client to be returned to the client and for the papers of the lawyer to be delivered to another lawyer or to be destroyed. In determining the method of disposition, the instructions and wishes of the client should be a dominant consideration.

DISCIPLINARY RULES

DR 4-101. PRESERVATION OF CONFIDENCES AND SECRETS OF A CLIENT.

(A) "Confidence" refers to information protected by the attorney-client privilege under applicable law, and "secret" refers to other information gained in the professional relationship that the client has requested be held inviolate or the disclosure of which would be embarrassing or would be likely to be detrimental to the client.

(B) Except when permitted under DR 4-101(C), a lawyer shall not knowingly: (1) Reveal a confidence or secret of his client. (2) Use a confidence or secret of his client to the disadvantage of the client.

(3) Use a confidence or secret of his client for the advantage of himself or of a third person, unless the client consents after full disclosure.

(C) A lawyer may reveal: (1) Confidences or secrets with the consent of the client or clients affected, but only after a full disclosure to them. (2) Confidences or secrets when permitted under Disciplinary Rules or required by law or court order. (3) The inten-

tion of his client to commit a crime and the information necessary to prevent the crime.

(4) Confidences or secrets necessary to establish or collect his fee or to defend himself or his employees or associates against an accusation of wrongful conduct.

(D) A lawyer shall exercise reasonable care to prevent his employees, associates, and others whose services are utilized by him from disclosing or using confidences or secrets of a client, except that a lawyer may reveal the information allowed by DR 4-101(C) through an employee.

CANON 5
A Lawyer Should Exercise Independent Professional Judgment on Behalf of a Client

ETHICAL CONSIDERATIONS
EC 5-1. The professional judgment of a lawyer should be exercised, within the bounds of the law, solely for the benefit of his client and free of compromising influences and loyalties. Neither his personal interests, the interests of other clients, nor the desires of third persons should be permitted to dilute his loyalty to his client.

Interests of a Lawyer That May Affect His Judgment

EC 5-2. A lawyer should not accept proffered employment if his personal interests or desires will, or there is a reasonable probability that they will, affect adversely the advice to be given or services to be rendered the prospective client. After accepting employment, a lawyer carefully should refrain from acquiring a property right or assuming a position that would tend to make his judgment less protective of the interests of his client.

EC 5-3. The self-interest of a lawyer resulting from his ownership of property in which his client also has an interest or which may affect property of his client may interfere with the exercise of free judgment on behalf of his client. If such interference would occur with respect to a prospective client, a lawyer should decline employment proffered by him. After accepting employment, a lawyer should not acquire property rights that would adversely affect his professional judgment in the representation of his client. Even if the property interests of a lawyer do not presently interfere with the exercise of his independent judgment, but the likelihood of interference can reasonably be foreseen by him, a lawyer should explain the situation to his client and should decline employment or withdraw unless the client consents to the continuance of the relationship after full disclosure. A lawyer should not seek to persuade his client to permit him to invest in an undertaking of his client nor make improper use of his professional relationship to influence his client to invest in an enterprise in which the lawyer is interested.

EC 5-4. If, in the course of his representation of a client, a lawyer is permitted to receive from his client a beneficial ownership in publication rights relating to the subject matter of the employment, he may be tempted to subordinate the interests of his client to his own anticipated pecuniary gain. For example, a lawyer in a criminal case who obtains from his client television, radio, motion picture, newspaper, magazine, book, or other publication rights with respect to the case may be influenced, consciously or unconsciously, to a course of conduct that will enhance the value of his publication rights to the prejudice of his client. To prevent these potentially differing interests, such arrangements should be scrupulously avoided prior to the termination of all aspects of the matter giving rise to the employment, even though his employment has previously ended.

EC 5-5. A lawyer should not suggest to the lawyer's client that a gift be made to the lawyer or for the lawyer's benefit. If a lawyer accepts a gift from the lawyer's client, the lawyer is peculiarly susceptible to the charge that the lawyer unduly influenced or overreached the client. If a client voluntarily offers to make a gift to the client's lawyer, the lawyer may accept the gift, but before doing so, the lawyer should urge that the client secure disinterested advice from an independent, competent person who is cognizant of all the circumstances. Unless the client is related by blood or marriage, a lawyer should insist that an instrument in which the lawyer's client desires to name the lawyer beneficially be prepared by another lawyer selected by the client.

EC 5-6. A lawyer should not consciously influence a client to name him as executor, trustee, or lawyer in an instrument. In those cases where a client wishes to name his lawyer as such, care should be taken by the lawyer to avoid even the appearance of impropriety.

EC 5-7. The possibility of an adverse effect upon the exercise of free judgment by a lawyer on behalf of his client during litigation generally makes it undesirable for the lawyer to acquire a proprietary interest in the cause of his client or otherwise to become financially interested in the outcome of the litigation. However, it is not improper for a lawyer to protect his right to collect a fee for his services by the assertion of legally permissible liens, even though by doing so he may acquire an interest in the outcome of litigation. Although a contingent fee arrangement gives a lawyer a financial interest in the outcome of litigation, a reasonable contingent fee is permissible in civil cases because it may be the only means by which a layman can obtain the services of a lawyer of his choice. But a lawyer, because he is in a better position to evaluate a cause of action, should enter into a contingent fee arrangement only in those instances where the arrangement will be beneficial to the client.

EC 5-8. A financial interest in the outcome of litigation also results if monetary advances are made by the lawyer to his client. Although this assistance generally is not encouraged, there are instances when it is not improper to make loans to a client. For example, the advancing or guaranteeing of payment of the costs and expenses of litigation by a lawyer may be the only way a client can enforce his cause of action, but the ultimate liability for such costs and expenses must be that of the client.

EC 5-9. Occasionally a lawyer is called upon to decide in a particular case whether he will be a witness or an advocate. If a lawyer is both counsel and witness, he becomes more easily impeachable for interest and thus may be a less effective witness. Conversely, the opposing counsel may be handicapped in challenging the credibility of the lawyer when the lawyer also appears as an advocate in the case. An advocate who becomes a witness is in the unseemly and ineffective position of arguing his own credibility. The roles of an advocate and of a witness are inconsistent; the function of an advocate is to advance or argue the cause of another, while that of a witness is to state facts objectively.

EC 5-10. Problems incident to the lawyer-witness relationship arise at different stages; they relate either to whether a lawyer should accept employment or should withdraw from employment. Regardless of when the problem arises, his decision is to be governed by the same basic considerations. It is not objectionable for a lawyer who is a potential witness to be an advocate if it is unlikely that he will be called as a witness because his testimony would be merely cumulative or if his testimony will relate only to an uncontested issue. In the exceptional situation where it will be manifestly unfair to the client for the lawyer to refuse employment or to withdraw when he will likely be a witness on a contested issue, he may serve as advocate even though he may be a witness. In making such decision, he should determine the personal or financial sacrifice of the client that may result from his refusal of employment or withdrawal therefrom, the materiality of his testimony, and the effectiveness of his representation in view of his personal involvement. In weighing these factors, it should be clear that refusal or withdrawal will impose an unreasonable hardship upon the client before the lawyer accepts or continues the employment. Where the question arises, doubts should be resolved in favor of the lawyer testifying and against his becoming or continuing as an advocate.

EC 5-11. A lawyer should not permit his personal interests to influence his advice relative to a suggestion by his client that additional counsel be employed. In like manner, his personal interests should not deter him from suggesting that additional counsel be employed; on the contrary, he should be alert to the desirability of recommending additional counsel when, in his judgment, the proper representation of his client requires it. However, a lawyer should advise his client not to employ additional counsel suggested by the client if the lawyer believes that such employment would be a disservice to the client, and he should disclose the reasons for his belief.

EC 5-12. Inability of co-counsel to agree on a matter vital to the representation of their client requires that their disagreement be submitted by them jointly to their client for his resolution, and the decision of the client shall control the action to be taken.

EC 5-13. A lawyer should not maintain membership in or be influenced by any organization of employees that undertakes to prescribe, direct, or suggest when or how he should fulfill his professional obligations to a person or organization that employs him as a lawyer. Although it is not necessarily improper for a lawyer employed by a corporation or similar entity to be a member of an organization of employees, he should be vigilant to safeguard his fidelity as a lawyer to his employer free from outside influences.

Interests of Multiple Clients

EC 5-14. Maintaining the independence of professional judgment required of a lawyer precludes his acceptance or continuation of employment that will adversely affect his judgment on behalf of or dilute his loyalty to a client. This problem arises whenever a lawyer is asked to represent two or more clients who may have differing interests, whether such interests be conflicting, inconsistent, diverse, or otherwise discordant.

EC 5-15. If a lawyer is requested to undertake or to continue representation of multiple clients having potentially differing interests, he must weigh carefully the possibility that his judgment may be impaired or his loyalty divided if he accepts or continues the employment. He should resolve all doubts against the propriety of the representation. A lawyer should never represent in litigation multiple clients with differing interests; and there are few situations in which he would be justified in representing in litigation multiple clients with potentially differing interests. If a lawyer accepted such employment and the interests did become actually differing, he would have to withdraw from employment with likelihood of resulting hardship on the clients; and for this reason it is preferable that he refuse the employment initially. On the other hand, there are many instances in which a lawyer may properly serve multiple clients having potentially differing interests in matters not involving litigation. If the interests vary only slightly, it is generally likely that the lawyer will not be subjected to an adverse influence and that he can retain his independent judgment on behalf of each client; and if the interests become differing, withdrawal is less likely to have a disruptive effect upon the causes of his clients.

EC 5-16. A lawyer representing a fiduciary that owes fiduciary duties to third parties does not solely by representation of the fiduciary engage in multiple representation even if the third parties' interests conflict with the interests of the fiduciary or other third parties. As used in this Ethical Consideration, "fiduciary" includes only a trustee under an express trust or an executor, administrator, or personal representative.

EC 5-17. In those instances in which a lawyer is justified in representing two or more clients having differing interests, it is nevertheless essential that each client be given the opportunity to evaluate his need for representation free of any potential conflict and to obtain other counsel if he so desires. Thus before a lawyer may represent multiple clients, he should explain fully to each client the implications of the common representation and should accept or continue employment only if the clients consent. If there are present other circumstances that might cause any of the multiple clients to question the undivided loyalty of the lawyer, he should also advise all of the clients of those circumstances.

EC 5-18. Typically recurring situations involving potentially differing interests are those in which a lawyer is asked to represent co-defendants in a criminal case, co-plaintiffs in a personal injury case, an insured and his insurer, and beneficiaries of the estate of a decedent. Whether a lawyer can fairly and adequately protect the interests of multiple clients in these and similar situations depends upon an analysis of each case. In certain circumstances, there may exist little chance of the judgment of the lawyer being adversely affected by the slight possibility that the interests will become actually differing; in other circumstances, the chance of adverse effect upon his judgment is not unlikely.

EC 5-19. A lawyer employed or retained by a corporation or similar entity owes his allegiance to the entity and not to a stockholder, director, officer, employee, representative, or other person connected with the entity. In advising the entity, a lawyer should keep paramount its interests and his professional judgment should not be influenced by the personal desires of any person or organization. Occasionally, a lawyer for an entity is requested by a stockholder, director, officer, employee, representative, or other person connected with the entity to represent him in an individual capacity; in such case the lawyer may serve the individual only if the lawyer is convinced that differing interests are not present.

EC 5-20. A lawyer may represent several clients whose interests are not actually or potentially differing. Nevertheless, he should explain any circumstances that might cause a client to question his undivided loyalty. Regardless of the belief of a lawyer that he may properly represent multiple clients, he must defer to a client who holds the contrary belief and withdraw from representation of that client.

EC 5-21. A lawyer is often asked to serve as an impartial arbitrator or mediator in matters which involve present or former clients. He may serve in either capacity if he first discloses such present or former relationships. After a lawyer has undertaken to act as an impartial arbitrator or mediator, he should not thereafter represent in the dispute any of the parties involved.

Desires of Third Persons

EC 5-22. The obligation of a lawyer to exercise professional judgment solely on behalf of his client requires that he disregard the desires of others that might impair his free judgment. The desires of a third person will seldom adversely affect a lawyer unless that person is in a position to exert strong eco-

nomic, political, or social pressures upon the lawyer. These influences are often subtle, and a lawyer must be alert to their existence. A lawyer subjected to outside pressures should make full disclosure of them to his client; and if he or his client believes that the effectiveness of his representation has been or will be impaired thereby, the lawyer should take proper steps to withdraw from representation of his client.

EC 5-23. Economic, political, or social pressures by third persons are less likely to impinge upon the independent judgment of a lawyer in a matter in which he is compensated directly by his client and his professional work is exclusively with his client. On the other hand, if a lawyer is compensated from a source other than his client, he may feel a sense of responsibility to someone other than his client.

EC 5-24. A person or organization that pays or furnishes lawyers to represent others possesses a potential power to exert strong pressures against the independent judgment of those lawyers. Some employers may be interested in furthering their own economic, political, or social goals without regard to the professional responsibility of the lawyer to his individual client. Others may be far more concerned with establishment or extension of legal principles than in the immediate protection of the rights of the lawyer's individual client. On some occasions, decisions on priority of work may be made by the employer rather than the lawyer with the result that prosecution of work already undertaken for clients is postponed to their detriment. Similarly, an employer may seek, consciously or unconsciously, to further its own economic interests through the actions of the lawyers employed by it. Since a lawyer must always be free to exercise his professional judgment without regard to the interests or motives of a third person, the lawyer who is employed by one to represent another must constantly guard against erosion of his professional freedom.

EC 5-25. To assist a lawyer in preserving his professional independence, a number of courses are available to him. For example, a lawyer should not practice with or in the form of a professional legal corporation, even though the corporate form is permitted by law, if any director, officer, or stockholder of it is a non-lawyer. Although a lawyer may be employed by a business corporation with non-lawyers serving as directors or officers, and they necessarily have the right to make decisions of business policy, a lawyer must decline to accept direction of his professional judgment from any layman. Various types of legal aid offices are administered by boards of directors composed of lawyers and laymen. A lawyer should not accept employment from such an organization unless the board sets only broad policies and there is no interference in the relationship of the lawyer and the individual client he serves. Where a lawyer is employed by an organization, a written agreement that defines the relationship between him and the organization and provides for his independence is desirable since it may serve to prevent misunderstanding as to their respective roles. Although other innovations in the means of supplying legal counsel may develop, the responsibility of the lawyer to maintain his professional independence remains constant, and the legal profession must insure that changing circumstances do not result in loss of the professional independence of the lawyer.

DISCIPLINARY RULES

DR 5-101. REFUSING EMPLOYMENT WHEN THE INTERESTS OF THE LAWYER MAY IMPAIR THE LAWYER'S INDEPENDENT PROFESSIONAL JUDGMENT.

(A)(1) Except with the consent of the client after full disclosure, a lawyer shall not accept employment if the exercise of professional judgment on behalf of the client will be or reasonably may be affected by the lawyer's financial, business, property, or personal interests. (2) Notwithstanding the consent of the client, a lawyer shall not knowingly prepare, draft, or supervise the preparation or execution of a will, codicil, or inter vivos trust for a client in which any of the following are named as beneficiary: (a) the lawyer; (b) the lawyer's law partner or a shareholder of the lawyer's firm; (c) an associate, paralegal, law clerk, or other employee in the lawyer's firm or office; (d) a lawyer acting "of counsel" in the lawyer's firm; (e) the spouses, siblings, natural or adoptive children, or natural or adoptive parents of any of those described in divisions (A)(2)(a) through (d) of this rule. (3) Division (A)(2) of this rule shall not apply if the client is related by blood or marriage to the beneficiary within the third degree of relationship as defined by the law of Ohio.

(B) A lawyer shall not accept employment in contemplated or pending litigation if the lawyer knows or it is obvious that the lawyer or a lawyer in the firm ought to be called as a witness, except that the lawyer may undertake the employment and the lawyer or a lawyer in the firm may testify: (1) If the testimony will relate solely to an uncontested matter. (2) If the testimony will relate solely to a matter of formality and there is no reason to believe that substantial evidence will be offered in opposition to the testimony. (3) If the testimony will relate solely to the nature and value of legal services rendered in the case by the lawyer or the firm to the client. (4) As to any matter, if refusal would work a substantial hardship on the client because of the distinctive value of the lawyer or the firm as counsel in the particular case.

DR 5-102. WITHDRAWAL AS COUNSEL WHEN THE LAWYER BECOMES A WITNESS.

(A) If, after undertaking employment in contemplated or pending litigation, a lawyer learns or it is obvious that he or a lawyer in his firm ought to be called as a witness on behalf of his client, he shall withdraw from the conduct of the trial and his firm, if any, shall not continue representation in the trial, except that he may continue the

representation and he or a lawyer in his firm may testify in the circumstances enumerated in DR 5-101(B)(1) through (4).

(B) If, after undertaking employment in contemplated or pending litigation, a lawyer learns or it is obvious that he or a lawyer in his firm may be called as a witness other than on behalf of his client, he may continue the representation until it is apparent that his testimony is or may be prejudicial to his client.

DR 5-103. AVOIDING ACQUISITION OF INTEREST IN LITIGATION.

(A) A lawyer shall not acquire a proprietary interest in the cause of action or subject matter of litigation the lawyer is conducting for a client, except that a lawyer may: (1) Acquire a lien granted by law to secure the lawyer's fee or expenses. (2) Contract with a client for a reasonable contingent fee in a civil case.

(B) While representing a client in connection with contemplated or pending litigation, a lawyer shall not advance or guarantee financial assistance to the client, except that a lawyer may advance or guarantee the expenses of litigation, including court costs, expenses of investigation, expenses of medical examination, and costs of obtaining and presenting evidence, the repayment of which may be contingent on the outcome of the matter.

DR 5-104. LIMITING BUSINESS RELATIONS WITH A CLIENT.

(A) A lawyer shall not enter into a business transaction with a client if they have differing interests therein and if the client expects the lawyer to exercise his professional judgment therein for the protection of the client, unless the client has consented after full disclosure.

(B) Prior to conclusion of all aspects of the matter giving rise to his employment, a lawyer shall not enter into any arrangement or understanding with a client or a prospective client by which he acquires an interest in publication rights with respect to the subject matter of his employment or proposed employment.

DR 5-105. REFUSING TO ACCEPT OR CONTINUE EMPLOYMENT IF THE INTERESTS OF ANOTHER CLIENT MAY IMPAIR THE INDEPENDENT PROFESSIONAL JUDGMENT OF THE LAWYER.

(A) A lawyer shall decline proffered employment if the exercise of his independent professional judgment in behalf of a client will be or is likely to be adversely affected by the acceptance of the proffered employment, except to the extent permitted under DR 5-105(C).

(B) A lawyer shall not continue multiple employment if the exercise of his independent professional judgment in behalf of a client will be or is likely to be adversely affected by his representation of another client, except to the extent permitted under DR 5-105(C).

(C) In the situations covered by DR 5-105(A) and (B), a lawyer may represent multiple clients if it is obvious that he can adequately represent the interest of each and if each consents to the representation after full disclosure of the possible effect of such representation on the exercise of his independent professional judgment on behalf of each.

(D) If a lawyer is required to decline employment or to withdraw from employment under DR 5-105, no partner or associate of his or his firm may accept or continue such employment.

DR 5-106. SETTLING SIMILAR CLAIMS OF CLIENTS.

(A) A lawyer who represents two or more clients shall not make or participate in the making of an aggregate settlement of the claims of or against his clients, unless each client has consented to the settlement after being advised of the existence and nature of all the claims involved in the proposed settlement, of the total amount of the settlement, and of the participation of each person in the settlement.

DR 5-107. AVOIDING INFLUENCE BY OTHERS THAN THE CLIENT.

(A) Except with the consent of his client after full disclosure, a lawyer shall not: (1) Accept compensation for his legal services from one other than his client. (2) Accept from one other than his client any thing of value related to his representation of or his employment by his client.

(B) A lawyer shall not permit a person who recommends, employs, or pays him to render legal services for another to direct or regulate his professional judgment in rendering such legal services.

(C) A lawyer shall not practice with or in the form of a professional corporation or association authorized to practice law for a profit, if: (1) A non-lawyer owns any interest therein, except that a fiduciary representative of the estate of a lawyer may hold the stock or interest of the lawyer for a reasonable time during administration; (2) A non-lawyer is a corporate director or officer thereof; or (3) A non-lawyer has the right to direct or control the professional judgment of a lawyer.

CANON 6
A Lawyer Should Represent a Client Competently

ETHICAL CONSIDERATIONS
EC 6-1. Because of his vital role in the legal process, a lawyer should act with competence and proper care in representing clients. He should strive to become and remain proficient in his practice and should accept employment only in matters which he is or intends to become competent to handle.
EC 6-2. A lawyer is aided in attaining and maintaining his competence by keeping abreast of current legal literature and developments, participating in continuing legal education programs, concentrating in particular areas of the law, and by utilizing other available means. He has the additional ethical obligation to assist in improving the legal profession, and he may do so by participating in bar activities

intended to advance the quality and standards of members of the profession. Of particular importance is the careful training of his younger associates and the giving of sound guidance to all lawyers who consult him. In short, a lawyer should strive at all levels to aid the legal profession in advancing the highest possible standards of integrity and competence and to meet those standards himself.
EC 6-3. While the licensing of a lawyer is evidence that he has met the standards then prevailing for admission to the bar, a lawyer generally should not accept employment in any area of the law in which he is not qualified. However, he may accept such employment if in good faith he expects to become qualified through study and investigation, as long as such preparation would not result in unreasonable delay or expense to his client. Proper preparation and representation may require the association by the lawyer of professionals in other disciplines. A lawyer offered employment in a matter in which he is not and does not expect to become so qualified should either decline the employment or, with the consent of his client, accept the employment and associate a lawyer who is competent in the matter.
EC 6-4. Having undertaken representation, a lawyer should use proper care to safeguard the interests of his client. If a lawyer has accepted employment in a matter beyond his competence but in which he expected to become competent, he should diligently

undertake the work and study necessary to qualify himself. In addition to being qualified to handle a particular matter, his obligation to his client requires him to prepare adequately for and give appropriate attention to his legal work.

EC 6-5. A lawyer should have pride in his professional endeavors. His obligation to act competently calls for higher motivation than that arising from fear of civil liability or disciplinary penalty.

EC 6-6. A lawyer should not seek, by contract or other means, to limit his or her individual liability to clients for malpractice. A lawyer who properly handles client affairs has no need to attempt to limit liability for professional activities, and a lawyer who does not properly handle client affairs should not be permitted to do so. A lawyer who is a stockholder in or is associated with a professional legal corporation may, however, limit his or her liability for malpractice of associates in the corporation, but only to the extent permitted by law. A lawyer who sells or purchases a law practice may enter into an agreement for contribution or indemnification with the other lawyer in accordance with DR 2-111.

DISCIPLINARY RULES
DR 6-101. FAILING TO ACT COMPETENTLY.
(A) A lawyer shall not: (1) Handle a legal matter which he knows or should know that he is not competent to handle, without associating with him a lawyer who is competent to handle it. (2) Handle a legal

matter without preparation adequate in the circumstances.
(3) Neglect a legal matter entrusted to him.

DR 6-102. LIMITING LIABILITY TO CLIENT.
(A) Except as permitted by DR 2-111(C), a lawyer shall not attempt to exonerate himself or herself from or limit his or her liability to a client for personal malpractice.

CANON 7
A Lawyer Should Represent a Client Zealously Within the Bounds of the Law

ETHICAL CONSIDERATIONS
EC 7-1. The duty of a lawyer, both to his client and to the legal system, is to represent his client zealously within the bounds of the law, which includes Disciplinary Rules and enforceable professional regulations. The professional responsibility of a lawyer derives from his membership in a profession which has the duty of assisting members of the public to secure and protect available legal rights and benefits. In our government of laws and not of men, each member of our society is entitled to have his conduct judged and regulated in accordance with the law; to seek any lawful objective through legally permissible means; and to present for adjudication any lawful claim, issue, or defense.
EC 7-2. The bounds of the law in a given case are often difficult to ascertain. The language of legislative enactments and judicial opinions may be uncertain as

applied to varying factual situations. The limits and specific meaning of apparently relevant law may be made doubtful by changing or developing constitutional interpretations, inadequately expressed statutes or judicial opinions, and changing public and judicial attitudes. Certainty of law ranges from well-settled rules through areas of conflicting authority to areas without precedent.

EC 7-3. Where the bounds of law are uncertain, the action of a lawyer may depend on whether he is serving as advocate or adviser. A lawyer may serve simultaneously as both advocate and adviser, but the two roles are essentially different. In asserting a position on behalf of his client, an advocate for the most part deals with past conduct and must take the facts as he finds them. By contrast, a lawyer serving as adviser primarily assists his client in determining the course of future conduct and relationships. While serving as advocate, a lawyer should resolve in favor of his client doubts as to the bounds of the law. In serving a client as adviser, a lawyer in appropriate circumstances should give his professional opinion as to what the ultimate decisions of the courts would likely be as to the applicable law.

Duty of the Lawyer to a Client

EC 7-4. The advocate may urge any permissible construction of the law favorable to his client, without regard to his professional opinion as to the likelihood that the construction will ultimately prevail. His conduct is within the bounds of the law, and therefore permissible, if the position taken is supported by the law or is supportable by a good faith argument for an extension, modification, or reversal of the law. However, a lawyer is not justified in asserting a position in litigation that is frivolous.

EC 7-5. A lawyer as adviser furthers the interest of his client by giving his professional opinion as to what he believes would likely be the ultimate decision of the courts on the matter at hand and by informing his client of the practical effect of such decision. He may continue in the representation of his client even though his client has elected to pursue a course of conduct contrary to the advice of the lawyer so long as he does not thereby knowingly assist the client to engage in illegal conduct or to take a frivolous legal position. A lawyer should never encourage or aid his client to commit criminal acts or counsel his client on how to violate the law and avoid punishment therefor.

EC 7-6. Whether the proposed action of a lawyer is within the bounds of the law may be a perplexing question when his client is contemplating a course of conduct having legal consequences that vary according to the client's intent, motive, or desires at the time of the action. Often a lawyer is asked to assist his client in developing evidence relevant to the state of mind of the client at a particular time. He may properly assist his client in the development and preservation of evidence of existing motive, intent, or desire; obviously, he may not do anything furthering the creation or preservation of false evidence. In many cases a lawyer may not be certain as to the state of mind of his client, and in those situations he should resolve reasonable doubts in favor of his client.

EC 7-7. In certain areas of legal representation not affecting the merits of the cause or substantially prejudicing the rights of a client, a lawyer is entitled to make decisions on his own. But otherwise the authority to make decisions is exclusively that of the client and, if made within the framework of the law, such decisions are binding on his lawyer. As typical examples in civil cases, it is for the client to decide whether he will accept a settlement offer or whether he will waive his right to plead an affirmative defense. A defense lawyer in a criminal case has the duty to advise his client fully on whether a particular plea to a charge appears to be desirable and as to the prospects of success on appeal, but it is for the client to decide what plea should be entered and whether an appeal should be taken.

EC 7-8. A lawyer should exert his best efforts to insure that decisions of his client are made only after the client has been informed of relevant considerations. A lawyer ought to initiate this decision-making process if the client does not do so. Advice of a lawyer to his client need not be confined to purely legal considerations. A lawyer should advise his client of the possible effect of each legal alternative. A lawyer should bring to bear upon this decision-making process the fullness of his experience as well as his objective viewpoint. In assisting his client to reach a proper decision, it is often desirable for a lawyer to point out those factors which may lead to a decision that is morally just as well as legally permissible. He may emphasize the possibility of harsh consequences that might result from assertion of legally permissible positions. In the final analysis, however, the lawyer should always remember that the decision whether to forego legally available objectives or methods because of non-legal factors is ultimately for the client and not for himself. In the event that the client in a non-adjudicatory matter insists upon a course of conduct that is contrary to the judgment and advice of the lawyer but not prohibited by Disciplinary Rules, the lawyer may withdraw from the employment.

EC 7-9. In the exercise of his professional judgment on those decisions which are for his determination in the handling of a legal matter, a lawyer should always act in a manner consistent with the best interests of his client. However, when an action in the best interest of his client seems to him to be unjust, he may ask his client for permission to forego such action.

EC 7-10. The duty of a lawyer to represent his client with zeal does not militate against his concurrent obligation to treat with consideration all persons involved in the legal process and to avoid the infliction of needless harm.

EC 7-11. The responsibilities of a lawyer may vary according to the intelligence, experience, mental condition or age of a client, the obligation of a public officer, or the nature of a particular proceeding. Examples include the representation of an illiterate or an incompetent, service as a public prosecutor or other government lawyer, and appearances before administrative and legislative bodies.

EC 7-12. Any mental or physical condition of a client that renders him incapable of making a considered judgment on his own behalf casts additional responsibilities upon his lawyer. Where an incompetent is acting through a guardian or other legal representative, a lawyer must look to such representative for those decisions which are normally the prerogative of the client to make. If a client under disability has no legal representative, his lawyer may be compelled in court proceedings to make decisions on behalf of the client. If the client is capable of understanding the matter in question or of contributing to the advancement of his interests, regardless of whether he is legally disqualified from performing certain acts, the lawyer should obtain from him all possible aid. If the disability of a client and the lack of a legal representative compel the lawyer to make decisions for his client, the lawyer should consider all circumstances then prevailing and act with care to safeguard and advance the interests of his client. But obviously a lawyer cannot perform any act or make any decision which the law requires his client to perform or make, either acting for himself if competent, or by a duly constituted representative if legally incompetent.

EC 7-13. The responsibility of a public prosecutor differs from that of the usual advocate; his duty is to seek justice, not merely to convict. This special duty exists because: (1) the prosecutor represents the sovereign and therefore should use restraint in the discretionary exercise of governmental powers, such as in the selection of cases to prosecute; (2) during trial the prosecutor is not only an advocate but he also may make decisions normally made by an individual client, and those affecting the public interest should be fair to all; and (3) in our system of criminal justice the accused is to be given the benefit of all reasonable doubts. With respect to evidence and witnesses, the prosecutor has responsibilities different from those of a lawyer in private practice: the prosecutor should make timely disclosure to the defense of available evidence, known to him, that tends to negate the guilt of the accused, mitigate the degree of the offense, or reduce the punishment. Further a prosecutor should not intentionally avoid pursuit of evidence merely because he believes it will damage the prosecution's case or aid the accused.

EC 7-14. A government lawyer who has discretionary power relative to litigation should refrain from instituting or continuing litigation that is obviously unfair. A government lawyer not having such discretionary power who believes there is lack of merit in a controversy submitted to him should so advise his superiors and recommend the avoidance of unfair litigation. A government lawyer in a civil action or administrative proceeding has the responsibility to seek justice and to develop a full and fair record, and he should not use his position or the economic power of the government to harass parties or to bring about unjust settlements or results.

EC 7-15. The nature and purpose of proceedings before administrative agencies vary widely. The proceedings may be legislative or quasi-judicial, or a combination of both. They may be ex parte in character, in which event they may originate either at the instance of the agency or upon motion of an interested party. The scope of an inquiry may be purely investigative or it may be truly adversary looking toward the adjudication of specific rights of a party or of classes of parties. The foregoing are but examples of some of the types of proceedings conducted by administrative agencies. A lawyer appearing before an administrative agency, regardless of the nature of the proceeding it is conducting, has the continuing duty to advance the cause of his client within the bounds of the law. Where the applicable rules of the agency impose specific obligations upon a lawyer, it is his duty to comply therewith, unless the lawyer has a legitimate basis for challenging the validity thereof. In all appearances before administrative agencies, a lawyer should identify himself, his client if identity of his client is not privileged, and the representative nature of his appearance. It is not improper, however, for a lawyer to seek from an agency information available to the public without identifying his client.

EC 7-16. The primary business of a legislative body is to enact laws rather than to adjudicate controversies, although on occasion the activities of a legislative body may take on the characteristics of an adversary proceeding, particularly in investigative and impeachment matters. The role of a lawyer supporting or opposing proposed legislation normally is quite different from his role in representing a person under investigation or on trial by a legislative body. When a lawyer appears in connection with proposed legislation, he seeks to affect the lawmaking process, but when he appears on behalf of a client in investigatory or impeachment proceedings, he is concerned with the protection of the rights of his client. In either event, he should identify himself and his client, if identity of his client is not privileged, and should comply with applicable laws and legislative rules.

EC 7-17. The obligation of loyalty to his client applies only to a lawyer in the discharge of his professional duties and implies no obligation to adopt a personal viewpoint favorable to the interests or desires of his client. While a lawyer must act always with circumspection in order that his conduct will not adversely affect the rights of a client in a matter he is then handling, he may take positions on public issues and espouse legal reforms he favors without regard to the individual views of any client.

EC 7-18. The legal system in its broadest sense functions best when persons in need of legal advice or assistance are represented by their own counsel. For this reason a lawyer should not communicate on the subject matter of the representation of his client with a person he knows to be represented in the matter by a lawyer, unless pursuant to law or rule of court or unless he has the consent of the lawyer for that person. If one is not represented by counsel, a lawyer representing another may have to deal directly with the unrepresented person; in such an instance, a lawyer should not undertake to give advice to the person who is attempting to represent himself, except that he may advise him to obtain a lawyer.

Duty of the Lawyer to the Adversary System of Justice

EC 7-19. Our legal system provides for the adjudication of disputes governed by the rules of substantive, evidentiary, and procedural law. An adversary presentation counters the natural human tendency to judge too swiftly in terms of the familiar that which is not yet fully known; the advocate, by his zealous preparation and presentation of facts and law, enables the tribunal to come to the hearing with an open and neutral mind and to render impartial judgments. The duty of a lawyer to his client and his duty to the legal system are the same: to represent his client zealously within the bounds of the law.

EC 7-20. In order to function properly, our adjudicative process requires an informed, impartial tribunal capable of administering justice promptly and efficiently according to procedures that command public confidence and respect. Not only must there be competent, adverse presentation of evidence and issues, but a tribunal must be aided by rules appropriate to an effective and dignified process. The procedures under which tribunals operate in our adversary system have been prescribed largely by legislative enactments, court rules and decisions, and administrative rules. Through the years certain concepts of proper professional conduct have become rules of law applicable to the adversary adjudicative process. Many of these concepts are the bases for standards of professional conduct set forth in the Disciplinary Rules.

EC 7-21. The civil adjudicative process is primarily designed for the settlement of disputes between parties, while the criminal process is designed for the protection of society as a whole. Threatening to use, or using, the criminal process to coerce adjustment of private civil claims or controversies is a subversion of that process; further, the person against whom the criminal process is so misused may be deterred from asserting his legal rights and thus the usefulness of the civil process in settling private disputes is impaired. As in all cases of abuse of judicial process, the improper use of criminal process tends to diminish public confidence in our legal system.

EC 7-22. Respect for judicial rulings is essential to the proper administration of justice; however, a litigant or his lawyer may, in good faith and within the framework of the law, take steps to test the correctness of a ruling of a tribunal.

EC 7-23. The complexity of law often makes it difficult for a tribunal to be fully informed unless the pertinent law is presented by the lawyers in the cause. A tribunal that is fully informed on the applicable law is better able to make a fair and accurate determination of the matter before it. The adversary system contemplates that each lawyer will present and argue the existing law in the light most favorable to his client. Where a lawyer knows of legal authority in the controlling jurisdiction directly adverse to the position of his client, he should inform the tribunal of its existence unless his adversary has done so; but, having made such disclosure, he may challenge its soundness in whole or in part.

EC 7-24. In order to bring about just and informed decisions, evidentiary and procedural rules have been established by tribunals to permit the inclusion of relevant evidence and argument and the exclusion of all other considerations. The expression by a lawyer of his personal opinion as to the justness of a cause, as to the credibility of a witness, as to the culpability of a civil litigant, or as to the guilt or innocence of an accused is not a proper subject for argument to the trier of fact. It is improper as to factual matters because admissible evidence possessed by a lawyer should be presented only as sworn testimony. It is improper as to all other matters because, were the rule otherwise, the silence of a lawyer on a given occasion could be construed unfavorably to his client. However a lawyer may argue, on his analysis of the evidence, for any position or conclusion with respect to any of the foregoing matters.

EC 7-25. Rules of evidence and procedure are designed to lead to just decisions and are part of the framework of the law. Thus while a lawyer may take steps in good faith and within the framework of the law to test the validity of rules, he is not justified in consciously violating such rules and he should be diligent in his efforts to guard against his unintentional violation of them. As examples, a lawyer should subscribe to or verify only those pleadings that he believes are in compliance with applicable law and rules; a lawyer should not make any prefatory statement before a tribunal in regard to the purported facts of the case on trial unless he believes that his statement will be supported by admissible evidence; a lawyer should not ask a witness a question solely for the purpose of harassing or embarrassing him; and a lawyer should not by subterfuge put before a jury matters which it cannot properly consider.

EC 7-26. The law and Disciplinary Rules prohibit the use of fraudulent, false, or perjured testimony or evidence. A lawyer who knowingly participates in introduction of such testimony or evidence is subject to discipline. A lawyer should, however, present any admissible evidence his client desires to have presented unless he knows, or from facts within his knowledge should know, that such testimony or evidence is false, fraudulent, or perjured.

EC 7-27. Because it interferes with the proper administration of justice, a lawyer should not suppress evidence that he or his client has a legal obligation to reveal or produce. In like manner, a lawyer should not advise or cause a person to secrete himself or to leave the jurisdiction of a tribunal for the purpose of making him unavailable as a witness therein.

EC 7-28. Witnesses should always testify truthfully and should be free from any financial inducements that might tempt them to do otherwise. A lawyer should not pay or agree to pay a non-expert witness an amount in excess of reimbursement for expenses and financial loss incident to his being a witness; however, a lawyer may pay or agree to pay an expert witness a reasonable fee for his services as an expert. But in no event should a lawyer pay or agree to pay a contingent fee to any witness. A lawyer should exercise reasonable diligence to see that his client and lay associates conform to these standards.

EC 7-29. To safeguard the impartiality that is essential to the judicial process, veniremen and jurors should be protected against extraneous influences. When impartiality is present, public confidence in the judicial system is enhanced. There should be no extrajudicial communication with veniremen prior to trial or with jurors during trial by or on behalf of a lawyer connected with the case. Furthermore, a lawyer who is not connected with the case should not communicate

with or cause another to communicate with a venireman or a juror about the case. After the trial, communication by a lawyer with jurors is permitted so long as he refrains from asking questions or making comments that tend to harass or embarrass the juror or to influence actions of the juror in future cases. Were a lawyer to be prohibited from communicating after trial with a juror, he could not ascertain if the verdict might be subject to legal challenge, in which event the invalidity of a verdict might go undetected. When an extrajudicial communication by a lawyer with a juror is permitted by law, it should be made considerately and with deference to the personal feelings of the juror.

EC 7-30. Vexatious or harassing investigations of veniremen or jurors seriously impair the effectiveness of our jury system. For this reason, a lawyer or anyone on his behalf who conducts an investigation of veniremen or jurors should act with circumspection and restraint.

EC 7-31. Communications with or investigations of members of families of veniremen or jurors by a lawyer or by anyone on his behalf are subject to the restrictions imposed upon the lawyer with respect to his communications with or investigations of veniremen and jurors.

EC 7-32. Because of his duty to aid in preserving the integrity of the jury system, a lawyer who learns of improper conduct by or towards a venireman, a juror, or a member of the family of either should make a prompt report to the court regarding such conduct.

EC 7-33. A goal of our legal system is that each party shall have his case, criminal or civil, adjudicated by an impartial tribunal. The attainment of this goal may be defeated by dissemination of news or comments which tend to influence judge or jury. Such news or comments may prevent prospective jurors from being impartial at the outset of the trial and may also interfere with the obligation of jurors to base their verdict solely upon the evidence admitted in the trial. The release by a lawyer of out-of-court statements regarding an anticipated or pending trial may improperly affect the impartiality of the tribunal. For these reasons, standards for permissible and prohibited conduct of a lawyer with respect to trial publicity have been established.

EC 7-34. The impartiality of a public servant in our legal system may be impaired by the receipt of gifts or loans. A lawyer, therefore, is never justified in making a gift or a loan to a judge, a hearing officer, or an official or employee of a tribunal.

EC 7-35. All litigants and lawyers should have access to tribunals on an equal basis. Generally, in adversary proceedings a lawyer should not communicate with a judge relative to a matter pending before, or which is to be brought before, a tribunal over which he presides in circumstances which might have the effect or give the appearance of granting undue advantage to one party. For example, a lawyer should not communicate with a tribunal by

a writing unless a copy thereof is promptly delivered to opposing counsel or to the adverse party if he is not represented by a lawyer. Ordinarily an oral communication by a lawyer with a judge or hearing officer should be made only upon adequate notice to opposing counsel, or, if there is none, to the opposing party. A lawyer should not condone or lend himself to private importunities by another with a judge or hearing officer on behalf of himself or his client.

EC 7-36. Judicial hearings ought to be conducted through dignified and orderly procedures designed to protect the rights of all parties. Although a lawyer has the duty to represent his client zealously, he should not engage in any conduct that offends the dignity and decorum of proceedings. While maintaining his independence, a lawyer should be respectful, courteous, and above-board in his relations with a judge or hearing officer before whom he appears. He should avoid undue solicitude for the comfort or convenience of judge or jury and should avoid any other conduct calculated to gain special consideration.

EC 7-37. In adversary proceedings, clients are litigants and though ill feeling may exist between clients, such ill feeling should not influence a lawyer in his conduct, attitude, and demeanor towards opposing lawyers. A lawyer should not make unfair or derogatory personal reference to opposing counsel. Haranguing and offensive tactics by lawyers interfere with the orderly administration of justice and have no proper place in our legal system. EC 7-38. A lawyer should be courteous to opposing counsel and should accede to reasonable requests regarding court proceedings, settings, continuances, waiver of procedural formalities, and similar matters which do not prejudice the rights of his client. He should follow local customs of courtesy or practice, unless he gives timely notice to opposing counsel of his intention not to do so. A lawyer should be punctual in fulfilling all professional commitments.

EC 7-39. In the final analysis, proper functioning of the adversary system depends upon cooperation between lawyers and tribunals in utilizing procedures which will preserve the impartiality of tribunals and make their decisional processes prompt and just, without impinging upon the obligation of the lawyer to represent their clients zealously within the framework of the law.

DISCIPLINARY RULES

DR 7-101. REPRESENTING A CLIENT ZEALOUSLY.

(A) A lawyer shall not intentionally: (1) Fail to seek the lawful objectives of his client through reasonably available means permitted by law and the Disciplinary Rules, except as provided by DR 7-101(B). A lawyer does not violate this Disciplinary Rule, however, by acceding to reasonable requests of opposing counsel which do not prejudice the rights of his client, by being punctual in fulfilling all professional commitments, by avoiding offensive tactics, or by treating with courtesy and consideration all persons involved in the legal process. (2) Fail to carry out a contract of employment entered into with a client for professional services, but he may withdraw as permitted under DR 2-110, DR 5102, and DR 5-105. (3) Prejudice or damage his client during the course of the professional relationship, except as required under DR 7-102(B).

(B) In his representation of a client, a lawyer may: (1) Where permissible, exercise his professional judgment to waive or fail to assert a right or position of his client. (2) Refuse to aid or participate in conduct that he believes to be unlawful, even though there is some support for an argument that the conduct is legal.

DR 7-102. REPRESENTING A CLIENT WITHIN THE BOUNDS OF THE LAW.

(A) In his representation of a client, a lawyer shall not: (1) File a suit, assert a position, conduct a defense, delay a trial, or take other action on behalf of his client when he knows or when it is obvious that such action would serve merely to harass or maliciously injure another. (2) Knowingly advance a claim or defense that is unwarranted under existing law, except that he may advance such claim or defense if it can be supported by good faith argument for an extension, modification, or reversal of existing law. (3) Conceal or knowingly fail to disclose that which he is required by law to reveal.

(4) Knowingly use perjured testimony or false evidence. (5) Knowingly make a false statement of law or fact. (6) Participate in the creation or preservation of evidence when he knows or it is obvious that the evidence is false. (7) Counsel or assist his client in conduct that the lawyer knows to be illegal or fraudulent. (8) Knowingly engage in other illegal conduct or conduct contrary to a Disciplinary Rule.

(B) A lawyer who receives information clearly establishing that: (1) His client has, in the course of the representation, perpetrated a fraud upon a person or tribunal, shall promptly call upon his client to rectify the same, and if his client refuses or is unable to do so, he shall reveal the fraud to the affected person or tribunal.

(2) A person other than his client has perpetrated a fraud upon a tribunal shall promptly reveal the fraud to the tribunal.

DR 7-103. PERFORMING THE DUTY OF PUBLIC PROSECUTOR OR OTHER GOVERNMENT LAWYER.

(A) A public prosecutor or other government lawyer shall not institute or cause to be instituted criminal charges when he knows or it is obvious that the charges are not supported by probable cause.

(B) A public prosecutor or other government lawyer in criminal litigation shall make timely disclosure to counsel for the defendant, or to the defendant if he has no counsel, of the existence of evidence, known to the prosecutor or other government lawyer, that tends to negate the guilt of the accused, mitigate the degree of the offense, or reduce the punishment.

DR 7-104. COMMUNICATING WITH ONE OF ADVERSE INTEREST.

(A) During the course of his representation of a client a lawyer shall not: (1) Communicate or cause another to communicate on the subject of the representation with a party he knows to be represented by a lawyer in that matter unless he has the prior consent of the lawyer representing such other party or is authorized by law to do so. (2) Give advice to a person who is not represented by a lawyer, other than the advice to secure counsel, if the interests of such person are or have a reasonable possibility of being in conflict with the interests of his client.

DR 7-105. THREATENING CRIMINAL PROSECUTION.

(A) A lawyer shall not present, participate in presenting, or threaten to present criminal charges solely to obtain an advantage in a civil matter.

DR 7-106. TRIAL CONDUCT.

(A) A lawyer shall not disregard or advise his client to disregard a standing rule of a tribunal or a ruling of a tribunal made in the course of a proceeding, but he may take appropriate steps in good faith to test the validity of such rule or ruling.

(B) In presenting a matter to a tribunal, a lawyer shall disclose:

(1) Legal authority in the controlling jurisdiction known to him to be directly adverse to the position of his client and which is not disclosed by opposing counsel. (2) Unless privileged or irrelevant, the identities of the clients he represents and of the persons who employed him. (C) In appearing in his professional capacity before a tribunal, a lawyer shall not: (1) State or allude to any matter that he has no reasonable basis to believe is relevant to the case or that will not be supported by admissible evidence.(2) Ask any question that he has no reasonable basis to believe is relevant to the case and that is intended to degrade a witness or other person. (3) Assert his personal knowledge of the facts in issue, except when testifying as a witness. (4) Assert his personal opinion as to the justness of a cause, as to the credibility of a witness, as to the culpability of a civil litigant, or as to the guilt or innocence of an accused; but he may argue, on his analysis of the evidence, for any position or conclusion with respect to the matters stated herein. (5) Fail to comply with known local customs of courtesy or practice of the bar or a particular tribunal without giving to opposing counsel timely notice of his intent not to comply.(6) Engage in undignified or discourteous conduct which is degrading to a tribunal. (7) Intentionally or habitually violate any established rule of procedure or of evidence.

DR 7-107. TRIAL PUBLICITY.

(A) A lawyer who is participating or has participated in the investigation or litigation of a matter shall not make an extrajudicial statement that a reasonable person would expect to be disseminated by means of public communication if the lawyer knows or reasonably should know that it will have a substantial likelihood of materially prejudicing an adjudicative proceeding in the matter.

(B) Notwithstanding division (A) of this rule, a lawyer may state any of the following: (1) The claim, offense, or defense involved and, except when prohibited by law, the identity of the persons involved; (2) Information contained in a public record; (3) That an investigation of a matter is in progress; (4) The scheduling or result of any step in litigation; (5) A request for assistance in obtaining evidence and information necessary to obtain evidence;

(6) A warning of danger concerning the behavior of a person involved, when there is reason to believe that there exists the likelihood of substantial harm to an individual or to the public interest;

(7) In a criminal case, in addition to divisions (B)(1) to (6) of this rule, any of the following: (a) The identity, residence, occupation, and family status of the accused; (b) If the accused has not been apprehended, information necessary to aid in apprehension of that person; (c) The fact, time, and place of arrest; (d) The identity of investigating and arresting officers or agencies and the length of the investigation.

(C) Notwithstanding division (A) of this rule, a lawyer may make a statement that a reasonable lawyer would believe is required to protect a client from the substantial undue prejudicial effect of recent publicity not initiated by the lawyer or the lawyer's client. A statement made pursuant to this division shall be limited to the information necessary to mitigate the recent adverse publicity. (D) No lawyer associated in a firm or government agency with a lawyer subject to division (A) of this rule shall make a statement prohibited by division (A) of this rule.

DR 7-108. COMMUNICATION WITH OR INVESTIGATION OF JURORS.

(A) Before the trial of a case a lawyer connected therewith shall not communicate with or cause another to communicate with anyone be knows to be a member of the venire from which the jury will be selected for the trial of the case. (B) During the trial of a case: (1) A lawyer connected therewith shall not communicate with or cause another to communicate with any member of the jury. (2) A lawyer who is not connected therewith shall not communicate with or cause another to communicate with a juror concerning the case. (C) DR 7-108(A) and (B) do not prohibit a lawyer from communicating with veniremen or jurors in the course of official proceedings. (D) After discharge of the jury from further consideration of a case with which the lawyer was connected, the lawyer shall not ask questions of or make comments to a member of that jury that are calculated merely to harass or embarrass the juror or

to influence his actions in future jury service. (E) A lawyer shall not conduct or cause, by financial support or otherwise, another to conduct a vexatious or harassing investigation of either a venireman or a juror. (F) All restrictions imposed by DR 7-108 upon a lawyer also apply to communications with or investigations of members of a family of a venireman or a juror. (G) A lawyer shall reveal promptly to the court improper conduct by a venireman or a juror, or by another toward a venireman or a juror or a member of his family, of which the lawyer has knowledge.

DR 7-109. CONTACT WITH WITNESSES.

(A) A lawyer shall not suppress any evidence that he or his client has a legal obligation to reveal or produce. (B) A lawyer shall not advise or cause a person to secrete himself or to leave the jurisdiction of a tribunal for the purpose of making him unavailable as a witness therein. (C) A lawyer shall not pay, offer to pay, or acquiesce in the payment of compensation to a witness contingent upon the content of his testimony or the outcome of the case. But a lawyer may advance, guarantee, or acquiesce in the payment of: (1) Expenses reasonably incurred by a witness in attending or testifying. (2) Reasonable compensation to a witness for his loss of time in attending or testifying. (3) A reasonable fee for the professional services of an expert witness.

DR 7-110. CONTACT WITH OFFICIALS.

(A) A lawyer shall not give or lend any thing of value to a judge, official, or employee of a tribunal.

(B) In an adversary proceeding, a lawyer shall not communicate, or cause another to communicate, as to the merits of the cause with a judge or an official before whom the proceeding is pending, except:

(1) In the course of official proceedings in the cause.

(2) In writing if he promptly delivers a copy of the writing to opposing counsel or to the adverse party if he is not represented by a lawyer. (3) Orally upon adequate notice to opposing counsel or to the adverse party if he is not represented by a lawyer. (4) As otherwise authorized by law.

DR 7-111. CONFIDENTIAL INFORMATION

(A)(1) A lawyer shall not disclose or cause to be disclosed, without appropriate authorization, information regarding the probable or actual decision in a case or legal proceeding pending before a court, including the vote of a justice, judge, or court in a case pending before the Supreme Court, a court of appeals, or a panel of judges of a trial court, prior to the announcement of the decision by the court or journalization of an opinion, entry, or other document reflecting that decision under either of the following circumstances:

(a) The probable or actual decision is confidential because of statutory or rule provisions; (b) The probable or actual decision clearly has been designated to the justice or judge as confidential when confidentiality is warranted because of the status of the proceedings or the circumstances under which the information was received and preserving confidentiality is necessary to the proper conduct of court business. (2) Nothing in division (A)(1) of this rule shall prohibit the disclosure of any of the following: (a) A decision that has been announced on the record or in open court, but that has not been journalized in a written opinion, entry, or other document;

(b) Information regarding the probable or actual decision in a pending case or legal proceeding to a justice, judge, or employee of the court; (c) Other information that is a matter of public record or that may be disclosed pursuant to law. (B)(1) No lawyer shall obtain or attempt to obtain information, without appropriate authorization, from a justice, judge, or court employee regarding the probable or actual decision in a case or legal proceeding pending before a court, including the vote of a justice or judge in a case pending before the Supreme Court or a court of appeals, prior to announcement of the decision by the court or journalization of an opinion, entry, or other document reflecting that decision under either of the following circumstances: (a) The probable or actual decision is confidential because of statutory or rule provisions; (b) The probable or actual decision clearly has been designated to the justice or judge as confidential when confidentiality is warranted because of the status of the proceedings or the circumstances under which the information was received and preserving confidentiality is necessary to the proper conduct of court business.

(2) Nothing in division (B)(1) of this rule shall prohibit a lawyer from obtaining or attempting to obtain either of the following: (a) A decision that has been announced on the record or in open court, but that has not been journalized in a written opinion, entry, or other document; (b) Information regarding the probable or actual decision in a pending case or legal proceeding from a justice, judge, or other employee of the court in which the lawyer is employed; (c) Other information that is a matter of public record or that may be disclosed pursuant to law.

(C) The imposition of discipline upon a lawyer for violation of division (A) or (B) of this rule shall not preclude prosecution for a violation of any applicable provision of the Revised Code, including, but not limited to, division (B) of section 102.03 of the Revised Code.

CANON 8
A Lawyer Should Assist in Improving the Legal System

ETHICAL CONSIDERATIONS
EC 8-1. Changes in human affairs and imperfections in human institutions make necessary constant efforts to maintain and improve our legal system. This system should function in a manner that commands public respect and fosters the use of legal remedies to achieve redress of grievances. By reason of education and experience, lawyers are especially qualified to recognize deficiencies in the legal system and to initiate corrective measures therein. Thus they should participate in proposing and supporting legislation and programs to improve the system, without regard to the general interests or desires of clients or former clients.

EC 8-2. Rules of law are deficient if they are not just, understandable, and responsive to the needs of society. If a lawyer believes that the existence or absence of a rule of law, substantive or procedural, causes or contributes to an unjust result, he should endeavor by lawful means to obtain appropriate changes in the law. He should encourage the simplification of laws and the repeal or amendment of laws that are outmoded. Likewise, legal procedures should be improved whenever experience indicates a change is needed.

EC 8-3. The fair administration of justice requires the availability of competent lawyers. Members of the public should be educated to recognize the existence of legal problems and the resultant need for legal services, and should be provided methods for intelligent selection of counsel. Those persons unable to pay for legal services should be provided needed services. Clients and lawyers should not be penalized by undue geographical restraints upon representation in legal matters, and the bar should address itself to improvements in licensing, reciprocity, and admission procedures consistent with the needs of modern commerce.

EC 8-4. Whenever a lawyer seeks legislative or administrative changes, he should identify the capacity in which he appears, whether on behalf of himself, a client, or the public. A lawyer may advocate such changes on behalf of a client even though he does not agree with them. But when a lawyer purports to act on behalf of the public, he should espouse only those changes which he conscientiously believes to be in the public interest.

EC 8-5. Fraudulent, deceptive, or otherwise illegal conduct by a participant in a proceeding before a tribunal or legislative body is inconsistent with fair administration of justice, and it should never be participated in or condoned by lawyers. Unless constrained by his obligation to preserve the confidences and secrets of his client, a lawyer should reveal to appropriate authorities any knowledge he may have of such improper conduct.

EC 8-6. Judges and administrative officials having adjudicatory powers ought to be persons of integrity, competence, and suitable temperament. Generally, lawyers are qualified, by personal observation or investigation, to evaluate the qualifications of persons seeking or being considered for such public offices, and for this reason they have a special responsibility to aid in the selection of only those who are qualified. It is the duty of lawyers to endeavor to prevent political considerations from outweighing judicial fitness in the selection of judges. Lawyers should protest earnestly against the appointment or election of those who are unsuited for the bench and should strive to have elected or appointed thereto only those who are willing to forego pursuits, whether of a business, political, or other nature, that may interfere with the free and fair consideration of questions presented for adjudication. Adjudicatory officials, not being wholly free to defend themselves, are entitled to receive the support of the bar against unjust criticism. While a lawyer as a citizen has a right to criticize such officials publicly, he should be certain of the merit of his complaint, use appropriate language, and avoid petty criticisms, for unrestrained and intemperate statements tend to lessen public confidence in our legal system. Criticisms motivated by reasons other than a desire to improve the legal system are not justified.

EC 8-7. Since lawyers are a vital part of the legal system, they should be persons of integrity, of professional skill, and of dedication to the improvement of the system. Thus a lawyer should aid in establishing, as well as enforcing, standards of conduct adequate to protect the public by insuring that those who practice law are qualified to so.

EC 8-8. Lawyers often serve as legislators or as holders of other public offices. This is highly desirable, as lawyers are uniquely qualified to make significant contributions to the improvement of the legal system. A lawyer who is a public officer, whether full or part-time, should not engage in activities in which his personal or professional interests are or foreseeably may be in conflict with his official duties.

EC 8-9 The advancement of our legal system is of vital importance in maintaining the rule of law and in facilitating orderly changes; therefore, lawyers should encourage, and should aid in making, needed changes and improvements.

DISCIPLINARY RULES
DR 8-101. ACTION AS A PUBLIC OFFICIAL.

(A) A lawyer who holds public office shall not: (1) Use his public position to obtain, or attempt to obtain, a special advantage in legislative matters for himself or for a client under circumstances where he knows or it is obvious that such action is not in the public interest.
(2) Use his public position to influence, or attempt to influence, a tribunal to act in favor of himself or of a client.
(3) Accept any thing of value from any person when the lawyer knows or it is obvious that the offer is for the purpose of influencing his action as a public official.

DR 8-102. STATEMENTS CONCERNING JUDGES AND OTHER ADJUDICATORY OFFICERS.

(A) A lawyer shall not knowingly make false statements of fact concerning the qualifications of a candidate for election or appointment to a judicial office.
(B) A lawyer shall not knowingly make false accusations against a judge or other adjudicatory officer.

CANON 9
A Lawyer Should Avoid Even the Appearance of Professional Impropriety

ETHICAL CONSIDERATIONS

EC 9-1. Continuation of the American concept that we are to be governed by rules of law requires that the people have faith that justice can be obtained through our legal system. A lawyer should promote public confidence in our system and in the legal profession.

EC 9-2. Public confidence in law and lawyers may be eroded by irresponsible or improper conduct of a lawyer. On occasion, ethical conduct of a lawyer may appear to laymen to be unethical. In order to avoid misunderstandings and hence to maintain confidence, a lawyer should fully and promptly inform his client of material developments in the matters being handled for the client. While a lawyer should guard against otherwise proper conduct that has a tendency to diminish public confidence in the legal system or in the legal profession his duty to clients or to the public should never be subordinate merely because the full discharge of his obligation may be misunderstood or may tend to subject him or the legal profession to criticism. When explicit ethical guidance does not exist, a lawyer should determine his conduct by acting in a manner that promotes public confidence in the integrity and efficiency of the legal system and the legal profession.

EC 9-3. After a lawyer leaves judicial office or other public employment, he should not accept employment in connection with any matter in which he had substantial responsibility prior to his leaving, since to accept employment would give the appearance of impropriety even if none exists.

EC 9-4. Because the very essence of the legal system is to provide procedures by which matters can be presented in an impartial manner so that they may be decided solely upon the merits, any statement or suggestion by a lawyer that he can or would attempt to circumvent those procedures is detrimental to the legal system and tends to undermine public confidence in it.

EC 9-5. Separation of the funds of a client from those of his lawyer not only serves to protect the client but also avoids even the appearance of impropriety, and therefore commingling of such funds should be avoided.

EC 9-6. Every lawyer owes a solemn duty to uphold the integrity and honor of his profession; to encourage respect for the law and for the courts and the judges thereof; to observe the Code of Professional Responsibility; to act as a member of a learned profession, one dedicated to public service; to cooperate with his brother lawyers in supporting the organized bar through the devoting of his time, efforts, and financial support as his professional standing and ability reasonably permit; to conduct himself so as to reflect credit on the legal profession and to inspire the confidence, respect, and trust of his clients and of the public; and to strive to avoid not only professional impropriety but also the appearance of impropriety.

DISCIPLINARY RULES

DR 9-101. AVOIDING EVEN THE APPEARANCE OF IMPROPRIETY.

(A) A lawyer shall not accept private employment in a matter upon the merits of which he has acted in a judicial capacity.

(B) A lawyer shall not accept private employment in a matter in which he had substantial responsibility while he was a public employee.

(C) A lawyer shall not state or imply that he is able to influence improperly or upon irrelevant grounds any tribunal, legislative body, or public official.

DR 9-102. PRESERVING IDENTITY OF FUNDS AND PROPERTY OF A CLIENT.

(A)   All funds of clients paid to a lawyer or law firm, other than advances for costs and expenses, shall be deposited in one or more identifiable bank accounts maintained in the state in which the law office is situated and no funds belonging to the lawyer or law firm shall be deposited therein except as follows: (1) Funds reasonably sufficient to pay bank charges may be deposited therein. (2) Funds belonging in part to a client and in part presently or potentially to the lawyer or law firm must be deposited therein, but the portion belonging to the lawyer or law firm may be withdrawn when due unless the right of the lawyer or law firm to receive it is disputed by the client, in which event the disputed portion shall not be withdrawn until the dispute is finally resolved. (B) A lawyer shall: (1) Promptly notify a client of the receipt of his funds, securities, or other properties. (2) Identify and label securities and properties of a client promptly upon receipt and place them in a safe deposit box or other place of safekeeping as soon as practicable. (3) Maintain complete records of all funds, securities, and other properties of a client coming into the possession of the lawyer and render appropriate accounts to his client regarding them. (4) Promptly pay or deliver to the client as requested by a client the funds, securities, or other properties in the possession of the lawyer which the client is entitled to receive.

(C) A lawyer, law firm, or estate of a deceased lawyer who sells a law practice shall transfer all funds held pursuant to DR 9-102(A) to the lawyer or law firm purchasing the law practice at the time client files are transferred.

(D) Nothing in the Code of Professional Responsibility shall be interpreted to prohibit compliance by a lawyer, a law firm, or an ancillary business related to the practice of law in which the lawyer is a principal with the provisions of sections 3953.231, 4705.09, and 4705.10 of the Revised Code and any rules adopted by the Ohio Legal Assistance Foundation pursuant to section 120.52 of the Revised Code.

(E) No lawyer, law firm, or ancillary business related to the practice of law shall fail to do any of the following:

(1) Maintain funds of clients or third persons in an interest-bearing trust account that is established in an eligible depository institution as required by sections 3953.231, 4705.09, and 4705.10 of the Revised Code or any rules adopted by the Ohio Legal Assistance Foundation pursuant to section 120.52 of the Revised Code; (2) Notify the Ohio Legal Assistance Foundation, in a manner required by rules adopted by the Ohio Legal Assistance Foundation pursuant to section 120.52 of the Revised Code, of the existence of an interest-bearing trust account; (3) Comply with the reporting requirement contained in Gov. Bar R. VI, Section 1(F).

DEFINITIONS*

As used in the Disciplinary Rules of the Code of Professional Responsibility:

(1) "Differing interests" include every interest that will adversely affect either the judgment or the loyalty of a lawyer to a client, whether it be a conflicting, inconsistent, diverse, or other interest.

(2) "Law firm" includes a legal professional association, corporation, legal clinic, limited liability company, registered partnership, or any other organization under which a lawyer may engage in the practice of law pursuant to the Supreme Court Rules for the Government of the Bar of Ohio.

(3) "Person" includes a corporation, an association, a trust, a

partnership, and any other organization or legal entity.

(4)   "Professional legal corporation" means a corporation, or an association treated as a corporation, authorized by law to practice law for profit.

(5)   "State" includes the District of Columbia, Puerto Rico, and other federal territories and possessions.

(6)   "Tribunal" includes all courts and all other adjudicatory bodies.

(7)   "A Bar association" includes a bar association of specialists as referred to in DR 2-105(A)(1) or (4).

(8)   "Qualified legal assistance organization" means an office or organization of one of the four types listed in DR 2-103(D)(1)-(4), inclusive that meets all the requirements thereof.

(9)   "Ancillary business related to the practice of law" includes, but is not limited to, a title insurance company that is owned, operated, or owned and operated by a lawyer or law firm and that is subject to section 3953.231 of the Revised Code.

* "Confidence" and "secret" are defined in DR 4-101(A).

–Appendix D–

RULES OF PROFESSIONAL CONDUCT

As stated in the text of this book, the American Bar Association developed both the Model Rules and Model Code of Professional Conduct. Most states have adopted some form of either the Rules or the Code. While some states have made substantial changes to the ABA's versions, many states' versions have been adopted with little or no changes whatsoever. The state presented here, West Virginia, is an examples of a state that has adopted a comparable version.

Counselor.
2.1 Advisor.
2.2 Intermediary.
2.3 Evaluation for use by third persons.

Advocate.
3.1 Meritorious claims and contentions.
3.2 Expediting litigation.
3.3 Candor toward the tribunal.
3.4 Fairness to opposing party and counsel.
3.5 Impartiality and decorum in the tribunal.
3.6 Trial publicity.
3.7 Lawyer as witness.
3.8 Special responsibilities of a prosecutor.
3.9 Advocate in nonadjudicative proceedings.

Transactions with Persons Other than Clients.
4.1 Truthfulness in statements to others.
4.2 Communication with person represented by counsel.
4.3 Dealing with unrepresented person.
4.4 Respect for rights of third persons.

Law Firms and Associations.
5.1 Responsibilities of a partner or supervisory lawyer.
5.2 Responsibilities of a subordinate lawyer.
5.3 Responsibilities regarding non-lawyer assistants.
5.4 Professional independence of a lawyer.
5.5 Unauthorized practice of law.
5.6 Restrictions on right to practice.
5.7 Limited liability legal practice.

Public Service.
6.1 Pro bono publico service.
6.2 Accepting appointments.
6.3 Membership in legal services organization.
6.4 Law reform activities affecting client interests.

Information About Legal Services.
7.1 Communications concerning a lawyer's services.
7.2 Advertising.
7.3 Direct contact with prospective clients.
7.4 Communication of fields of practice.
7.5 Firm names and letterheads.

Maintaining the Integrity of the Profession.
8.1 Bar admission and disciplinary matters.
8.2 Judicial and legal officials.
8.3 Reporting professional misconduct.
8.4 Misconduct.
8.5 Jurisdiction.

PREAMBLE, SCOPE AND TERMINOLOGY.
Preamble: A Lawyer's Responsibilities.

A lawyer is a representative of clients, an officer of the legal system and a public citizen having special responsibility for the quality of justice.

As a representative of clients, a lawyer performs various functions. As advisor, a lawyer provides a client with an informed understanding of the client's legal rights and obligations and explains their practical implications. As advocate, a lawyer zealously asserts the client's position under the rules of the adversary system. As negotiator, a lawyer seeks a result advantageous to the client but consistent with requirements of honest dealing with others. As intermediary between clients, a lawyer seeks to reconcile their divergent interests as an advisor and, to a limited extent, as a spokesperson for each client. A lawyer acts as evaluator by examining a client's legal affairs and reporting about them to the client or to others.

In all professional functions a lawyer should be competent, prompt and diligent. A lawyer should maintain communications with a client concerning the representation. A lawyer should keep in confidence information relating to representation of a client except so far as disclosure is required or permitted by the Rules of Professional Conduct or other law.

A lawyer's conduct should conform to the requirements of the law, both in professional service to clients and in the lawyer's business and personal affairs. A lawyer should use the law's procedures only for legitimate purposes and not to harass or intimidate others. A lawyer should demonstrate respect for the legal system and for those who serve it, including judges, other lawyers and public officials. While it is a lawyer's duty, when necessary, to challenge the rectitude of official action, it is also a lawyer's duty to uphold legal process.

As a public citizen, a lawyer should seek improvement of the law, the administration of justice and the quality of service rendered by the legal profession. As a member of a learned profession, a lawyer should cultivate knowledge of the law beyond its use for clients, employ that knowledge in reform of the law and work to strengthen legal education. A lawyer should be mindful of deficiencies in the administration of justice and of the fact that the poor, and sometimes persons who are not poor, cannot afford adequate legal assistance, and should therefore devote professional time and civic influence in their behalf. A lawyer should aid the legal profession in pursuing these objectives and should help the bar regulate itself in the public interest.

Many of a lawyer's professional responsibilities are prescribed in the Rules of Professional Conduct, as well as substantive and procedural law. However, a lawyer is also guided by personal conscience and the approbation of professional peers. A lawyer should strive to attain the highest level of skill, to improve the law and the legal profession and to exemplify the legal profession's ideals of public service. A lawyer's responsibilities as a representative of clients, an officer of the legal system and a public citizen are usually harmonious. Thus, when an opposing party is well represented, a lawyer can be a zealous advocate on behalf of a client and at the same time assume that justice is being done. So also, a lawyer can be sure that preserving client confidences ordinarily serves the public interest because people are more likely to seek legal advice, and thereby heed their legal obligations, when they know their communications will be private. In the nature of law practice, however, conflicting responsibilities are encountered. Virtually all difficult ethical problems arise from conflict between a lawyer's responsibilities to clients, to the legal system and to the lawyer's own interest in remaining an upright person while earning a satisfactory living.

The Rules of Professional Conduct prescribe terms for resolving such conflicts. Within the framework of these Rules many difficult issues of professional discretion can arise. Such issues must be resolved through the exercise of sensitive professional and moral judgment guided by the basic principles underlying the Rules. The legal profession is largely self-governing. Although other professions also have been granted powers of self-government, the legal profession is unique in this respect because of the close relationship between the profession and processes of government and law enforcement. This connection is manifested in the fact that ultimate authority over the legal profession is vested largely in the courts. To the extent that lawyers meet the obligations of their professional calling, the occasion for government regulation is obviated. Self-regulation also helps maintain the legal profession's independence from government domination.

An independent legal profession is an important force in preserving government under law, for abuse of legal authority is more readily challenged by a profession whose members are not dependent on government for the right of practice. The legal profession's relative autonomy carries with it special responsibilities of self-government. The profession has a responsibility to assure that its regulations are conceived in the public interest and not in furtherance of parochial or self-interested concerns of the bar. Every lawyer is responsible for observance of the Rules of Professional Conduct. A lawyer should also aid in securing their observance by other lawyers. Neglect of these responsibilities compromises the independence of the profession and the public interest which it serves. Lawyers play a vital role in the preservation of society. The fulfillment of this role requires an understanding by lawyers of their relationship to our legal system. The Rules of Professional Conduct, when properly applied, serve to define that relationship.

Scope.

The Rules of Professional Conduct are rules of reason. They should be interpreted with reference to the purposes of legal representation and of the law itself. Some of the Rules are imperatives, cast in the terms "shall" or "shall not." These define proper conduct for purposes of professional discipline. Others, generally cast in the term "may," are permissive and define areas under the Rules in which the lawyer has professional discretion. No disciplinary action should be taken when the lawyer chooses not to act or acts within the bounds of such discretion. Other Rules define the nature of relationships between the lawyer and others. The Rules are thus partly obligatory and disciplinary and partly constitutive and descriptive in that they define a lawyer's professional role. Many of the Comments use the term "should." Comments do not add obligations to the Rules but provide guidance for practicing in compliance with the Rules.

The Rules presuppose a larger legal context shaping the lawyer's role. That context includes court rules and statutes relating to matters of licensure, laws defining specific obligations of lawyers and substantive and procedural law in general. Compliance with the Rules, as with all law in an open society, depends primarily upon understanding and voluntary compliance, secondarily upon reinforcement by peer and public opinion and finally, when necessary, upon enforcement through disciplinary proceedings. The Rules do not, however, exhaust the moral and ethical considerations that should inform a lawyer for no worthwhile human activity can be completely defined by legal rules. The Rules simply provide a framework for the ethical practice of law.

Furthermore, for purposes of determining the lawyer's authority and responsibility, principles of substantive law external to these Rules determine whether a client-lawyer relationship exists. Most of the duties flowing from the client-lawyer relationship attach only after the client has requested the lawyer to render legal services and the lawyer has agreed to do so. But there are some duties, such as that of confidentiality under Rule 1.6, that may attach when the lawyer agrees to consider whether a client-lawyer relationship shall be established. Whether a client-lawyer relationship exists for any specific purpose can depend on the circumstances and may be a question of fact.

Under various legal provisions, including constitutional, statutory and common law, the responsibilities of government lawyers may include authority concerning legal matters that ordinarily reposes in the client in private client-lawyer relationships. For example, a lawyer for a government agency may have authority on behalf of the government to decide upon settlement or whether to appeal from an adverse judgment. Such authority in various respects is generally vested in the attorney general and the state's attorney in state government, and their federal counterparts, and the same may be true of other government law officers. Also, lawyers under the supervision of these officers may be authorized to represent several government agencies in intragovernmental legal controversies in circumstances where a private lawyer could not represent multiple private clients. They also may have authority to represent the "public interest" in circumstances where a private lawyer would not be authorized to do so. These Rules do not abrogate any such authority.

Failure to comply with an obligation or prohibition imposed by a Rule is a basis for invoking the disciplinary process. The Rules presuppose that disciplinary assessment of a lawyer's conduct will be made on the basis of the facts and circumstances as they existed at the time of the conduct in question and in recognition of the fact that a lawyer often has to act upon uncertain or incomplete evidence of the situation. Moreover, the Rules presuppose that whether or not discipline should be imposed for a violation, and the severity of a sanction, depend on all the circumstances. such as the willfulness and seriousness of the violation, extenuating factors and whether there have been previous violations.

Violation of a Rule should not give rise to a cause of action nor should it create any presumption that a legal duty has been breached. The Rules are designed to provide guidance to lawyers and to provide a structure for regulating conduct through disciplinary agencies. They are not designed to be a basis for civil liability. Furthermore, the purpose of the Rules can be subverted when they are invoked by opposing parties as procedural weapons. The fact that a Rule is a just basis for a lawyer's self-assessment, or for sanctioning a lawyer under the administration of a disciplinary authority, does not imply that an antagonist in a collateral proceeding or transaction has standing to seek enforcement of the Rule. Accordingly, nothing in the Rules should be deemed to augment any substantive legal duty of lawyers or the extra-disciplinary consequences of violating such a duty.

Moreover, these Rules are not intended to govern or affect judicial application of either the attorney-client or work product privilege. Those privileges were developed to promote compliance with law and fairness in litigation. In reliance on the attorney-client privilege, clients are entitled to expect that communications within the scope of the privilege will be protected against compelled disclosure. The attorney-client privilege is that of the client and not of the lawyer. The fact that in exceptional situations the lawyer under the Rules has a limited discretion to disclose a client confidence does not vitiate the proposition that, as a general matter, the client has a reasonable expectation that information relating to the client will not be voluntarily disclosed and that disclosure of such information may be judicially compelled only in accordance with recognized exceptions to the attorney-client and work product privileges.

The lawyer's exercise of discretion not to disclose information under Rule 1.6 should not be subject to reexamination. Permitting such reexamination would be incompatible with the general policy of promoting compliance with law through assurances that communications will be protected against disclosure.

The Comment accompanying each Rule explains and illustrates the meaning and purpose of the Rule. The Preamble and this note on Scope provide general orientation. The Comments are intended as guides to interpretation, but the text of each Rule is authoritative. Research notes were prepared to compare counterparts in the ABA Model Code of Professional Responsibility (adopted 1969, as amended) and to provide selected references to other authorities. The notes have not been adopted, do not constitute part of the Model Rules, and are not intended to affect the application or interpretation of the Rules and Comments.

Terminology.
"Belief" or "believes" denotes that the person involved actually supposed the fact in question to be true. A person's belief may be inferred from circum- stances.

"Consult" or "consultation" denotes communication of information reasonably sufficient to permit the client to appreciate the significance of the matter in question.

"Firm" or "law firm" denotes a lawyer or lawyers in a private firm, lawyers employed in the legal department of a corporation or other organization and lawyers employed in a legal service organization.

"Fraud" or "fraudulent" denotes conduct having a purpose to deceive and not merely negligent misrepresentation or failure to apprise another of relevant information.

"Knowingly," "known," or "knows" denotes actual knowledge of the fact in question. A person's knowledge may be inferred from circumstances.

"Partner" denotes a member of a partnership and a shareholder in a law firm organized as a professional corporation.

"Reasonable" or "reasonably" when used in relation to conduct by a lawyer denotes the conduct of a reasonably prudent and competent lawyer.

"Reasonable belief" or "reasonably believes" when used in reference to a lawyer denotes that the lawyer believes the matter in question and that the circumstances are such that the belief is reasonable.

"Reasonably should know" when used in reference to a lawyer denotes that a lawyer of reasonable prudence and competence would ascertain the matter in question.

"Substantial" when used in reference to degree or extent denotes a material matter of clear and weighty importance.

CLIENT-LAWYER RELATIONSHIP.

Rule 1.1. Competence.

A lawyer shall provide competent representation to a client. Competent representation requires the legal knowledge, skill, thoroughness and preparation reasonably necessary for the representation.

Rule 1.2. Scope of representation.

(a) A lawyer shall abide by a client's decisions concerning the objectives of representation, subject to paragraphs (c), (d) and (e), and shall consult with the client as to the means by which they are to be pursued. A lawyer shall abide by a client's decision whether to accept an offer of settlement of a matter. In a criminal case, the lawyer shall abide by the client's decision, after consultation with the lawyer, as to a plea to be entered, whether to waive jury trial and whether the client will testify.

(b) A lawyer's representation of a client, including representation by appointment, does not constitute an endorsement of the client's political, economic, social or moral views or activities.

(c) A lawyer may limit the objectives of the representation if the client consents after consultation.

(d) A lawyer shall not counsel a client to engage, or assist a client, in conduct that the lawyer knows is criminal or fraudulent, but a lawyer may discuss the legal consequences of any proposed course of conduct with a client and may counselor assist a client to make a good faith effort to determine the validity, scope, meaning or application of the law.

(e) When a lawyer knows that a client expects assistance not permitted by the rules of professional conductor other law, the lawyer shall consult with the client regarding the relevant limitations on the lawyer's conduct.

Rule 1.3. Diligence.

A lawyer shall act with reasonable diligence and promptness in representing a client.

Rule 1.4. Communication.

(a) A lawyer shall keep a client reasonably informed about the status of a matter and promptly comply with reasonable requests for information.

(b) A lawyer shall explain a matter to the extent reasonably necessary to permit the client to make informed decisions regarding the representation.

Rule 1.5. Fees.

(a) A lawyer's fee shall be reasonable. The factors to be considered in determining the reasonableness of a fee include the following:

(1) the time and labor required, the novelty and difficulty of the questions involved, and skill requisite to perform the legal service properly;

(2) the likelihood, if apparent to the client, that the acceptance of the particular employment will preclude other employment by the lawyer;

(3) the fee customarily charged in the locality for similar legal services;

(4) the amount involved and results obtained;

(5) the time limitations imposed by the client or by the circumstances;

(6) the nature and length of the professional relationship with the client;

(7) the experience, reputation, and ability of the lawyer or lawyers performing the services; and

(8) whether the fee is fixed or contingent.

(b) When the lawyer has not regularly represented the client, the basis or rate of the fee shall be communicated to the client, preferably in writing, before or within a reasonable time after commencing the representation.

(c) A fee may be contingent on the outcome of the matter for which the service is rendered, except in a matter in which a contingent fee is prohibited by paragraph (d) or other law. A contingent fee agreement shall be in writing and shall state the method by which the fee is to be determined, including the percentage or percentages that shall accrue to the lawyer in the event of settlement, trial or appeal, litigation and other expenses to be deducted from the recovery, and whether such expenses are to be deducted before or after the contingent fee is calculated. Upon conclusion of a contingent fee matter, the lawyer shall provide the client with a written statement stating the outcome of the matter and, if there is a recovery, showing the remittance to the client and the method of its determination.

(d) A lawyer shall not enter into an arrangement for, charge, or collect:

(1) any fee in a domestic relations matter, the payment or amount of which is contingent upon the securing of a divorce or upon the amount of alimony or support, or property settlement in lieu thereof; or

(2) a contingent fee for representing a defendant in a criminal case.

(e) A division of a fee between lawyers who are not in the same firm may be made only if:

(1) the division is in proportion to the services performed by each lawyer or, by written agreement with the client, each lawyer assumes joint responsibility for the representations;

(2) the client is advised of and does not object to the participation of all the lawyers involved; and

(3) the total fee is reasonable.

(4) The requirements of "services performed" and "joint responsibility" shall be satisfied in contingent fee cases when: (1) a lawyer who is regularly engaged in the full time practice of law evaluates a case and forwards it to another lawyer who is more experienced in the area or field of law being referred; (2) the client is advised that the lawyer who is more experienced in the area or field of law being referred will be primarily responsible for the litigation and that there will be a division of fees; and, (3) the total fee charged the client is reasonable and in keeping with what is usually charged for such matters in the community.

Rule 1.6. Confidentiality of information.

(a) A lawyer shall not reveal information relating to representation of a client unless the client consents after consultation, except for disclosures that are impliedly authorized in order to carry out the representation, and except as stated in paragraph (b).

(b) A lawyer may reveal such information to the extent the lawyer reasonably believes necessary :

(1) to prevent the client & from committing a criminal act; or

(2) to establish a claim or defense on behalf of the lawyer in a controversy between the lawyer and the client, to establish a defense to a criminal charge or civil claim against the lawyer based upon conduct in which the client was involved, or to respond to allegations in any proceeding concerning the lawyer's representation of a client.

Rule 1.7. Conflict of interest: General rules.

(a) A lawyer shall not represent a client if the representation of that client will be directly adverse to another client, unless:

(1) the lawyer reasonably believes the representation will not adversely affect the relationship with the other client; and

(2) each client consents after consultation.

(b) A lawyer shall not represent a client if the representation of that client may be materially limited by the lawyer's responsibilities to another client or to a third person, or by the lawyer's own interests, unless:

(1) the lawyer reasonably believes the representation will not be adversely affected; and

(2) the client consents after consultation. When representation of multiple clients in a single matter is undertaken, the consultation shall include explanation of the implications of the common representation and the advantage and risks involved.

Rule 1.8. Conflict of interest: Prohibited transactions.

(a) A lawyer shall not enter into a business transaction with a client or knowingly acquire an ownership, possessory, security or other pecuniary interest adverse to a client unless:

(1) the transaction and terms on which the lawyer acquires the interest are fair and reasonable to the client and are fully disclosed and transmitted in writing to the client in a manner which can be reasonably understood by the client;

(2) the client is given a reasonable opportunity to seek the advice of independent counsel in the transaction; and

(3) the client consents in writing thereto.

(b) A lawyer shall not use information relating to representation of a client to the disadvantage of the client unless the client consents after consultation, except as permitted or required by Rule 1.6 or Rule 3.3.

(c) A lawyer shall not prepare an instrument giving the lawyer or a person related to the lawyer as parent, child, sibling, or spouse any substantial gift from a client, including a testamentary gift, except where the client is related to the donee.

(d) Prior to the conclusion of representation of a client, a lawyer shall not make or negotiate an agreement giving the lawyer literary or media rights to a portrayal or account based in substantial part on information relating to the representation.

(e) A lawyer shall not provide financial assistance to a client in connection with pending or contemplated litigation, except that:

(1) a lawyer may advance court costs and expenses of litigation, the repayment of which may be contingent on the outcome of the matter; and

(2) a lawyer representing an indigent client may pay court costs and expenses of litigation on behalf of the client.

(f) A lawyer shall not accept compensation for representing a client from one other than the client unless:

(1) the client consents after consultation;

(2) there is no interference with the lawyer's independence of professional judgment or with the client-lawyer relationship; and

(3) information relating to representation of a client is protected as required by Rule 1.6.

(g) A lawyer who represents two or more clients shall not participate in making an aggregate settlement of the claims of or against the clients, or in a criminal case an aggregated agreement as to guilty or nolo contendere pleas, unless each client consents after consultation, including disclosure of the existence and nature of all the claims or pleas involved and of the participation of each person in the settlement.

(h) A lawyer shall not make an agreement prospectively limiting the lawyer's liability to a client for malpractice unless permitted by law and the client is independently represented in making the agreement, or settle a claim for such liability with an unrepresented client or former client without first advising that person in writing that independent representation is appropriate in connection therewith.

(i) A lawyer related to another lawyer as parent, child, sibling or spouse or a lawyer sharing living quarters with another lawyer shall not represent a client in a representation directly adverse to a person who the lawyer knows is represented by the other lawyer except upon consent by the client after consultation regarding the relationship.

(j) A lawyer shall not acquire a proprietary interest in the cause of action or subject matter of litigation the lawyer is conducting for a client, except that the lawyer may:

(1) acquire a lien granted by law to secure the lawyer's fee or expenses; and

(2) contract with a client for a reasonable contingent fee in a civil case.

(k) A lawyer shall not pay, offer to pay, or acquiesce in the payment of compensation to a witness or to anyone referring a lawyer to a witness, contingent upon the content of the witness's testimony or the outcome of the case. But a lawyer may advance, guarantee, or acquiesce in the payment of:

(1) expenses reasonably incurred by a witness in attending or testifying.

(2) reasonable compensation to a witness for his loss of time in attending or testifying.

(3) a reasonable fee for the professional services of an expert witness.

Rule 1.9. Conflict of interest: Former client.

A lawyer who has formerly represented a client in a matter shall not thereafter:

(a) represent another person in the same or substantially related matter in which that person's interest are materially adverse to the interests of the former client unless the former client consents after consultation; or

(b) use information relating to the representation to the disadvantage of the former client except as Rule 1.6 or Rule 3.3 would permit or require with respect to a client or when the information has become generally known.

Rule 1.10. Imputed disqualification: General rule.

(a) While lawyers are associated in a firm, none of them shall knowingly represent a client when anyone of them practicing alone would be prohibited from doing so by Rules 1.7, 1.8(c), 1.9 or 2.2.

(b) When a lawyer becomes associated with a firm, the firm may not knowingly represent a person in the same or a substantially related matter in which that lawyer, or a firm with which the lawyer was associated, had previously represented a client whose interests are materially adverse to that person and about whom the lawyer had acquired information protected by Rules 1.6

and 1.9(b) that is material to the matter.

(c) When a lawyer has terminated an association with a firm, the firm is not prohibited from thereafter representing a person with interests materially adverse to those of a client represented by the formerly associated lawyer unless:

(1) the matter is the same or substantially related to that in which the formerly associated lawyer represented the client; and

(2) any lawyer remaining in the firm has information protected by Rules 1.6 and 1.9(b) that is material to the matter.

(d) A disqualification prescribed by this rule may be waived by the affected client under the conditions stated in Rule 1.7.

Rule 1.11. Successive government and private employment.

(a) Except as law may otherwise expressly permit, a lawyer shall not represent a private client in connection with a matter in which the lawyer participated personally and substantially as a public officer or employee, unless the appropriate government agency consents after consultation. No lawyer in a firm with which that lawyer is associated may knowingly undertake or continue representation in such a matter unless:

(1) the disqualified lawyer is screened from any participation in the matter and is apportioned no part of the fee therefrom; and

(2) written notice is promptly given to the appropriate government agency to enable it to ascertain

compliance with the provisions of this rule.

(b) Except as law may otherwise expressly permit, a lawyer having information that the lawyer knows is confidential government information about a person acquired when the lawyer was a public officer or employee, may not represent a private client whose interests are adverse to that person in a matter in which the information could be used to the material disadvantage of that person. A firm with which that lawyer is associated may undertake or continue representation in the matter only if the disqualified lawyer is screened from any participation in the matter and is apportioned no part of the fee therefrom.

(c) Except as law may otherwise expressly permit, a lawyer serving as a public officer or employee shall not:

(1) participate in a matter in which the lawyer participated personally and substantially while in private practice or nongovernmental employment, unless under applicable law no one is, or by lawful delegation may be authorized to act in the lawyer's stead in the matter; or

(2) negotiate for private employment with any person who is involved as a party or as attorney for a party in a matter in which the lawyer is participating personally and substantially, except that a lawyer serving as law clerk to a judge, other adjudicative officer or arbitrator may negotiate for private employment as permitted by Rule

1.12(b) and subject to the conditions stated in Rule 1.12(b).

(d) As used in this Rule, the term "matter" includes:

(1) any judicial or other proceeding, application, request for a ruling or other determination, contract, claim, controversy, investigation, charge, accusation, arrest or other particular matter involving a specific party or parties, and

(2) any other matter covered by the conflict of interest rules of the appropriate government agency.

(e) As used in this Rule, the term "confidential government information" means information which has been obtained under governmental authority and which, at the time this rule is applied, the government is prohibited by law from disclosing to the public or has a legal privilege not to disclose, and which is not otherwise available to the public.

Rule 1.12. Former judge or arbitrator.

(a) Except as stated in paragraph (d), a lawyer shall not represent anyone in connection with a matter in which the lawyer participated personally and substantially as a judge or other adjudicative officer, arbitrator or law clerk to such a person, unless all parties to the proceeding consent after consultation.

(b) A lawyer shall not negotiate for employment with any person who is involved as a party or as attorney for a party in a matter in which the lawyer is participating personally and substantially as a judge or other adjudicative officer, or arbitrator. A lawyer serving as a law clerk to a judge, other adjudicative officer or arbitrator may negotiate for employment with a party or attorney involved in a matter in which the clerk is participating personally and substantially, but only after the lawyer has notified the judge, other adjudicative officer or arbitrator.

(c) If a lawyer is disqualified by paragraph (a), no lawyer in a firm with which that lawyer is associated may knowingly undertake or continue representation in the matter unless:

(1) the disqualified lawyer is screened from any participation in the matter and is apportioned no part of the fee therefrom; and

(2) written notice is promptly given to the appropriate tribunal to enable it to ascertain compliance with the provisions of this rule.

(d) An arbitrator selected as a partisan of a party in a multimember arbitration panel is not prohibited from subsequently representing that party.

Rule 1.13. Organization as client.

(a) A lawyer employed or retained by an organization represents the organization acting through its duly authorized constituents.

(b) If a lawyer for an organization knows that an officer, employee or other person associated with the organization is engaged in action, intends to act or refuses to act in a matter related to the representation that is a violation of a legal obligation to the organization, or a violation of law which reasonably might be imputed to the organization, and is likely to result in substantial injury to the organiza-

tion, the lawyer shall proceed as is reasonably necessary in the best interest of the organization. In determining how to proceed, the lawyer shall give due consideration to the seriousness of the violation and its consequences, the scope and nature of the lawyer's representation, the responsibility in the organization and the apparent motivation of the person involved, the policies of the organization concerning such matters and any other relevant considerations. Any measures taken shall be designed to minimize disruption of the organization and the risk of revealing information relating to the representation to persons outside the organization. Such measures may include among others:

(1) asking reconsideration of the matter;

(2) advising that a separate legal opinion on the matter be sought for presentation to appropriate authority in the organization; and

(3) referring the matter to higher authority in the organization, including, if warranted by the seriousness of the matter, referral to the highest authority that can act in behalf of the organization as determined by applicable law.

(c) If, despite the lawyer's efforts in accordance with paragraph (b), the highest authority that can act on behalf of the organization insists upon action, or a refusal to act, that is clearly a violation of law and is likely to result in substantial injury to the organization, the lawyer may resign in accordance with Rule 1.16.

(d) In dealing with an organization's directors, officers, employees, members, shareholders or other constituents, a lawyer shall explain the identity of the client when it is apparent that the organization's interests are adverse to those of the constituents with whom the lawyer is dealing.

(e) A lawyer representing an organization may also represent any of its directors, officers, employees, members, shareholders or other constituents, subject to the provisions of Rule 1.7. If the organization's consent to the dual representation is required by Rule 1.7, the consent shall be given by an appropriate official of the organization other than the individual who is to be represented, or by the shareholders.

Rule 1.14. Client under a disability.

(a) When a client's ability to make adequately considered decisions in connection with the representation is impaired, whether because of minority, mental disability or for some other reason, the lawyer shall, as far as reasonably possible, maintain a normal client-lawyer relationship with the client.

(b) A lawyer may seek the appointment of a guardian or take other protective action with respect to a client, only when the lawyer reasonably believes that the client cannot adequately act in the client's own interest.

Rule 1.15. Safekeeping property.

(a) A lawyer shall hold property of clients or third persons that is in a lawyer's possession in connection with a representation separate from the lawyer's own property. Funds shall be kept in a separate account designated as a "client's trust account" in an institution whose accounts are federally insured and maintained in the state where the lawyer's office is situated, or in a separate account elsewhere with the consent of the client or third person. Other property shall be identified as such and appropriately safeguarded. Complete records of such account funds and other property shall be kept by the lawyer and shall be preserved for a period of five years after termination of the representation.

(b) Upon receiving funds or other property in which a client or third person has an interest, a lawyer shall promptly notify the client or third person. Except as stated in this rule or otherwise permitted by law or by agreement with the client, a lawyer shall promptly deliver to the client or third person any funds or other property that the client or third person is entitled to receive and, upon request by the client or third person, shall promptly render a full accounting regarding such property.

(c) When in the course of representation a lawyer is in possession of property in which both the lawyer and another person claim interests, the property shall be kept separate by the lawyer until there is an accounting and severance of their interests. If a dispute arises concerning their respective interests, the portion in dispute shall be kept separate by the lawyer until the dispute is resolved.

(d) A lawyer who receives client funds that are nominal in amount or are expected to be held for a brief period shall establish and maintain a pooled, interest-bearing, federally-insured depository account for the deposit of such funds, in compliance with the following provisions: (1) the account shall include only such client funds that are so nominal in amount or are expected to be held for such a brief period of time that administrative expenses would exceed interest earned from the investment thereof;

(2) no interest from such account shall be made available to the lawyer;

(3) funds deposited in such account must be available for withdrawal or transfer on demand, subject only to any notice period which the depository institution is required to observe by law or regulation;

(4) the lawyer shall direct the depository institution:

(i) to remit interest, on at least a quarterly basis, net any customary service charges or fees in accordance with the depository institution's standard accounting practice, to the West Virginia Bar Foundation, Inc.; and

(ii) to transmit with each remittance to the West Virginia Bar Foundation, Inc., a statement showing the name of the lawyer or law firm on whose account the remittance is sent and the rate of interest applied, with a copy of such statement to be transmitted to such lawyer or law firm; and,

(5) the lawyer shall review the account at reasonable intervals to determine whether circumstances warrant further action with respect to the funds of any client.

(e) A lawyer may not be charged with any breach of the Rules of Professional Conduct or other ethical violation with regard to either the good faith determination of whether client funds are nominal in amount or are expected to be held for a brief period or the failure to establish and maintain a pooled, interest-bearing, federally-insured depository account for the deposit of such funds in accordance with Rule 1.15(d).

(f) All interest transmitted to the West Virginia Bar Foundation, Inc., shall be distributed by that entity as follows: (1) an annual fee not to exceed fifty thousand dollars shall be retained by the West Virginia Bar Foundation, Inc., for administration of the fund, with a detailed annual accounting of services performed in consideration for such fee to be filed for public inspection with the Supreme Court of Appeals; (2) special grants not to exceed fifteen percent of the fund's annual receipts to WV CASA Network, coordinating agency for court-appointed special advocate programs, in the amount of forty-seven percent of special grant funds available; to the West Virginia Fund for Law in the Public Interest, Inc., to provide summer legal interns to West Virginia's four legal services organizations, in the amount of twenty percent of special grant funds available; to the Appalachian Center for Law and Public Service, a West Virginia University College of Law public service program providing legal services for the poor, in the amount of eight percent of special grant funds available; and to the Elder Law Program of the North Central West Virginia Legal Aid Society, Inc., in the amount of twenty-five percent of special grant funds available; and (3) the remaining funds to West Virginia's four legal services organizations in accordance with their percentage of poor population served using the most recent Bureau of the Census statistics or such other method of distribution as may hereinafter be adopted by order of the Supreme Court of Appeals. Any funds distributed by the West Virginia Bar Foundation, Inc., pursuant to this subdivision shall not be used by the recipient organization to support any lobbying activities.

Rule 1.16. Declining or terminating representation.

(a) Except as stated in paragraph (c), a lawyer shall not represent a client or, where representation has commenced, shall withdraw from the representation of a client if

(1) the representation will result in violation of the rules of professional conduct or other law;

(2) the lawyer's physical or mental condition materially impairs the lawyer's ability to represent the client; or

(3) the lawyer is discharged

(b) Except as stated in paragraph (c), a lawyer may withdraw from representing a client if withdrawal can be accomplished without material adverse effect on the interests of the client, or if:

(1) the client persists in a Course of action involving the lawyer's ser-

vices that the lawyer reasonably believes is criminal or fraudulent;

(2) the client has used the lawyer's services to perpetrate a crime or fraud;

(3) the client insists upon pursuing an objective that the lawyer considers repugnant or imprudent;

(4) the client fails substantially to fulfill an obligation to the lawyer regarding the lawyer's services and has been given reasonable warning that the lawyer will withdraw unless the obligations is fulfilled;

(5) the representation will result in an unreasonable financial burden on the lawyer or has been rendered unreasonably difficult by the client; or

(6) other good cause for withdrawal exists.

(c) When ordered to do so by a tribunal, a lawyer shall continue representation notwithstanding good cause for terminating the representation.

(d) Upon termination of representation, a lawyer shall take steps to the extent reasonably practicable to protect a client's interests, such as giving reasonable notice to the client, allowing time for employment of other counsel, surrendering papers and property to which the client is entitled and refunding any advance payment of fee that has not been earned. The lawyer may retain papers relating to the client to the extent permitted by other law.

Rule 1.17. Sale of law practice.

A lawyer or a law firm may sell or purchase a law practice, including good will, if the following conditions are satisfied:

(a) The seller ceases to engage in the private practice of law in West Virginia;

(b) The practice is sold as an entirety to another lawyer or law firm;

(c) Actual written notice is given to each of the seller's clients regarding:

(1) the proposed sale;

(2) the terms of any proposed change in the fee arrangement authorized by paragraph (d);

(3) the client's right to retain other counsel take possession of the file; and

(4) the fact that the client's consent to the sale will be presumed if the client does not take any action or does not otherwise object within ninety (90) days of receipt of the notice.

If a client cannot be given notice, the representation of that client may be transferred to the purchaser only upon entry of an order so authorizing by a court having jurisdiction. The seller may disclose to the court in camera information relating to the representation only to the extent necessary to obtain an order authorizing the transfer of a file.

(d) The fees charged clients shall not be increased by reasons of the sale. The purchaser may, however, refuse to undertake representation unless the client consents to pay the purchaser fees at a rate not exceeding the fees charged by the purchaser for rendering substantially similar services prior to the initiation of the purchase negotiations.

COUNSELOR.

Rule 2.1. Advisor.

In representing a client, a lawyer shall exercise independent professional judgment and render candid advice. In rendering advice, a lawyer may refer not only to law but to other considerations such as moral, economic, social and political factors, that may be relevant to the client's situation.

Rule 2.2. Intermediary.

(a) A lawyer may act as intermediary between clients if:

(1) the lawyer consults with each client concerning the implications of the common representation, including the advantages and risks involved, and the effect on the attorney-client privileges, and obtains each client's consent to the common representation;

(2) the lawyer reasonably believes that the matter can be resolved on terms compatible with the client's best interests, that each client will be able to make adequately informed decisions in the matter and that there is little risk of material prejudice to the interests of any of the clients if the contemplated resolution is unsuccessful; and

(3) the lawyer reasonably believes that the common representation can be undertaken impartially and without improper effect on other responsibilities the lawyer has to any of the clients.

(b) While acting as intermediary, the lawyer shall consult with each client concerning the decisions to be made and the considerations relevant in making them, so that each client can make adequately informed decisions.

(c) A lawyer shall withdraw as intermediary if any of the clients so requests, or if any of the conditions stated in paragraph (a) is no longer satisfied. Upon withdrawal, the lawyer shall not continue to represent any of the clients in the matter that was the subject of the intermediation.

Rule 2.3. Evaluation for use by third persons.

(a) A lawyer may undertake an evaluation of a matter affecting a client for the use of someone other than the client if:

(1) the lawyer reasonably believes that making the evaluation is compatible with other aspects of the lawyer's relationship with the client; and

(2) the client consents after consultation.

(b) Except as disclosure is required in connection with a report of an evaluation, information relating to the evaluation is otherwise protected by Rule 1.6.

(c) In reporting an evaluation the lawyer shall indicate any material limitations that were imposed on the scope of the inquiry or on the disclosure of information.

ADVOCATE.

Rule 3.1. Meritorious claims and contentions.

A lawyer shall not bring or defend a proceeding, or assert or controvert an issue therein, unless there is a basis for doing so that is not frivolous, which includes a good faith

argument for an extension, modification or reversal of existing law. A lawyer for the defendant in a criminal proceeding, or the respondent in a proceeding that could result in incarceration, may nevertheless so defend the proceeding as to require that every element of the case be established.

Rule 3.2. Expediting litigation.

A lawyer shall make reasonable efforts to expedite litigation consistent with the interest of the client.

Rule 3.3. Candor toward the tribunal.

(a) A lawyer shall not knowingly:

(1) make a false statement of material fact or law to a tribunal;

(2) fail to disclose a material fact to a tribunal when disclosure is necessary to avoid assisting a criminal or fraudulent act by the client;

(3) fail to disclose to the tribunal legal authority in the controlling jurisdic- tion known to the lawyer to be directly adverse to the position of the client and not disclosed by opposing counsel; or

(4) offer evidence that the lawyer knows to be false. If a lawyer has offered material evidence and comes to know of its falsity, the lawyer shall take reasonable remedial measures.

(b) The duties stated in paragraph (a) continue to the conclusion of the proceeding, and apply even if compliance requires disclosure of information otherwise protected by Rule 1.6.

(c) A lawyer may refuse to offer evidence that the lawyer reasonably believes is false.

(d) In an ex parte proceeding, a lawyer shall inform the tribunal of all material facts known to the lawyer which will enable the tribunal to make an informed decision. whether or not the facts are adverse.

Rule 3.4. Fairness to opposing party and counsel.

A lawyer shall not:

(a) unlawfully obstruct another party's access to evidence or unlawfully alter, destroy or conceal a document or other material having potential evidentiary value. A lawyer shall not counselor assist another person to do any such act;

(b) falsify evidence, counselor assist a witness to testify falsely, or offer an inducement to a witness that is prohibited by law;

(c) knowingly disobey an obligation under the rules of a tribunal except for an open refusal based on an assertion that no valid obligation exists;

(d) in pretrial procedure, make a frivolous discovery request or fail to make reasonably diligent effort to comply with a legally proper discovery request by an opposing party;

(e) in trial, allude to any matter that the lawyer does not reasonably believe is relevant or that will not be supported by admissible evidence, assert personal knowledge of facts in issue except when testifying as a witness, or state a personal opinion as to the justness of a cause, the credibility of a witness, the culpability of a civil litigant or the guilt or innocence of an accused; or

(f) request a person other than a client to refrain from voluntarily giving relevant information to another party unless:

(1) the person is a relative or an employee or other agent of a client; and

(2) the lawyer reasonably believes that the person's interests will not be adversely affected by refraining from giving such information.

Rule 3.5. Impartiality and decorum in the tribunal.

A lawyer shall not:

(a) seek to influence a judge, juror, prospective juror or other official by means prohibited by law;

(b) communicate ex parte with such a person except as permitted by law; or

(c) engage in conduct intended to disrupt a tribunal.

Rule 3.6. Trial publicity.

(a) A lawyer shall not make an extrajudicial statement that a reasonable person would expect to be disseminated by means of public communication if the lawyer knows or reasonably should know that it will have a substantial likelihood of materially prejudicing an adjudicative proceeding.

(b) A statement referred to in paragraph (a) ordinarily is likely to have such an effect when it refers to a civil matter triable to a jury, a criminal matter, or any other proceeding that could result in incarceration, and the statement relates to:

(1) the character, credibility, reputation or criminal record of a party,

suspect in a criminal investigation or witness, or the identity of a witness, or the expected testimony of a party or witness;

(2) in a criminal case or proceeding that could result in incarceration, the possibility of a plea of guilty to the offense or the existence or contents of any confession, admission, or statement given by a defendant or suspect or that person's refusal or failure to make a statement:

(3) the performance or results of any examination or test or the refusal or failure of a person to submit to an examination or test, or the identity or nature of physical evidence expected to be presented;

(4) any opinion as to the guilt or innocence of a defendant or suspect in a criminal case or proceeding that could result in incarceration;

(5) information the lawyer knows or reasonably should know is likely to be inadmissible as evidence in a trial and would if disclosed create a substantial risk of prejudicing an impartial trial; or

(6) the fact that a defendant has been charged with a crime, unless there is included therein a statement explaining that the charge is merely an accusation and that the defendant is presumed innocent until and unless proven guilty.

(c) Notwithstanding paragraphs (a) and (b) (1-5), a lawyer involved in the investigation or litigation of a matter may state without elaboration:

(1) the general nature of the claim or defense;

(2) the information contained in a public record;

(3) that an investigation of the matter is in progress, including the general scope of the investigation, the offense or claim or defense involved and, except when prohibited by law, the identity of the persons involved;

(4) the scheduling or result of any step in litigation;

(5) a request for assistance in obtaining evidence and information necessary thereto;

(6) a warning of danger concerning the behavior of a person involved, when there is reason to believe that there exists the likelihood of substantial harm to an individual or to the public interest; and

(7) in a criminal case:

(i) the identity, residence, occupation and family status of the accused;

(ii) if the accused has not been apprehended, information necessary to aid in apprehension of that person;

(iii) the fact, time and place of arrest; and

(iv) the identity of investigating and arresting officers or agencies and the length of the investigation.

Rule 3.7. Lawyer as witness.

(a) A lawyer shall not act as advocate at a trial in which the lawyer is likely to be a necessary witness except where:

(1) the testimony relates to an uncontested issue;

(2) the testimony relates to the nature and value of legal services rendered in the case; or

(3) disqualification of the lawyer would work substantial hardship on the client.

(b) A lawyer may act as advocate in a trial in which another lawyer in the lawyer's firm is likely to be called as a witness unless precluded from doing so by Rule 1.7 or Rule 1.9.

Rule 3.8. Special responsibilities of a prosecutor.
The prosecutor in a criminal case shall:
(a) refrain from prosecuting a charge that the prosecutor knows is not supported by probable cause;
(b) make reasonable efforts to assure that the accused has been advised of the right to, and the procedure for obtaining, counsel and has been given reasonable opportunity to obtain counsel;
(c) not seek to obtain from an unrepresented accused a waiver of important pretrial rights, such as the right to a preliminary hearing;
(d) make timely disclosure to the defense of all evidence or information known to the prosecutor that tends to negate the guilt of the accused or mitigates the offense, and, in connection with sentencing, disclose to the defense and to the tribunal all unprivileged mitigating information known to the prosecutor, except when the prosecutor is relieved of this responsibility by a protective order of the tribunal; and
(e) exercise reasonable care to prevent investigators, law enforcement personnel, employees or other persons assisting or associated with the prosecutor in a criminal case from making an extrajudicial statement that the prosecutor would be prohibited from making under Rule 3.6.

Rule 3.9. Advocate in nonadjudicative proceedings.
A lawyer representing a client before a legislative or administrative tribunal in a nonadjudicative proceeding shall disclose that the appearance is in a representative capacity and shall conform to the provisions of Rules 3.3(a) through (c), 3.4(a) through (c), and 3.5.

TRANSACTIONS WITH PERSONS OTHER THAN CLIENTS.

Rule 4.1. Truthfulness in statements to others.
In the course of representing a client a lawyer shall not knowingly:
(a) make a false statement of material fact or law to a third person; or
(b) fail to disclose a material fact to a third person when disclosure is necessary to avoid assisting a criminal or fraudulent act by a client, unless disclosure is prohibited bv Rule 1.6.

Rule 4.2. Communication with person represented by counsel.
In representing a client, a lawyer shall not communicate about the subject of the representation with a party the lawyer knows to be represented by another lawyer in the matter, unless the lawyer has the consent of the other lawyer or is authorized by law to do so.

Rule 4.3. Dealing with unrepresented person.
In dealing on behalf of a client with a person who is not represented by counsel, a lawyer shall not state or imply that the lawyer is disinterested. When the lawyer knows or

reasonably should know that the unrepresented person misunderstands the lawyer's role in the matter, the lawyer shall make reasonable efforts to correct the misunderstanding.

Rule 4.4. Respect for rights of third persons.

In representing a client, a lawyer shall not use means that have no substantial purpose other than to embarrass, delay, or burden a third person, or use methods of obtaining evidence that violate the legal rights of such a person.

LAW FIRMS AND ASSOCIATIONS.

Rule 5.1. Responsibilities of a partner or supervisory lawyer.

(a) A partner in a law firm shall make reasonable efforts to ensure that the firm has in effect measures giving reasonable assurance that all lawyers in the firm conform to the Rules of Professional Conduct.

(b) A lawyer having direct supervisory authority over another lawyer shall make reasonable efforts to ensure that the other lawyer conforms to the Rules of Professional Conduct.

(c) A lawyer shall be responsible for another lawyer's violation of the Rules of Professional Conduct if:

(1) the lawyer orders or, with knowledge of the specific conduct, ratifies the conduct involved; or

(2) the lawyer is a partner in the law firm in which the other lawyer practices, or has direct supervisory authority over the other lawyer, and knows of the conduct at a time when its consequences can be avoided or mitigated but fails to take reasonable remedial action.

Rule 5.2. Responsibilities of a subordinate lawyer.

(a) A lawyer is bound by the Rules of Professional Conduct notwithstanding that the lawyer acted at the direction of another person.

(b) A subordinate lawyer does not violate the Rules of Professional Conduct if that lawyer acts in accordance with a supervisory lawyer's reasonable resolution of an arguable question of professional duty.

Rule 5.3. Responsibilities regarding nonlawyer assistants.

With respect to a nonlawyer employed or retained by or associated with a lawyer:

(a) a partner in a law firm shall make reasonable efforts to ensure that the firm has in effect measures giving reasonable assurance that the person's conduct is compatible with the professional obligations of the lawyer;

(b) a lawyer having direct supervisory authority over the nonlawyer shall make reasonable efforts to ensure that the person's conduct is compatible with the professional obligations of the lawyer; and

(c) a lawyer shall be responsible for conduct of such a person that would be a violation of the Rules of Professional Conduct if engaged in by a lawyer if:

(1) the lawyer orders or, with the knowledge of the specific conduct, ratifies the conduct involved; or

(2) the lawyer is a partner in the law firm in which the person is employed, or has direct supervisory authority over the person, and knows of the conduct at a time when its consequences can be avoided or mitigated but fails to take reasonable remedial action.

Rule 5.4. Professional independence of a lawyer.
(a) A lawyer or law firm shall not share legal fees with a nonlawyer, except that:
(1) an agreement by a lawyer with the lawyer's firm, partner or associate may provide for the payment of money, over a reasonable period of time after the lawyer's death, to the lawyer's estate or to one or more specified persons;
(2) a lawyer who undertakes to complete unfinished legal business of a deceased lawyer may pay to the estate of the deceased lawyer that proportion of the total compensation which fairly represents the services rendered by the deceased lawyer;
(3) a lawyer or law firm purchasing the practice of a deceased, disabled or disappeared lawyer may, pursuant to the provisions of Rule 1.17, pay to the estate or other representative of that lawyer an agreed-upon purchase price; and
(4) a lawyer or law firm may include nonlawyer employees in a compensation or retirement plan, even though the plan is based in whole or in part on a profit-sharing arrangement.
(b) A lawyer shall not form a partnership with a nonlawyer if any of

the activities of the partnership consist of the practice of law.
(c) A lawyer shall not permit a person who recommends, employs, or pays the lawyer to render legal service for another to direct or regulate the lawyer's professional judgment in rendering such legal services.
(d) A lawyer shall not practice with or in the form of a professional corporation or association authorized to practice law for a profit, if:
(1) a nonlawyer owns any interest therein, except that a fiduciary representative of the estate of a lawyer may hold the stock or interest of the lawyer for a reasonable time during administration;
(2) a nonlawyer is a corporate director or officer thereof; or
(3) a nonlawyer has the right to direct or control the professional judgment of a lawyer.

Rule 5.5. Unauthorized practice of law.
A lawyer shall not:
(a) practice law in a jurisdiction where doing so violates the regulation of the legal profession in that jurisdiction; or
(b) assist a person who is not a member of the bar in the performance of activity that constitutes the unauthorized practice of law.

Rule 5.6. Restrictions on right to practice.
A lawyer shall not participate in offering or making:
(a) a partnership or employment agreement that restricts the right of a lawyer to practice after termination of the relationship, except an

agreement concerning benefits upon retirement; or

(b) an agreement in which a restriction on the lawyer's right to practice is part of the settlement of a controversy between private parties.

Rule 5.7. Limited liability legal practice.

(a) A lawyer may be a member of a law firm that is organized as a limited liability company or registered limited liability partnership (collectively, "limited liability organizations") solely to render professional legal services under the laws of West Virginia, including, but not limited to, the Uniform Limited Liability Act, W. Va. Code §§ 31B-1-101, et seq., and the Uniform Partnership Act, W. Va. Code §§ 47B-1-1, et seq., and may practice in or as such a limited liability organization, provided that such lawyer is otherwise licensed to practice in West Virginia and such law firm is registered pursuant to rules promulgated by The West Virginia State Bar.

(b) Nothing in this rule or the laws under which a lawyer or law firm is organized shall relieve a lawyer from personal liability for the acts, errors, and omissions of such lawyer arising out of the performance of professional legal services.

(c) Law firms wishing to practice as limited liability organizations under this rule shall comply with the rules of The West Virginia State Bar with regard to registration of limited liability organizations.

(d) A law firm organized as a limited liability organization under the laws of any other state or jurisdiction of the United States solely for the purpose of rendering professional legal services and authorized to do business in West Virginia and which has at least one lawyer licensed to practice law in West Virginia may register in West Virginia as a limited liability organization under this rule by registering pursuant to rules promulgated by The West Virginia State Bar.

PUBLIC SERVICE.

Rule 6.1. Pro bono publico service.
A lawyer should render public interest legal service. A lawyer may discharge this responsibility by providing professional services at no fee or a reduced fee to persons of limited means or to public service or charitable groups or organization, by service in activities for improving the law, the legal system or the legal profession, and by financial support for organizations that provide legal service to persons of limited means.

Rule 6.2. Accepting appointments.
A lawyer shall not seek to avoid appointment by a tribunal to represent a person except for good cause, such as:

(a) representing the client is likely to result in violation of the Rules of Professional Conduct or other law;

(b) representing the client is likely to result in an unreasonable financial burden on the lawyer; or

(c) the client or the cause is so repugnant to the lawyer as to be likely to impair the client-lawyer relationship or the lawyer's ability to represent the client.

Rule 6.3. Membership in legal services organization.

A lawyer may serve as a director, officer or member of a legal services organization, apart from the law firm in which the lawyer practices, notwithstanding that the organization serves persons having interests adverse to a client of the lawyer. The lawyer shall not knowingly participate in a decision or action of the organization:

(a) if participating in the decision or action would be incompatible with the lawyer's obligations to a client under Rule 1.7; or

(b) where the decision or action could have a material adverse affect on the representation of a client of the organization whose interests are adverse to a client of the lawyer.

Rule 6.4. Law reform activities affecting client interests.

A lawyer may serve as a director, officer or member of an organization involved in reform of the law or its administration notwithstanding that the reform may affect the interests of a client of the lawyer. When the lawyer knows that the interests of a client may be materially benefitted by a decision in which the lawyer participates, the lawyer shall disclose that fact but need not identify the client.

INFORMATION ABOUT LEGAL SERVICES

Rule 7.1. Communications concerning a lawyer's services.

A lawyer shall not make a false or misleading communication about the lawyer or the lawyer's services. A communication is false or misleading if it:

(a) contains a material misrepresentation of fact or law, or omits a fact necessary to make the statement considered as a whole not materially misleading;

(b) is likely to create an unjustified expectation about results the lawyer can achieve, or states or implies that the lawyer can achieve results by means that violate the Rules of Professional Conduct or other law; or

(c) compares the lawyer's services with other lawyer's services, unless the comparison can be factually substantiated.

Rule 7.2. Advertising.

(a) Subject to the requirements of Rules 7.1 and 7.3, a lawyer may advertise services through public media, such as a telephone directory, legal directory, newspaper or other periodical, outdoor advertising, radio or television, or through written or recorded communication.

(b) A copy or recording of an advertisement or communication shall be kept for two years after its last dissemination along with a record of when and where it was used.

(c) A lawyer shall not give anything of value to a person for recommending the lawyer's services, except that a lawyer may pay the reasonable cost of advertisements or communications permitted by this rule; may pay the usual charges of a not-for-profit lawyer referral service or other legal service organization; and may pay for a law practice in accordance with Rule 1.17.

(d) Any communication made pursuant to this rule shall include the name of at least one lawyer responsible for its content.

Rule 7.3. Direct contact with prospective clients.

(a) A lawyer shall not by in-person or telephone contact solicit professional employment from a prospective client with whom the lawyer has no family or prior professional relationship when a motive for the lawyer's doing so is the lawyer's pecuniary gain.

(b) A lawyer shall not solicit professional employment from a prospective client by written or recorded communication or by in-person or telephone contact even when not otherwise prohibited by paragraph (a), if:

(1) the prospective client has made known to the lawyer a desire not to be solicited by the lawyer; or

(2) the solicitation involves coercion, duress or harassment.

(c) Every written or recorded communication from a lawyer soliciting professional employment from a prospective client known to be in need of legal services in a particular matter shall include the words" Advertising Material" on the outside envelope and at the beginning and ending of any recorded com-

munication and shall be maintained as required by Rule 7.2(b).

Rule 7.4. Communication of fields of practice.

A lawyer may communicate the fact that the lawyer does or does not practice in particular fields of law. A lawyer shall not state or imply that the lawyer is a specialist except as follows:

(a) a lawyer admitted to engage in patent practice before the United States Patent and Trademark Office may use the designation "Patent Attorney" or a substantially similar designation;

(b) a lawyer engaged in Admiralty practice may use the designation "Admiralty'" "Proctor in Admiralty" or a substantially similar designation.

Rule 7.5. Firm names and letterheads.

(a) A lawyer shall not use a firm name, letterhead or other professional designation that violates Rule 7.1. A trade name may be used by a lawyer in private practice if it does not imply a connection with a government agency or with a public or charitable legal services organization and is not otherwise in violation of Rule 7.1.

(b) A law firm with offices in more than one jurisdiction may use the same name in each jurisdiction, but identification of the lawyers in an office of the firm shall indicate the jurisdictional limitations on those not licensed to practice in the jurisdiction where the office is located.

(c) The name of a lawyer holding a public office shall not be used in the name of a law firm, or in communications on its behalf, during any substantial period in which the lawyer is not actively and regularly practicing with the firm.

(d) Lawyers may state or imply that they practice in a partnership or other organization only when that is the fact.

MAINTAINING THE INTEGRITY OF THE PROFESSION.

Rule 8.1. Bar admission and disciplinary matters.

An applicant for admission to the bar, or a lawyer in connection with a bar admission application or in connection with a disciplinary matter, shall not:

(a) knowingly make a false statement of material fact; or

(b) fail to disclose a fact necessary to correct a misapprehension known by the person to have arisen in the matter, or knowingly fail to respond to a lawful demand for information from an admissions or disciplinary authority, except that this rule does not require disclosure of information otherwise protected by Rule 1.6.

Rule 8.2. Judicial and legal officials.

(a) A lawyer shall not make a statement that the lawyer knows to be false or with reckless disregard as to its truth or falsity concerning the qualifications or integrity of a judge, adjudicatory officer or public legal officer, or of a candidate for election or appointment to judicial or legal office.

(b) A lawyer who is a candidate for judicial office shall comply with the applicable provisions of the Code of Judicial Conduct.

Rule 8.3. Reporting professional misconduct.

(a) A lawyer having knowledge that another lawyer has committed a violation of the Rules of Professional Conduct that raises a substantial question as to that lawyer's honesty, trustworthiness or fitness as a lawyer in other respects, shall inform the appropriate professional authority.

(b) A lawyer having knowledge that a judge has committed a violation of applicable rules of judicial conduct that raises a substantial question as to the judge's fitness for office shall inform the appropriate authority.

(c) This Rule does not require disclosure of information otherwise protected by Rule 1.6.

(d) This Rule shall not apply to members of the West Virginia State Bar Committee on Assistance, and Intervention, the Committee on Lawyer Assistance, or the Lawyer Intervention Panel, or to a Committee's or Panel's intervenors and representatives, to the extent that they are acting in their official capacities as members, intervenors, or representatives of a Committee or Panel. However, the Committees, the Panel, and their intervenors and representatives shall not be relieved of the duty to inform the Ethics Commit tee of the State Bar of on-going or prospective violations of Rule 8.4(b), (c), or (d), unless the impaired lawyer agrees to discontinue the violation and to seek a program of rehabilitation, as prescribed by a Committee or Panel.

Rule 8.4. Misconduct.

It is professional misconduct for a lawyer to:

(a) violate or attempt to violate the Rules of Professional Conduct, knowingly assist or induce another to do so, or do so through the acts of another;

(b) commit a criminal act that reflects adversely on the lawyer's honesty, trustworthiness or fitness as a lawyer in other respects;

(c) engage in conduct involving dishonesty, fraud, deceit or misrepresentation;

(d) engage in conduct that is prejudicial to the administration of justice;

(e) state or imply an ability to influence improperly a government agency or official;

(f) knowingly assist a judge or judicial officer in conduct that is a violation of applicable rules of judicial conduct or other law; or

(g) have sexual relations with a client whom the lawyer personally represents during the legal representation unless a consensual sexual relationship existed between them at the commencement of the lawyer/client relationship. For purposes of this rule, "sexual relations" means sexual intercourse or any touching of the sexual or other intimate parts of a client or causing such client to touch the sexual or other intimate parts of the lawyer for the purpose of arousing or gratifying the sexual desire of either party or as a means of abuse.

Rule 8.5. Jurisdiction.

A lawyer admitted to practice in this jurisdiction is subject to the disciplinary authority of this jurisdiction although engaged in practice elsewhere.

−Appendix E−

STATUTES OF LIMITATIONS TO SUE FOR MALPRACTICE

This appendix contains the time frame in which you must bring a malpractice claim to court or have it barred by a statute of limitations. The material presented is a general reference for each state along with the statutory citation where the rule can be found. The length of time is indicated after the state name. Some states have multiple rules, so there may be more than one time frame given.

NOTE: *These are general limitations periods. Your matter could have a special exemption or other circumstance that could shorten or extend the limitations period. If you believe that you have a malpractice action, speak with an attorney immediately to determine the actual length of time you have to file suit.*

ALABAMA (TWO YEARS)
Ala. Code Sec. 6-5-574.

Statute of limitations

All legal service liability actions against a legal service provider must be commenced within two years after the act or omission or failure giving rise to the claim, and not afterwards; provided, that if the cause of action is not discovered and could not reasonably have been discovered within such period, then the action may be commenced within six months from the date of such discovery or the date of discovery of facts which would reasonably lead to such discovery, whichever is earlier; provided, further, that in no event may the action be commenced more than four years after such act or omission or failure; except, that an act or omission or failure giving rise to a claim which occurred before August 1, 1987, shall not in any event be barred until the expiration of one year from such date.

ALASKA (TWO YEARS)
Alaska Stat. Sec. 09.10.070.

Actions for torts, for injury to personal property, for certain statutory liabilities, and against peace officers and coroners to be brought in two years

(a) Except as otherwise provided by law, a person may not bring an action (1) for libel, slander, assault, battery, seduction, or false imprisonment, (2) for personal injury or death, or injury to the rights of another not arising on contract and not specifically provided otherwise; (3) for taking, detaining, or injuring personal property, including an action for its specific recovery; (4) upon a statute for a forfeiture or penalty to the state; or (5) upon a liability created by statute, other than a penalty or forfeiture; unless the action is commenced within two years of the accrual of the cause of action.

ARIZONA (TWO YEARS)
Ariz. Rev. Stat Sec. 12-542.

Injury to person; injury when death ensues; injury to property; conversion of property; forcible entry and forcible detainer; two year limitation

Except as provided in section 12-551 there shall be commenced and prosecuted within two years after the cause of action accrues, and not afterward, the following actions:

1. For injuries done to the person of another including causes of action for medical malpractice as defined in section 12-561.

2. For injuries done to the person of another when death ensues from such injuries, which action shall be considered as accruing at the death of the party injured.

3. For trespass for injury done to the estate or the property of another.

4. For taking or carrying away the goods and chattels of another.

5. For detaining the personal property of another and for converting such property to one's own use.

6. For forcible entry or forcible detainer, which action shall be considered as accruing at the commencemet of the forcible entry or detainer.

ARKANSAS (THREE YEARS)
Ark. Code Ann. Sec. 16-56-105.

Actions with limitation of three years

The following actions shall be commenced within three (3) years after the cause of action accrues:
(1) All actions founded upon any contract, obligation, or liability not under seal and not in writing, excepting such as are brought upon the judgment or decree of some court of record of the United States or of this or some other state;
(2) All actions for arrearages of rent not reserved by some instrument in writing, under seal;
(3) All actions founded on any contract or liability, expressed or implied;
(4) All actions for trespass on lands;
(5) All actions for libels;
(6) All actions for taking or injuring any goods or chattels.

CALIFORNIA (ONE YEAR AFTER DISCOVERY OR FOUR YEARS FROM ACT)
Cal. Civ. Proc. Code Sec. 340.6.

Action against attorney for wrongful act or omission, other than fraud

(a) An action against an attorney for a wrongful act or omission, other than for actual fraud, arising in the performance of professional services shall be commenced within one year after the plaintiff discovers, or through the use of reasonable diligence should have discovered, the facts constituting the wrongful act or omission, or four years from the date of the wrongful act or omission, whichever occurs first. In no event shall the time for commencement of legal action exceed four years except that the period shall be tolled during the time that any of the following exist:

(1) The plaintiff has not sustained actual injury;

(2) The attorney continues to represent the plaintiff regarding the specific subject matter in which the alleged wrongful act or omission occurred;

(3) The attorney willfully conceals the facts constituting the wrongful act or omission when such facts are known to the attorney, except that this subdivision shall toll only the four-year limitation; and

(4) The plaintiff is under a legal or physical disability which restricts the plaintiff's ability to commence legal action.

(b) In an action based upon an instrument in writing, the effective date of which depends upon some act or event of the future, the period of limitations provided for by this section shall commence to run upon the occurrence of such act or event.

COLORADO (TWO YEARS)
Colo. Rev. Stat. Sec. 13-80-102.

General limitation of actions - two years

(1) The following civil actions, regardless of the theory upon which suit is brought, or against whom suit is brought, shall be com-

menced within two years after the cause of action accrues, and not thereafter:

Tort actions, including but not limited to actions for negligence, trespass, malicious abuse of process, malicious prosecution, outrageous conduct, interference with relationships, and tortious breach of contract; except that this paragraph (a) does not apply to any tort action arising out of the use or operation of a motor vehicle as set forth in section 13-80-101 (1) (n).

CONNECTICUT (THREE YEARS)
Conn. Gen. Stat. Sec. 52-577

Action founded upon a tort

No action founded upon a tort shall be brought but within three years from the date of the act or omission complained of.

DELAWARE (THREE YEARS)
10 Del. Code Ann. Tit. 10, Sec. 8106.

Actions subject to 3-year limitation

No action to recover damages for trespass, no action to regain possession of personal chattels, no action to recover damages for the detention of personal chattels, no action to recover a debt not evidenced by a record or by an instrument under seal, no action based on a detailed statement of the mutual demands in the nature of debit and credit between parties arising out of contractual or fiduciary relations, no action based on a promise, no action based on a statute, and no action to recover damages caused by an injury unaccompanied with force or resulting indirectly from the act of the defendant shall be brought after the expiration of 3 years from the accruing of the cause of such action; subject, however, to the provisions of §§ 8108-8110, 8119 and 8127 of this title.

DISTRICT OF COLUMBIA (THREE YEARS)

D.C. Code Ann. Sec 12-301(8).

Limitation of time for bringing actions

Except as otherwise specifically provided by law, actions for the following purposes may not be brought after the expiration of the period specified below from the time the right to maintain the action accrues:

(8) for which a limitation is not otherwise specially prescribed -- 3 years.

FLORIDA (TWO YEARS FROM DISCOVERY)

Fla. Stat. Ann. 95.11(4)(a).

Limitations other than for the recovery of real property

(4) WITHIN TWO YEARS.

(a) An action for professional malpractice, other than medical malpractice, whether founded on contract or tort; provided that the period of limitations shall run from the time the cause of action is discovered or should have been discovered with the exercise of due diligence. However, the limitation of actions herein for professional malpractice shall be limited to persons in privity with the professional.

GEORGIA (FOUR YEARS/TWO YEARS)

Ga. Code Ann. Sec. 9-3-25.

Open accounts; breach of certain contracts; implied promise; exception

All actions upon open account, or for the breach of any contract not under the hand of the party sought to be charged, or upon any implied promise or undertaking shall be brought within four years after the right of action accrues. However, this Code section shall not apply to actions for the breach of contracts for the sale of goods under Article 2 of Title 11.

Ga. Code Ann. Sec. 9-3-33.

Injuries to the person; injuries to reputation; loss of consortium; exception

Actions for injuries to the person shall be brought within two years after the right of action accrues, except for injuries to the reputation, which shall be brought within one year after the right of action accrues, and except for actions for injuries to the person involving loss of consortium, which shall be brought within four years after the right of action accrues.

HAWAII (SIX YEARS)

Haw. Rev. Stat. Sec. 657-1.

Six years

The following actions shall be commenced within six years next after the cause of action accrued, and not after:

(1) Actions for the recovery of any debt founded upon any contract, obligation, or liability, excepting such as are brought upon the judgment or decree of a court; excepting further that actions for the recovery of any debt founded upon any contract, obligation, or liability made pursuant to chapter 577A shall be governed by chapter 577A;

IDAHO (TWO YEARS)

Idaho Code Sec. 5-219(4).

Actions against officers, for penalties, on bonds, and for professional malpractice or for personal injuries

Within two (2) years:

4. An action to recover damages for professional malpractice, or for an injury to the person, or for the death of one caused by the wrongful act or neglect of another, including any such action arising from breach of an implied warranty or implied covenant; provided, however, when the action is for damages arising out of the placement and inadvertent, accidental or unintentional leaving of any foreign object in the body of any person by reason of the professional malpractice of any hospital, physician or other person or institution practicing any of the healing arts or when the fact of damage has, for the purpose of escaping responsibility therefor, been fraudulently and knowingly concealed from the injured party by an alleged wrongdoer standing at the time of the wrongful act, neglect or breach in a professional or commercial relationship with the injured party, the same shall be deemed to accrue when the injured party knows or in the exercise of reasonable care should have been put on inquiry regarding the condition or matter complained of; but in all other actions, whether arising from professional malpractice or otherwise, the cause of action shall be deemed to have accrued as of the time of the occurrence, act or omission complained of, and the limitation period shall not be extended by reason of any continuing consequences or damages resulting therefrom or any continuing professional or commercial relationship between the injured party and the alleged wrongdoer, and, provided

further, that an action within the foregoing foreign object or fraudulent concealment exceptions must be commenced within one (1) year following the date of accrual as aforesaid or two (2) years following the occurrence, act or omission complained of, whichever is later. The term "professional malpractice" as used herein refers to wrongful acts or omissions in the performance of professional services by any person, firm, association, entity or corporation licensed to perform such services under the law of the state of Idaho. This subsection shall not affect the application of section 5-243, Idaho Code, except as to actions arising from professional malpractice. Neither shall this subsection be deemed or construed to amend, or repeal section 5-241, Idaho Code.

ILLINOIS (TWO YEARS OF DISCOVERY, SIX YEARS FROM ACT)

735 ILCS 5/13-214.3.

Attorneys

Sec. 13-214.3. Attorneys. (a) In this Section: "attorney" includes (i) an individual attorney, together with his or her employees who are attorneys, (ii) a professional partnership of attorneys, together with its employees, partners, and members who are attorneys, and (iii) a professional service corporation of attorneys, together with its employees, officers, and shareholders who are attorneys; and "non-attorney employee" means a person who is not an attorney but is employed by an attorney.

(b) An action for damages based on tort, contract, or otherwise (i) against an attorney arising out of an act or omission in the performance of professional services or (ii) against a non-attorney employee arising out of an act or omission in the course of his or her employment by an attorney to assist the attorney in performing professional services must be commenced within 2 years from the time the person bringing the action knew or reasonably should have known of the injury for which damages are sought.

(c) An action described in subsection (b) may not be commenced in any event more than 6 years after the date on which the act or omission occurred.

(d) (Blank.)

(e) If the person entitled to bring the action is under the age of majority or under other legal disability at the time the cause of action accrues, the period of limitations shall not begin to run until majority is attained or the disability is removed.

(f) The provisions of Public Act 86-1371 creating this Section apply to all causes of action accruing on or after its effective date.

(g) This amendatory Act of 1995 applies to all actions filed on or after its effective date. If, as a result of this amendatory Act of 1995, the action is either barred or there remains less than 2 years to bring the action, then the individual may bring the action within 2 years of the effective date of this amendatory Act of 1995.

INDIANA (TWO YEARS)

Ind. Code Sec. 34-11-2-4.

Injury to person or character -- Injury to personal property -- Forfeiture of penalty given by statute

An action for:

(1) injury to person or character,

(2) injury to personal property; or

(3) a forfeiture of penalty given by statute;

must be commenced within two (2) years after the cause of action accrues.

IOWA (FIVE YEARS)

Iowa Code Sec. 614.1(4)

Period

Actions may be brought within the times herein limited, respectively, after their causes accrue, and not afterwards, except when otherwise specially declared:

4. Unwritten contracts -- injuries to property -- fraud -- other actions. Those founded on unwritten contracts, those brought for injuries to property, or for relief on the ground of fraud in cases heretofore solely cognizable in a court of chancery, and all other actions not otherwise provided for in this respect, within five years, except as provided by subsections 8 and 10.

KANSAS (THREE YEARS/TWO YEARS)

Kan. Stat. Ann. Sec. 60-512.

Actions limited to three years

The following actions shall be brought within three (3) years: (1) All actions upon contracts, obligations or liabilities expressed or implied but not in writing. (2) An action upon a liability created by a statute other than a penalty or forfeiture.

Kan. Stat. Ann. Sec. 60-513.

Actions limited to two years.

(a) The following actions shall be brought within two years:

(1) An action for trespass upon real property.

(2) An action for taking, detaining or injuring personal property, including actions for the specific recovery thereof.

(3) An action for relief on the ground of fraud, but the cause of action shall not be deemed to have accrued until the fraud is discovered.
(4) An action for injury to the rights of another, not arising on contract, and not herein enumerated.
(5) An action for wrongful death.
(6) An action to recover for an ionizing radiation injury as provided in K.S.A. 60-513a, 60-513b and 60-513c, and amendments thereto.
(7) An action arising out of the rendering of or failure to render professional services by a health care provider, not arising on contract.

(b) Except as provided in subsections (c) and (d), the causes of action listed in subsection (a) shall not be deemed to have accrued until the act giving rise to the cause of action first causes substantial injury, or, if the fact of injury is not reasonably ascertainable until some time after the initial act, then the period of limitation shall not commence until the fact of injury becomes reasonably ascertainable to the injured party, but in no event shall an action be commenced more than 10 years beyond the time of the act giving rise to the cause of action.

KENTUCKY (ONE YEAR)
Ky. Rev. Stat. Ann. Sec. 413.245.

Actions for professional service malpractice

Notwithstanding any other prescribed limitation of actions which might otherwise appear applicable, except those provided in KRS 413.140, a civil action, whether brought in tort or contract, arising out of any act or omission in rendering, or failing to render, professional services for others shall be brought within one (1) year from the date of the occurrence or from the date when the cause of action was, or reasonably should have been, discovered by the party injured. Time shall not commence against a party under legal disability until removal of the disability.

LOUISIANA (ONE YEAR FROM DISCOVERY, THREE YEARS FROM ACT)
La. Rev. Stat. Ann. Sec. 5605

Actions for legal malpractice

A. No action for damages against any attorney at law duly admitted to practice in this state, any partnership of such attorneys at law, or any professional corporation, company, organization, association, enterprise, or other commercial business or professional combination authorized by the laws of this state to engage in the practice of law, whether based upon tort, or breach of contract, or otherwise, arising out of an engagement to provide legal services shall be brought unless filed in a court of competent jurisdiction and proper venue within one year from the date of the alleged act, omission, or neglect, or within one year from the date that the alleged act, omission, or neglect is discovered or should have been discovered; however, even as to actions filed within one year from the date of such discovery, in all events such actions shall be filed at the latest within three years from the date of the alleged act, omission, or neglect.

B. The provisions of this Section are remedial and apply to all causes of action without regard to the date when the alleged act, omission, or neglect occurred. However, with respect to any alleged act, omission, or neglect occurring prior to September 7,

1990, actions must, in all events, be filed in a court of competent jurisdiction and proper venue on or before September 7, 1993, without regard to the date of discovery of the alleged act, omission, or neglect. The one-year and three-year periods of limitation provided in Subsection A of this Section are peremptive periods within the meaning of Civil Code Article 3458 and, in accordance with Civil Code Article 3461, may not be renounced, interrupted, or suspended.

C. Notwithstanding any other law to the contrary, in all actions brought in this state against any attorney at law duly admitted to practice in this state, any partnership of such attorneys at law, or any professional law corporation, company, organization, association, enterprise, or other commercial business or professional combination authorized by the laws of this state to engage in the practice of law, the prescriptive and peremptive period shall be governed exclusively by this Section.

D. The provisions of this Section shall apply to all persons whether or not infirm or under disability of any kind and including minors and interdicts.

E. The peremptive period provided in Subsection A of this Section shall not apply in cases of fraud, as defined in Civil Code Article 1953.

MAINE (SIX YEARS)
Me. Rev. Stat. Ann. Tit. 14, Sec. 752.

Six years

All civil actions shall be commenced within 6 years after the cause of action accrues and not afterwards, except actions on a judg-

ment or decree of any court of record of the United States, or of any state or of a justice of the peace in this State, and except as otherwise specially provided.

MARYLAND (THREE YEARS)
Md. Crts and Jud. Proceedings Code Ann. § 5-101.

Three-year limitation in general

A civil action at law shall be filed within three years from the date it accrues unless another provision of the Code provides a different period of time within which an action shall be commenced.

MASSACHUSETTS (THREE YEARS)
Mass. Gen. Laws ch. 260, Sec. 4.

Limitation of Three Years; Limitation of One Year for Certain Action

Actions of contract or tort for malpractice, error or mistake against attorneys, certified public accountants and public accountants, actions for assault and battery, false imprisonment, slander, libel, actions against sheriffs, deputy sheriffs, constables or assignees in insolvency for the taking or conversion of personal property, actions of tort for injuries to the person against counties, cities and towns, and actions of contract or tort for malpractice, error or mistake against hairdressers, operators and shops registered under sections eighty-seven T to eighty-seven JJ, inclusive of chapter one hundred and twelve, actions of tort for bodily injuries or for death the payment of judgments in which is required to be secured by chapter ninety and also actions of tort for bodily injuries or for death or for damage to property against officers and employees of the commonwealth, of the metropolitan district commission, and of any county, city or town, arising out of the operation of motor or other vehicles owned by the commonwealth, including those under the control of said commission, or by any such county, city or town, suits by judgment creditors in such actions of tort under section one hundred and thirteen of chapter one hundred and seventy-five and clause (9) of section three of chapter two hundred and fourteen and suits on motor vehicle liability bonds under section thirty-four G of said chapter ninety shall be commenced only within three years next after the cause of action accrues.

Actions of contract or tort for malpractice, error or mistake against physicians, surgeons, dentists, optometrists, hospitals and sanitoria shall be commenced only within three years after the cause of action accrues, but in no event shall any such action be commenced more than seven years after occurrence of the act or omission which is the alleged cause of the injury upon which such action is based except where the action is based upon the leaving of a foreign object in the body.

For the purposes only of this section, an officer or soldier of the military forces of the commonwealth, as defined in chapter thirty-three, shall while performing any lawfully ordered military duty be deemed to be an officer or employee of the commonwealth.

MICHIGAN (TWO YEARS)
Mich. Comp. Laws Sec. 600.5805(6).

Injuries to persons or property; limitations

A person shall not bring or maintain an action to recover damages for injuries to persons or property unless, after the claim first accrued to the plaintiff or to someone through whom the plaintiff claims, the action is commenced within the periods of time prescribed by this section.

(6) Except as otherwise provided in this chapter, the period of limitations is 2 years for an action charging malpractice.

MINNESOTA (SIX YEARS)
Minn. Stat. Sec. 541.05

Various cases, six years

Subdivision 1. Six-year limitation. Except where the Uniform Commercial Code otherwise prescribes, the following actions shall be commenced within six years:

(1) upon a contract or other obligation, express or implied, as to which no other limitation is expressly prescribed;

(2) upon a liability created by statute, other than those arising upon a penalty or forfeiture or where a shorter period is provided by section 541.07;

(3) for a trespass upon real estate;

(4) for taking, detaining, or injuring personal property, including actions for the specific recovery thereof;

(5) for criminal conversation, or for any other injury to the person or rights of another, not arising on contract, and not hereinafter enumerated;

(6) for relief on the ground of fraud, in which case the cause of action shall not be deemed to have accrued until the discovery by the aggrieved party of the facts constituting the fraud;

(7) to enforce a trust or compel a trustee to account, where the trustee has neglected to discharge the trust, or claims to have fully performed it, or has repudiated the trust relation;

(8) against sureties upon the official bond of any public officer, whether of the state or of any county, town, school district, or a

municipality therein; in which case the limitation shall not begin to run until the term of such officer for which the bond was given shall have expired;

(9) for damages caused by a dam, used for commercial purposes; or

(10) for assault, battery, false imprisonment, or other tort, resulting in personal injury, if the conduct that gives rise to the cause of action also constitutes domestic abuse as defined in section 518B.01.

Subd. 2. Strict liability. Unless otherwise provided by law, any action based on the strict liability of the defendant and arising from the manufacture, sale, use or consumption of a product shall be commenced within four years.

MISSISSIPPI (THREE YEARS)

Miss. Code Ann. Sec. 5-1-49.

Limitations applicable to actions not otherwise specifically provided for

(1) All actions for which no other period of limitation is prescribed shall be commenced within three (3) years next after the cause of such action accrued, and not after.

(2) In actions for which no other period of limitation is prescribed and which involve latent injury or disease, the cause of action does not accrue until the plaintiff has discovered, or by reasonable diligence should have discovered, the injury.

(3) The provisions of subsection (2) of this section shall apply to all pending and subsequently filed actions.

MISSOURI (FIVE YEARS)

Mo. Rev. Stat. Sec. 516.120.

What actions within five years

Within five years:

(1) All actions upon contracts, obligations or liabilities, express or implied, except those mentioned in section 516.110, and except upon judgments or decrees of a court of record, and except where a different time is herein limited;

(2) An action upon a liability created by a statute other than a penalty or forfeiture;

(3) An action for trespass on real estate;

(4) An action for taking, detaining or injuring any goods or chattels, including actions for the recovery of specific personal property, or for any other injury to the person or rights of another, not arising on contract and not herein otherwise enumerated;

(5) An action for relief on the ground of fraud, the cause of action in such case to be deemed not to have accrued until the discovery by the aggrieved party, at any time within ten years, of the facts constituting the fraud.

MONTANA (THREE YEARS FROM DISCOVERY, TEN YEARS FROM ACT)

Mont. Code Ann. Sec. 27-2-206

Actions for legal malpractice

An action against an attorney licensed to practice law in Montana or a paralegal assistant or a legal intern employed by an attorney based upon the person's alleged professional negligent act or for error or omission in the person's practice must be commenced within 3 years after the plaintiff discovers or through the use of reasonable diligence should have discovered the act, error, or omission, whichever occurs last, but in no case may the action be commenced after 10 years from the date of the act, error, or omission.

NEBRASKA (TWO YEARS IF KNOWN, ONE YEAR FROM DISCOVERY, TEN YEARS MAXIMUM)
Neb. Rev. Stat. Sec. 25-222.

Actions on professional negligence

Any action to recover damages based on alleged professional negligence or upon alleged breach of warranty in rendering or failure to render professional services shall be commenced within two years next after the alleged act or omission in rendering or failure to render professional services providing the basis for such action; Provided, if the cause of action is not discovered and could not be reasonably discovered within such two-year period, then the action may be commenced within one year from the date of such discovery or from the date of discovery of facts which would reasonably lead to such discovery, whichever is earlier; and provided further, that in no event may any action be commenced to recover damages for professional negligence or breach of warranty in rendering or failure to render professional services more than ten years after the date of rendering or failure to render such professional service which provides the basis for the cause of action.

NEVADA (TWO YEARS FROM DISCOVERY, FOUR YEARS FROM ACT)
Nev. Rev. Stat. Sec 11.207.

Malpractice actions against attorneys and veterinarians

1. An action against an attorney or veterinarian to recover damages for malpractice, whether based on a breach of duty or contract, must be commenced within 4 years after the plaintiff sustains damage or within 2 years after the plaintiff discovers or through the use of reasonable diligence should have discovered the material facts which constitute the cause of action, whichever occurs earlier.

2. This time limitation is tolled for any period during which the attorney or veterinarian conceals any act, error or omission upon which the action is founded and which is known or through the use of reasonable diligence should have been known to him.

NEW HAMPSHIRE (THREE YEARS)
N.H. Rev. Stat. Ann. Sec. 508:4.

Personal Actions

I. Except as otherwise provided by law, all personal actions, except actions for slander or libel, may be brought only within 3 years of the act or omission complained of, except that when the injury and its causal relationship to the act or omission were not discovered and could not reasonably have been discovered at the time of the act or omission, the action shall be commenced within 3 years of the time the plaintiff discovers, or in the exercise of reasonable diligence should have discovered, the injury and its causal relationship to the act or omission complained of.

II. Personal actions for slander or libel, unless otherwise provided by law, may be brought only within 3 years of the time the cause of action accrued.

NEW JERSEY (SIX YEARS)
N.J. Stat. Ann. Sec. 2A:14-1.

6 years

Every action at law for trespass to real property, for any tortious injury to real or personal property, for taking, detaining, or converting personal property, for replevin of goods or chattels, for any tortious injury to the rights of another not stated in sections 2A:14-2 and 2A:14-3 of this Title, or for recovery upon a contractual claim or liability, express or implied, not under seal, or upon an account other than one which concerns the trade or merchandise between merchant and merchant, their factors, agents and servants, shall be commenced within 6 years next after the cause of any such action shall have accrued.

NEW MEXICO (FOUR YEARS)
N.M. Stat. Ann. Sec. 37-1-4.

Accounts and unwritten contracts; injuries to property; conversion; fraud; unspecified actions

Those founded upon accounts and unwritten contracts; those brought for injuries to property or for the conversion of personal property or for relief upon the ground of fraud, and all other actions not herein otherwise provided for and specified within four years.

NEW YORK (SIX YEARS/THREE YEARS)
N.Y. CPLR Law Sec. 213.

Actions to be commenced within six years: where not otherwise provided for; on contract; on sealed instrument; on bond or note, and mortgage upon real property; by state based on misappropriation of public property; based on mistake; by corporation against director, officer or stockholder; based on fraud

The following actions must be commenced within six years:

1. an action for which no limitation is specifically prescribed by law;
2. an action upon a contractual obligation or liability, express or implied, except as provided in section two hundred thirteen-a of this article or article 2 of the uniform commercial code or article 36-B of the general business law;
3. an action upon a sealed instrument;
4. an action upon a bond or note, the payment of which is secured by a mortgage upon real property, or upon a bond or note and mortgage so secured, or upon a mortgage of real property, or any interest therein;
5. an action by the state based upon the spoliation or other misappropriation of public property; the time within which the action must be commenced shall be computed from discovery by the state of the facts relied upon;
6. an action based upon mistake;
7. an action by or on behalf of a corporation against a present or former director, officer or stockholder for an accounting, or to procure a judgment on the ground of fraud, or to enforce a liability, penalty or forfeiture, or to recover damages for waste or for an injury to property or for an accounting in conjunction therewith.
8. an action based upon fraud; the time within which the action must be commenced shall be computed from the time the plaintiff or the person under whom he claims discovered the fraud, or could with reasonable diligence have discovered it.

N.Y. CPLR Law Sec. 214.

Actions to be commenced within three years: for non-payment of money collected on execution; for penalty created by statute; to recover chattel; for injury to property; for personal injury; for malpractice other than medical, dental or podiatric malpractice; to annul a marriage on the ground of fraud

The following actions must be commenced within three years:

1. an action against a sheriff, constable or other officer for the non-payment of money collected upon an execution;
2. an action to recover upon a liability, penalty or forfeiture created or imposed by statute except as provided in sections 213 and 215;
3. an action to recover a chattel or damages for the taking or detaining of a chattel;
4. an action to recover damages for an injury to property except as provided in section 214-c;
5. an action to recover damages for a personal injury except as provided in sections 214-b, 214-c and 215;
6. an action to recover damages for malpractice, other than medical, dental or podiatric malpractice, regardless of whether the underlying theory is based in contract or tort; and
7. an action to annul a marriage on the ground of fraud; the time within which the action must be commenced shall be computed from the time the plaintiff discovered the facts constituting the fraud, but if the plaintiff is a person other than the spouse whose consent was obtained by fraud, the time within which the action must be commenced shall be computed from the time, if earlier, that that spouse discovered the facts constituting the fraud.

NORTH CAROLINA (FOUR YEARS)
N.C. Gen. Stat. Sec. 1-15.

Statute runs from accrual of action

(a) Civil actions can only be commenced within the periods prescribed in this Chapter, after the cause of action has accrued, except where in special cases a different limitation is prescribed by statute.

(b) Repealed by Session Laws 1979, c. 654, s. 3.

(c) Except where otherwise provided by statute, a cause of action for malpractice arising out of the performance of or failure to perform professional services shall be deemed to accrue at the time of the occurrence of the last act of the defendant giving rise to the cause of action: Provided that whenever there is bodily injury to the person, economic or monetary loss, or a defect in or damage to property which originates under circumstances making the injury, loss, defect or damage not readily apparent to the claimant at the time of its origin, and the injury, loss, defect or damage is discovered or should reasonably be discovered by the claimant two or more years after the occurrence of the last act of the defendant giving rise to the cause of action, suit must be commenced within one year from the date discovery is made: Provided nothing herein shall be construed to reduce the statute of limitation in any such case below three years. Provided further, that in no event shall an action be commenced more than four years from the last act of the defendant giving rise to the cause of action: Provided further, that where damages are sought by reason of a foreign object, which has no therapeutic or diagnostic purpose or effect, having been left in the body, a person seeking damages for malpractice may commence an action therefor within one year after discovery thereof as hereinabove provided, but in no event may the action be commenced more than 10 years from the last act of the defendant giving rise to the cause of action.

NORTH DAKOTA (TWO YEARS)
N. D. Cent. Code Stat. Sec. 28-01-18 (3).

Actions having two-year limitations

The following actions must be commenced within two years after the claim for relief has accrued:

3. An action for the recovery of damages resulting from malpractice; provided, however, that the limitation of an action against a physician or licensed hospital will not be extended beyond six years of the act or omission of alleged malpractice by a nondiscovery thereof unless discovery was prevented by the fraudulent conduct of the physician or licensed hospital. This limitation is subject to the provisions of section 28-01-25.

OHIO (ONE YEAR)
§ 2305.11

Time limitations for bringing certain actions

(A) An action for libel, slander, malicious prosecution, or false imprisonment, an action for malpractice other than an action upon a medical, dental, optometric, or chiropractic claim, or an action upon a statute for a penalty or forfeiture shall be commenced within one year after the cause of action accrued, provided that an action by an employee for the payment of unpaid minimum wages, unpaid overtime compensation, or liquidated damages by reason of the nonpayment of minimum wages or overtime compensation shall be commenced

within two years after the cause of action accrued.

OKLAHOMA (TWO YEARS)
Okla. Stat. tit. 12, Sec. 95.

Limitation of other actions

Civil actions other than for the recovery of real property can only be brought within the following periods, after the cause of action shall have accrued, and not afterwards:

1. Within five (5) years: An action upon any contract, agreement, or promise in writing;
2. Within three (3) years: An action upon a contract express or implied not in writing; an action upon a liability created by statute other than a forfeiture or penalty; and an action on a foreign judgment;
3. Within two (2) years: An action for trespass upon real property; an action for taking, detaining, or injuring personal property, including actions for the specific recovery of personal property; an action for injury to the rights of another, not arising on contract, and not hereinafter enumerated; an action for relief on the ground of fraud--the cause of action in such case shall not be deemed to have accrued until the discovery of the fraud;
4. Within one (1) year: An action for libel, slander, assault, battery, malicious prosecution, or false imprisonment; an action upon a statute for penalty or forfeiture, except where the statute imposing it prescribes a different limitation.

OREGON (TEN YEARS)
Or. Rev. Stat. Sec.12.115.

Action for negligent injury to person or property

(1) In no event shall any action for negligent injury to person or property of another be commenced more than 10 years from the date of the act or omission complained of.
(2) Nothing in this section shall be construed to extend any period of limitation otherwise established by law, including but not limited to the limitations established by ORS 12.110.

PENNSYLVANIA (FOUR YEARS)
Pa. Stat. Ann. tit. 42 Sec. 5525.

Four year limitation

(a) General rule. Except as provided for in subsection (b), the following actions and proceedings must be commenced within four years:

(1) An action upon a contract, under seal or otherwise, for the sale, construction or furnishing of tangible personal property or fixtures.
(2) Any action subject to 13 Pa.C.S. § 2725 (relating to statute of limitations in contracts for sale).
(3) An action upon an express contract not founded upon an instrument in writing.
(4) An action upon a contract implied in law, except an action subject to another limitation specified in this subchapter.
(5) An action upon a judgment or decree of any court of the United States or of any state.
(6) An action upon any official bond of a public official, officer or employee.
(7) An action upon a negotiable or non-negotiable bond, note or other similar instrument in writing. Where such an instrument is payable upon demand, the time within which an action on it must be commenced shall be computed from the later of either demand or any payment of principal of or interest on the instrument.

(8) An action upon a contract, obligation or liability founded upon a writing not specified in paragraph (7), under seal or otherwise, except an action subject to another limitation specified in this subchapter.

(b) Special provisions. An action subject to section 8315 (relating to damages in actions for identity theft) must be commenced within four years of the date of the offense or four years from the date of the discovery of the identity theft by the plaintiff.

RHODE ISLAND (THREE YEARS)
R.I. Gen Laws Sec. 9-1-14.3.

Limitation on legal malpractice actions

Notwithstanding the provisions of §§ 9-1-13 and 9-1-14, an action for legal malpractice shall be commenced within three (3) years of the occurrence of the incident which gave rise to the action; provided, however, that:

(1) One who is under disability by reason of age, mental incompetence, or otherwise, and on whose behalf no action is brought within the period of three (3) years from the time of the occurrence of the incident, shall bring the action within three (3) years from the removal of the disability.
(2) In respect to those injuries due to acts of legal malpractice which could not in the exercise of reasonable diligence be discoverable at the time of the occurrence of the incident which gave rise to the action, suit shall be commenced within three (3) years of the time that the act or acts of legal malpractice should, in the exercise of reasonable diligence, have been discovered.

SOUTH CAROLINA
S.C. Code Ann. Sec. 5-3-530 (1).

Three years

Within three years:

(1) an action upon a contract, obligation, or liability, express or implied, excepting those provided for in Section 15-3-520.

SOUTH DAKOTA (THREE YEARS)
S.D. Codified Laws Sec. 15-2-14.2.

Time for bringing legal malpractice actions -- Prospective application

An action against a licensed attorney, his agent or employee, for malpractice, error, mistake or omission, whether based upon contract or tort, can be commenced only within three years after the alleged malpractice, error, mistake or omission shall have occurred. This section shall be prospective in application.

TENNESSEE (ONE YEAR)
Tenn. Code Ann. Sec. 28-3-104.

Personal tort actions

(a) The following actions shall be commenced within one (1) year after the cause of action accrued:

(1) Actions for libel, for injuries to the person, false imprisonment, malicious prosecution, breach of marriage promise;
(2) Actions and suits against attorneys or licensed public accountants or certified public accountants for malpractice, whether the actions are grounded or based in contract or tort;

(3) Civil actions for compensatory or punitive damages, or both, brought under the federal civil rights statutes; and
(4) Actions for statutory penalties.

(b) For the purpose of this section, in products liability cases:

(1) The cause of action for injury to the person shall accrue on the date of the personal injury, not the date of the negligence or the sale of a product;
(2) No person shall be deprived of the right to maintain a cause of action until one (1) year from the date of the injury; and
(3) Under no circumstances shall the cause of action be barred before the person sustains an injury.

TEXAS (TWO YEARS)
Tex. Civ. Prac. & Rem. Code Sec. 16.003.

Two-Year Limitations Period

Except as provided by Sections 16.010 and 16.0045, a person must bring suit for trespass for injury to the estate or to the property of another, conversion of personal property, taking or detaining the personal property of another, personal injury, forcible entry and detainer, and forcible detainer not later than two years after the day the cause of action accrues.

UTAH (FOUR YEARS)
Utah Code Ann. Sec. 78-12-25 (1).

Within four years

An action may be brought within four years:

(1) upon a contract, obligation, or liability not founded upon an instrument in writing;

also on an open account for goods, wares, and merchandise, and for any article charged on a store account; also on an open account for work, labor or services rendered, or materials furnished; provided, that action in all of the foregoing cases may be commenced at any time within four years after the last charge is made or the last payment is received;

VERMONT (SIX YEARS)
Vt. Stat. Ann. tit 12 Sec. 511.

Civil action

A civil action, except one brought upon the judgment or decree of a court of record of the United States or of this or some other state, and except as otherwise provided, shall be commenced within six years after the cause of action accrues and not thereafter.

VIRGINIA (FIVE YEARS/THREE YEARS)
Va. Code Ann. Sec. 8.01-246 (2).

Personal actions based on contracts

Subject to the provisions of § 8.01-243 regarding injuries to person and property and of § 8.01-245 regarding the application of limitations to fiduciaries, and their bonds, actions founded upon a contract, other than actions on a judgment or decree, shall be brought within the following number of years next after the cause of action shall have accrued:

2. In actions on any contract which is not otherwise specified and which is in writing and signed by the party to be charged thereby, or by his agent, within five years whether such writing be under seal or not;

Va. Code Ann. Sec. 8.01-246 (4)
4. In actions upon any unwritten contract, express or implied, within three years.

WASHINGTON (THREE YEARS/SIX YEARS)
Wash. Rev. Code Sec. 4.16.080 (3).

Actions limited to three years

The following actions shall be commenced within three years:

(3) Except as provided in RCW 4.16.040(2), an action upon a contract or liability, express or implied, which is not in writing, and does not arise out of any written instrument;

Wash. Rev. Code Sec. 4.16.040.

Actions limited to six years

The following actions shall be commenced within six years:

(1) An action upon a contract in writing, or liability express or implied arising out of a written agreement.
(2) An action upon an account receivable incurred in the ordinary course of business.
(3) An action for the rents and profits or for the use and occupation of real estate.

WEST VIRGINIA (TWO YEARS/FIVE YEARS/TEN YEARS)
W. Va. Code Sec. 55-2-12.

Personal actions not otherwise provided for

Every personal action for which no limitation is otherwise prescribed shall be brought: (a) Within two years next after the right to bring the same shall have accrued, if it be for damage to property; (b) within two years next after the right to bring the same shall have accrued if it be for damages for personal injuries; and (c) within one year next after the right to bring the same shall have accrued if it be for any other matter of such nature that, in case a party die, it could not have been brought at common law by or against his personal representative.

W. Va. Code Sec. 55-2-6.

Actions to recover on award or contract other than judgment or recognizance

Every action to recover money, which is founded upon an award, or on any contract other than a judgment or recognizance, shall be brought within the following number of years next after the right to bring the same shall have accrued, that is to say: If the case be upon an indemnifying bond taken under any statute, or upon a bond of an executor, administrator or guardian, curator, committee, sheriff or deputy sheriff, clerk or deputy clerk, or any other fiduciary or public officer, within ten years; if it be upon any other contract in writing under seal, within ten years; if it be upon an award, or upon a contract in writing, signed by the party to be charged thereby, or by his agent, but not under seal, within ten years; and if it be upon any other contract, express or implied, within five years, unless it be an action by one party against his copartner for a settlement of the partnership accounts, or upon accounts concerning the trade or merchandise between merchant and merchant, their factors or servants, where the action of account would lie, in either of which cases the action may be brought until the expiration of five years from a cessation of the

dealings in which they are interested together, but not after.

WISCONSIN
Wis. Stat. Sec. 893.53.

Action for injury to character or other rights

An action to recover damages for an injury to the character or rights of another, not arising on contract, shall be commenced within 6 years after the cause of action accrues, except where a different period is expressly prescribed, or be barred.

WYOMING
Wyo. Stat. Ann. Sec. 1-3-107.

Act, error or omission in rendering professional or health care services

(a) A cause of action arising from an act, error or omission in the rendering of licensed or certified professional or health care services shall be brought within the greater of the following times:

(i) Within two (2) years of the date of the alleged act, error or omission, except that a cause of action may be instituted not more than two (2) years after discovery of the alleged act, error or omission, if the claimant can establish that the alleged act, error or omission was:

   (A) Not reasonably discoverable within a two (2) year period; or
   (B) The claimant failed to discover the alleged act, error or omission within the two (2) year period despite the exercise of due diligence.

(ii) For injury to the rights of a minor, by his eighth birthday or within two (2) years of the date of the alleged act, error or omission, whichever period is greater, except that a cause of action may be instituted not more than two (2) years after discovery of the alleged act, error or omission, if the claimant can establish that the alleged act, error or omission was:

(A) Not reasonably discoverable within the two (2) year period; or

(B) That the claimant failed to discover the alleged act, error or omission within the two (2) year period despite the exercise of due diligence.

(iii) For injury to the rights of a plaintiff suffering from a legal disability other than minority, within one (1) year of the removal of the disability;

(iv) If under paragraph (i) or (ii) of this subsection, the alleged act, error or omission is discovered during the second year of the two (2) year period from the date of the act, error or omission, the period for commencing a lawsuit shall be extended by six (6) months.

(b) This section applies to all persons regardless of minority or other legal disability.

INDEX

duration of case, 56, 58, 69, 73, 78, 80, 82

E

economic injury, 12
ECs. *See ethical considerations*
effective representation, 37
embezzling client's funds, 51
employee supervision, 8
employment agreements. *See contracts*
enforcing judgments, 82
engagement letters. *See contracts*
equitable remedies, 25
escrow accounts, 49
estate and probate law, 16
ethical considerations (ECs), 66
ethical rules, 11, 12, 29, 30, 34
ethics rules, 61–68
excessive fees, 46, 47
excessive sentences, 15
expertise, 47, 48, 76, 78

F

fairness, 79
false evidence, 67
false statements, 67
family law, 16
Federal Mediation and Conciliation Service, 76
fee agreements. *See contracts*
fee dispute resolution, 52
filing
    cases, 57
    claims, 17
    documents, 17
    fees, 58, 59
fixed fees, 48
flat fees, 43, 45
foreseeability of harm, 10
formality, 58, 78, 79
former spouses, 16
future inheritances, 16

G

gambling, 7
general retainers, 45
general trial courts, 55, 57, 58, 60
good faith, 68, 73
good faith assessments, 5
grievance committees, 61–64
grievance procedures, 62
grievances, 15, 24, 49, 50, 51, 55, 61–63, 69, 70, 81
guardians, 16

H

hearings, 63, 76
hourly rates, 43, 45

I

immigration cases, 46
    permits, 15
immunity from liability, 67
immunity of judgment, 15
impartiality, 30, 32–34, 76
impropriety, 34, 35
imputation of mistakes, 8
incompetence, 38, 41, 67, 68
independent counsel, 70
indigent defendants, 37
ineffective assistance, 37–42
informed waivers, 35
insurance company clams, 31
interest, 29–36
interest on funds, 51
Interest on Lawyers' Trust Accounts (IOLTA), 51
Interest on Trust Accounts (IOTA), 51
investigation of client's claim, 18

J

jurisdiction, 17, 59
justices. *See small claims courts*

L

law libraries, 55, 59

ABOUT THE AUTHOR

Suzan Herskowitz Singer, born and raised in The Bronx, New York, received her B.A. from the University of Texas at Arlington and her J.D. from Texas Tech University School of Law. She has also authored Wills, Trusts and Estates and Legal Research Made Easy, in its 3rd edition and published by Sourcebooks. She is licensed to practice law in Virginia, West Virginia, Florida and Texas. She currently practices land use development law in Virginia.

Your #1 Source for Real World Legal Information...

Sphinx® Publishing
An Imprint of Sourcebooks, Inc.®

- Written by lawyers • Simple English explanation of the law
- Forms and instructions included

THE MOST VALUABLE PERSONAL
LEGAL FORMS YOU'LL EVER NEED, 2E

This book contains more than 100
ready-to-use forms. It includes such
forms as mortages, employment
applications, sales contracts, and
change of adddress.

288 pages; $26.95;
ISBN 1-57248-360-1

THE 529 COLLEGE SAVINGS PLAN

Demonstrates how everyone can save
for college—tax free. Explains the 529
Plan state requirements for all participating states and clarifies beneficiary
issues.

248 pages; $16.95;
ISBN 1-57248-238-9

What our customers say about our books:

"It couldn't be more clear for the layperson." —R.D.

"I want you to know I really appreciate your book. It has saved me a lot of time
and money." —L.T.

"Your real estate contracts book has saved me nearly $12,000.00 in closing costs
over the past year." —A.B.

"...many of the legal questions that I have had over the years were answered clearly
and concisely through your plain English interpretation of the law." —C.E.H.

"If there weren't people out there like you I'd be lost. You have the best books of
this type out there." —S.B.

"...your forms and directions are easy to follow." —C.V.M.

*Sphinx Publishing's Legal Survival Guides are directly available from
Sourcebooks, Inc., or from your local bookstores.*

*For credit card orders call 1–800–432-7444,
write P.O. Box 4410, Naperville, IL 60567-4410, or fax 630-961-2168*

SPHINX® PUBLISHING'S NATIONAL TITLES
Valid in All 50 States

LEGAL SURVIVAL IN BUSINESS

The Complete Book of Corporate Forms	$24.95
The Complete Patent Book	$26.95
The Entrepreneur's Internet Handbook	$21.95
How to Form a Limited Liability Company (2E)	$24.95
Incorporate in Delaware from Any State	$24.95
Incorporate in Nevada from Any State	$24.95
How to Form a Nonprofit Corporation (2E)	$24.95
How to Form Your Own Corporation (4E)	$26.95
How to Form Your Own Partnership (2E)	$24.95
How to Register Your Own Copyright (4E)	$24.95
How to Register Your Own Trademark (3E)	$21.95
Most Valuable Business Legal Forms	$21.95
You'll Ever Need (3E)	
Profit from Intellectual Property	$28.95
Protect Your Patent	$24.95
The Small Business Owner's	$21.95
Guide to Bankruptcy	

LEGAL SURVIVAL IN COURT

Crime Victim's Guide to Justice (2E)	$21.95
Grandparents' Rights (3E)	$24.95
Help Your Lawyer Win Your Case (2E)	$14.95
Jurors' Rights (2E)	$12.95
Legal Research Made Easy (3E)	$21.95
Winning Your Personal Injury Claim (2E)	$24.95
Your Rights When You Owe Too Much	$16.95

LEGAL SURVIVAL IN REAL ESTATE

Essential Guide to Real Estate Contracts (2E)	$18.95
Essential Guide to Real Estate Leases	$18.95
How to Buy a Condominium or Townhome (2E)	$19.95
How to Buy Your First Home	$18.95
Working with Your Homeowners Association	$19.95

LEGAL SURVIVAL IN PERSONAL AFFAIRS

The 529 College Savings Plan	$16.9
The Antique and Art Collector's Legal Guide	$24.9
Cómo Hacer su Propio Testamento	$16.9
Cómo Restablecer su propio Crédito y	$21.9
Renegociar sus Deudas	
Cómo Solicitar su Propio Divorcio	$24.9
The Complete Legal Guide to Senior Care	$21.9
Family Limited Partnership	$26.9
Gay & Lesbian Rights	$26.9
Guía de Inmigración a Estados Unidos (3E)	$24.9
Guía de Justicia para Víctimas del Crimen	$21.9
How to File Your Own Bankruptcy (5E)	$21.9
How to File Your Own Divorce (5E)	$26.9
How to Make Your Own Simple Will (3E)	$18.9
How to Write Your Own Living Will (3E)	$18.9
How to Write Your Own	$24.9
Premarital Agreement (3E)	
Inmigración a los EE. UU. Paso a Paso	$22.9
Living Trusts and Other Ways to	$24.9
Avoid Probate (3E)	
Manual de Beneficios para el Seguro Social	$18.9
Mastering the MBE	$16.9
Most Valuable Personal Legal Forms	$26.9
You'll Ever Need (2E)	
Neighbor v. Neighbor (2E)	$16.9
The Nanny and Domestic Help Legal Kit	$22.9
The Power of Attorney Handbook (4E)	$19.9
Repair Your Own Credit and Deal with Debt (2E)	$18.9
El Seguro Social Preguntas y Respuestas	$14.9
Sexual Harassment:Your Guide to Legal Action	$18.9
The Social Security Benefits Handbook (3E)	$18.9
Social Security Q&A	$12.9
Teen Rights	$22.9
Traveler's Rights	$21.9
Unmarried Parents' Rights (2E)	$19.9
U.S. Immigration Step by Step	$21.9
U.S.A. Immigration Guide (4E)	$24.9
The Visitation Handbook	$18.9
The Wills, Estate Planning and Trusts Legal Kit	&26.9
Win Your Unemployment	$21.9
Compensation Claim (2E)	
Your Right to Child Custody,	$24.9
Visitation and Support (2E)	

SPHINX® PUBLISHING ORDER FORM

SHIP TO:

	Terms	**F.O.B.**	Chicago, IL	**Ship Date**

Charge my: ☐ VISA ☐ MasterCard ☐ American Express   ☐ **Money Order or Personal Check**

Credit Card Number   **Expiration Date**

ISBN	Title	Retail	Qty	ISBN	Title	Retail
SPHINX PUBLISHING NATIONAL TITLES				1-57248-167-6	Most Val. Business Legal Forms You'll Ever Need (3E)	$21.95
1-57248-238-9	The 529 College Savings Plan	$16.95		1-57248-360-1	Most Val. Personal Legal Forms You'll Ever Need (2E)	$26.95
1-57248-349-0	The Antique and Art Collector's Legal Guide	$24.95				
1-57248-347-4	Attroney Responsibilities & Client Rights	$19.95		1-57248-098-X	The Nanny and Domestic Help Legal Kit	$22.95
1-57248-148-X	Cómo Hacer su Propio Testamento	$16.95		1-57248-089-0	Neighbor v. Neighbor (2E)	$16.95
1-57248-226-5	Cómo Restablecer su propio Crédito y Renegociar sus Deudas	$21.95		1-57248-169-2	The Power of Attorney Handbook (4E)	$19.95
				1-57248-332-6	Profit from Intellectual Property	$28.95
1-57248-147-1	Cómo Solicitar su Propio Divorcio	$24.95		1-57248-329-6	Protect Your Patent	$24.95
1-57248-166-8	The Complete Book of Corporate Forms	$24.95		1-57248-344-X	Repair Your Own Credit and Deal with Debt (2E)	$18.95
1-57248-229-X	The Complete Legal Guide to Senior Care	$21.95		1-57248-350-4	El Seguro Social Preguntas y Respuestas	$14.95
1-57248-201-X	The Complete Patent Book	$26.95		1-57248-217-6	Sexual Harassment: Your Guide to Legal Action	$18.95
1-57248-163-3	Crime Victim's Guide to Justice (2E)	$21.95		1-57248-219-2	The Small Business Owner's Guide to Bankruptcy	$21.95
1-57248-251-6	The Entrepreneur's Internet Handbook	$21.95		1-57248-168-4	The Social Security Benefits Handbook (3E)	$18.95
1-57248-346-6	Essential Guide to Real Estate Contracts (2E)	$18.95		1-57248-216-8	Social Security Q&A	$12.95
1-57248-160-9	Essential Guide to Real Estate Leases	$18.95		1-57248-221-4	Teen Rlghts	$22.95
1-57248-254-0	Family Limited Partnership	$26.95		1-57248-335-0	Traveler's Rights	$21.95
1-57248-331-8	Gay & Lesbian Rights	$26.95		1-57248-236-2	Unmarried Parents' Rights (2E)	$19.95
1-57248-139-0	Grandparents' Rights (3E)	$24.95		1-57248-218-4	U.S. Immigration Step by Step	$21.95
1-57248-188-9	Guía de Inmigración a Estados Unidos (3E)	$24.95		1-57248-161-7	U.S.A. Immigration Guide (4E)	$24.95
1-57248-187-0	Guía de Justicia para Víctimas del Crimen	$21.95		1-57248-192-7	The Visitation Handbook	$18.95
1-57248-103-X	Help Your Lawyer Win Your Case (2E)	$14.95		1-57248-225-7	Win Your Unemployment Compensation Claim (2E)	$21.95
1-57248-164-1	How to Buy a Condominium or Townhome (2E)	$19.95				
1-57248-328-8	How to Buy Your First Home	$18.95		1-57248-330-X	The Wills, Estate Planning and Trusts Legal Kit	&26.95
1-57248-191-9	How to File Your Own Bankruptcy (5E)	$21.95		1-57248-138-2	Winning Your Personal Injury Claim (2E)	$24.95
1-57248-343-1	How to File Your Own Divorce (5E)	$26.95		1-57248-333-4	Working with Your Homeowners Association	$19.95
1-57248-222-2	How to Form a Limited Liability Company (2E)	$24.95		1-57248-162-5	Your Right to Child Custody, Visitation and Support (2E)	$24.95
1-57248-231-1	How to Form a Nonprofit Corporation (2E)	$24.95				
1-57248-345-8	How to Form Your Own Corporation (4E)	$26.95		1-57248-157-9	Your Rights When You Owe Too Much	$16.95
1-57248-224-9	How to Form Your Own Partnership (2E)	$24.95		**CALIFORNIA TITLES**		
1-57248-232-X	How to Make Your Own Simple Will (3E)	$18.95		1-57248-150-1	CA Power of Attorney Handbook (2E)	$18.95
1-57248-200-1	How to Register Your Own Copyright (4E)	$24.95		1-57248-337-7	How to File for Divorce in CA (4E)	$26.95
1-57248-104-8	How to Register Your Own Trademark (3E)	$21.95		1-57248-145-5	How to Probate and Settle an Estate in CA	$26.95
1-57248-233-8	How to Write Your Own Living Will (3E)	$18.95		1-57248-336-9	How to Start a Business in CA (2E)	$21.95
1-57248-156-0	How to Write Your Own Premarital Agreement (3E)	$24.95		1-57248-194-3	How to Win in Small Claims Court in CA (2E)	$18.95
				1-57248-246-X	Make Your Own CA Will	$18.95
1-57248-230-3	Incorporate in Delaware from Any State	$24.95		1-57248-196-X	The Landlord's Legal Guide in CA	$24.95
1-57248-158-7	Incorporate in Nevada from Any State	$24.95		1-57248-241-9	Tenants' Rights in CA	$21.95
1-57248-250-8	Inmigración a los EE.UU. Paso a Paso	$22.95		**FLORIDA TITLES**		
1-57071-333-2	Jurors' Rights (2E)	$12.95		1-57071-363-4	Florida Power of Attorney Handbook (2E)	$16.95
1-57248-223-0	Legal Research Made Easy (3E)	$21.95		1-57248-176-5	How to File for Divorce in FL (7E)	$26.95
1-57248-165-X	Living Trusts and Other Ways to Avoid Probate (3E)	$24.95		1-57248-356-3	How to Form a Corporation in FL (6E)	$24.95
				1-57248-203-6	How to Form a Limited Liability Co. in FL (2E)	$24.95
1-57248-186-2	Manual de Beneficios para el Seguro Social	$18.95				
1-57248-220-6	Mastering the MBE	$16.95		**Form Continued on Following Page**		**SubTotal** _____

Qty	ISBN	Title	Retail
_____	1-57071-401-0	How to Form a Partnership in FL	$22.95
_____	1-57248-113-7	How to Make a FL Will (6E)	$16.95
_____	1-57248-088-2	How to Modify Your FL Divorce Judgment (4E)	$24.95
_____	1-57248-354-7	How to Probate and Settle an Estate in FL (5E)	$26.95
_____	1-57248-339-3	How to Start a Business in FL (7E)	$21.95
_____	1-57248-204-4	How to Win in Small Claims Court in FL (7E)	$18.95
_____	1-57248-202-8	Land Trusts in Florida (6E)	$29.95
_____	1-57248-338-5	Landlords' Rights and Duties in FL (9E)	$22.95

GEORGIA TITLES

Qty	ISBN	Title	Retail
_____	1-57248-340-7	How to File for Divorce in GA (5E)	$21.95
_____	1-57248-180-3	How to Make a GA Will (4E)	$21.95
_____	1-57248-341-5	How to Start a Business in Georgia (3E)	$21.95

ILLINOIS TITLES

Qty	ISBN	Title	Retail
_____	1-57248-244-3	Child Custody, Visitation, and Support in IL	$24.95
_____	1-57248-206-0	How to File for Divorce in IL (3E)	$24.95
_____	1-57248-170-6	How to Make an IL Will (3E)	$16.95
_____	1-57248-247-8	How to Start a Business in IL (3E)	$21.95
_____	1-57248-252-4	The Landlord's Legal Guide in IL	$24.95

MARYLAND, VIRGINIA AND THE DISTRICT OF COLUMBIA

Qty	ISBN	Title	Retail
_____	1-57248-240-0	How to File for Divorce in MD, VA and DC	$28.95

MASSACHUSETTS TITLES

Qty	ISBN	Title	Retail
_____	1-57248-128-5	How to File for Divorce in MA (3E)	$24.95
_____	1-57248-115-3	How to Form a Corporation in MA	$24.95
_____	1-57248-108-0	How to Make a MA Will (2E)	$16.95
_____	1-57248-248-6	How to Start a Business in MA (3E)	$21.95
_____	1-57248-209-5	The Landlord's Legal Guide in MA	$24.95

MICHIGAN TITLES

Qty	ISBN	Title	Retail
_____	1-57248-215-X	How to File for Divorce in MI (3E)	$24.95
_____	1-57248-182-X	How to Make a MI Will (3E)	$16.95
_____	1-57248-183-8	How to Start a Business in MI (3E)	$18.95

MINNESOTA TITLES

Qty	ISBN	Title	Retail
_____	1-57248-142-0	How to File for Divorce in MN	$21.95
_____	1-57248-179-X	How to Form a Corporation in MN	$24.95
_____	1-57248-178-1	How to Make a MN Will (2E)	$16.95

NEW JERSEY TITLES

Qty	ISBN	Title	Retail
_____	1-57248-239-7	How to File for Divorce in NJ	$24.95

NEW YORK TITLES

Qty	ISBN	Title	Retail
_____	1-57248-193-5	Child Custody, Visitation and Support in NY	$26.95
_____	1-57248-351-2	File for Divorce in NY	$26.95
_____	1-57248-249-4	How to Form a Corporation in NY (2E)	$24.95
_____	1-57248-095-5	How to Make a NY Will (2E)	$16.95
_____	1-57248-199-4	How to Start a Business in NY (2E)	$18.95
_____	1-57248-198-6	How to Win in Small Claims Court in NY (2E)	$18.95
_____	1-57248-197-8	Landlords' Legal Guide in NY	$24.95
_____	1-57071-188-7	New York Power of Attorney Handbook	$19.95
_____	1-57248-122-6	Tenants' Rights in NY	$21.95

NORTH CAROLINA TITLES

Qty	ISBN	Title	Retail
_____	1-57248-185-4	How to File for Divorce in NC (3E)	$22.95
_____	1-57248-129-3	How to Make a NC Will (3E)	$16.95
_____	1-57248-184-6	How to Start a Business in NC (3E)	$18.95
_____	1-57248-091-2	Landlords' Rights & Duties in NC	$21.95

OHIO TITLES

Qty	ISBN	Title	Retail
_____	1-57248-190-0	How to File for Divorce in OH (2E)	$24.95

Qty	ISBN	Title	R
_____	1-57248-174-9	How to Form a Corporation in OH	$24
_____	1-57248-173-0	How to Make an OH Will	$16

PENNSYLVANIA TITLES

Qty	ISBN	Title	R
_____	1-57248-242-7	Child Custody, Visitation and Support in PA	$26
_____	1-57248-211-7	How to File for Divorce in PA (3E)	$24
_____	1-57248-094-7	How to Make a PA Will (2E)	$16
_____	1-57248-357-1	How to Start a Business in PA (3E)	$21
_____	1-57248-245-1	The Landlord's Legal Guide in PA	$24

TEXAS TITLES

Qty	ISBN	Title	R
_____	1-57248-171-4	Child Custody, Visitation, and Support in TX	$22
_____	1-57248-172-2	How to File for Divorce in TX (3E)	$24
_____	1-57248-114-5	How to Form a Corporation in TX (2E)	$24
_____	1-57248-255-9	How to Make a TX Will (3E)	$16
_____	1-57248-214-1	How to Probate and Settle an Estate in TX (3E)	$24
_____	1-57248-228-1	How to Start a Business in TX (3E)	$18
_____	1-57248-111-0	How to Win in Small Claims Court in TX (2E)	$16
_____	1-57248-355-5	the Landlord's Legal Guide in TX	$24

SubTotal This page _____
SubTotal previous page _____
Shipping— $5.00 for 1st book, $1.00 each additional _____
Illinois residents add 6.75% sales tax _____
Connecticut residents add 6.00% sales tax _____

Total _____